AppleWorks™ Made Easy

Second Edition

AppleWorks™
Made Easy

Second Edition

Carole Boggs Matthews

Osborne **McGraw-Hill**
Berkeley, California

Published by
Osborne **McGraw-Hill**
2600 Tenth Street
Berkeley, California 94710
U.S.A.

For information on translations and book distributors outside of the
U.S.A., please write to Osborne **McGraw-Hill** at the above address.

Trademarks referenced in this book can be found on page 389.

AppleWorks™ Made Easy, Second Edition

34567890   DODO   898

ISBN 0-07-881260-7

Contents

Introduction

AppleWorks is an integrated business software package with three components: spreadsheet, data base, and word processor. Each of these is an important computer tools that contributes to your ability to increase productivity and make better decisions in your business or profession.

If you have purchased AppleWorks or are contemplating buying it to use in your business, *AppleWorks Made Easy* was written for you. It will help you learn how to use Apple-Works effectively in solving business problems and also to define the types of problems AppleWorks can address. *AppleWorks Made Easy* will help you whether you're a new user of AppleWorks or a somewhat experienced user who now wants to develop more advanced skills or get some new ideas on how you might apply the program.

Because the book is written for you, the business professional or small-business operator, the examples and exercises are designed to address real-life business problems, which you may find useful in and of themselves. The book is a tutorial in which you learn by performing exercises. It instructs you in a step-by-step manner, explaining not only what you should do, but also why, and what the implications of each procedure are. As you work with the examples, you will be able to compare the screens on your monitor with reproductions of the screen throughout the book, so that you will always be firmly anchored in the program.

AppleWorks Made Easy supplements Apple's own documentation, the *AppleWorks Tutorial* and *Using AppleWorks*, by continuing where that documentation leaves off. Whereas the Apple documentation presents you with short and simple exercises designed to help you use AppleWorks immediately,

AppleWorks Made Easy provides more substantial examples designed not only to get you started, but also to guide you in building your skills so that you can perform more advanced business tasks—all with clear, step-by-step instructions.

How This Book Is Organized

AppleWorks Made Easy is organized to allow you both flexibility and continuity in your approach to learning the program. The book allows you either to concentrate on learning one or two components thoroughly before going on to the third or else to gain a basic proficiency in each of the three components, which you then proceed to refine for all three.

Whichever approach you take, it's important to read Chapters 1 and 2, since they provide an introduction to Apple-Works and also a grounding in terminology and concepts that are used in the rest of the book. Every reader should also read the final chapter, Chapter 9, "Integration and Mail Merge: the Final Step," since this is where you will learn how to take advantage of AppleWorks' ability to integrate work done in the three components.

After Chapters 1 and 2, you have several choices. You can read Chapter 3, "Working With the Word Processor," Chapter 4, "Building a Data Base," and Chapter 5, "Building a Spreadsheet" in sequence; these chapters form a kind of natural group since they explain the essentials of using the three components. Alternatively, you can read any one of these chapters to find out how to use a particular component and then go on to read the corresponding chapter in the advanced group: Chapter 6, "Expanding Your Word Processing Skills," Chapter 7, "Expanding Your Data Base Skills," and Chapter 8, "Expanding Your Spreadsheet Skills." For example, you might be interested in first learning how to use AppleWorks' spreadsheet, and in delaying your work with the other components until later. In this case, you would read Chapters 1 and 2, and then skip to Chapter 5 to learn the fundamentals of using the spreadsheet. Then you would skip again to Chapter 8, "Expanding Your Spreadsheet Skills."

Some readers, of course, may wish to work with the chapters in the normal sequence, developing a basic and then a more sophisticated knowledge of all three components of the program. If you read in a straight sequence, you will find that the examples build nicely on each other.

A Brief Synopsis

Here is a brief synopsis of what you will learn in this book: Chapter 1 puts AppleWorks into the context of other software packages by explaining what integration is and why it's so important to you. Chapter 1 also explains the activities typically involved in word processing and building a data base or spreadsheet from a generic perspective. It then summarizes the features of AppleWorks' word processor, data base, and spreadsheet.

Chapter 2 introduces you to some of the basic elements of the AppleWorks environment that you will use each time you bring up the program. And in this chapter you will use the word processor to begin your hands-on practice with the program.

In Chapter 3 you will become familiar with the basics of word processing by writing a business letter and then turning it into a form letter.

Chapter 4, "Building a Data Base," is centered around two basic data base tasks: building a customer information file and then printing out a portion of that file as a simple customer telephone number list.

Chapter 5 teaches you the basics of the spreadsheet component by having you build a file of accounts receivable invoices from which you will proceed to format a report listing outstanding receivables.

Chapter 6 shows you how to perform advanced formatting functions in word processing, such as inserting page headers and footers and setting up automatic page numbering. In this chapter you will create the textual framework for a hypothetical business plan that outlines the vital facts about the proposed addition of a new store. Later, information created in both the data base and spreadsheet can be inserted into the business plan.

Like the earlier data base chapter, Chapter 4, Chapter 7 develops your data base skills through two separate tasks: first you'll generate mailing labels from the customer information file that you created in Chapter 4; then you'll create a more complex file of inventory items that will eventually be combined with the business plan. This chapter will also teach you more advanced skills for creating reports from the data base.

In Chapter 8 you'll prepare a sophisticated budget that allows you to use many advanced features of the spreadsheet. This chapter will teach you how to use the spreadsheet to perform mathematical calculations that normally take hours. It will also pass along some special techniques that will make your work with the spreadsheet even more efficient.

Chapter 9 is where we use AppleWorks' integration capability to pull everything together. In this chapter, you will learn how to integrate by combining the inventory list created in Chapter 7 and the budget created in Chapter 8 with the business plan created in Chapter 6. The second part of Chapter 9 shows you how to use the Mail Merge feature to merge a form letter with the data base file to generate customized letters for direct mailing operations.

Equipment You Will Need

You will need, of course, either an Apple IIe, IIc, or IIGS computer to use AppleWorks and this book. There are minor differences between the computers in the way that AppleWorks is used. The differences are noted in the text where they occur.

You must have at least 128K of memory in your computer to use AppleWorks version 2.0. With versions prior to 2.0, you must have at least 64K of memory in your computer, but 128K is recommended. With 128K of memory you will have 56K to build your files in AppleWorks. (If you have a standard, 256K Apple IIGS, the area available for files will be 125K.) This is equivalent to one word processing file with about 2,250 lines of text. That means a document with 60 lines per page can be about 37 pages long. If you're building a data base, 56K can handle about 1,350 records. Or 56K can contain a spreadsheet of about 2K per row, which translates to a worksheet of approximately 28 rows and 127 columns. If one large file is not convenient, you can store up to 12 smaller files in memory at one time.

The examples in this book were created on machines with the minimum amount of memory: 128K for version 2.0 of AppleWorks and 64K for versions prior to 2.0. Consequently, you may use this book for all versions of AppleWorks including 2.0. You may find that you have larger files than the minimum amount of memory can accommodate. Depending on which Apple computer you own, you can increase its available memory in different ways:

- With an Apple IIe you can add an Apple Memory Expansion card with between 256K and 1 megabyte of memory. AppleWorks automatically recognizes this memory and expands the available working memory to 250K. An alternative with the Apple IIe is to add an extended 80-column card with more than 64K of RAM. You will have to obtain software from the card manufacturer that modifies AppleWorks so that it recognizes this card. Manufacturers that provide this software include Apple Engineering and Checkmate Technology.

- With an Apple IIc you can add the Apple IIc Memory Expansion kit with between 256K and 1 megabyte of memory. This kit is functionally equivalent to the Apple Memory Expansion card for the Apple IIe. You can also purchase memory expansion kits from third parties, but you must obtain software from them that allows AppleWorks to recognize this memory. Again, manufacturers include Apple Engineering and Checkmate Technology.

- With an Apple IIGS you can add memory by using the memory expansion slot of the IIGS. A number of third parties, as well as Apple, manufacture IIGS memory expansion cards. AppleWorks automatically recognizes this added memory in the IIGS. You can also use an Apple IIe Memory Expansion card in the IIGS. As an example of the potential expansion of available memory, an Apple IIGS with a 1-megabyte memory expansion provides an AppleWorks working memory of 1149K.

If you have added 256K or more of memory to your computer, AppleWorks automatically loads the entire program into memory when it is started (unless you press the ESC key to stop it). This extra step, which takes 8 to 10 seconds, makes AppleWorks run significantly faster when you skip between sections. As a general rule, unless you are only performing a short task with AppleWorks, you should load the entire program into memory.

Another piece of equipment you will need is the 80-column Text Card, which allows you to see 80 characters per line across the monitor screen. Without it, you're restricted to 40 characters: this is not enough for AppleWorks.

In *AppleWorks Made Easy* we assume that your computer is equipped with two disk drives because this is much more convenient for business use. If you don't have two disk drives or a single disk drive accompanied by a hard disk, you will spend much time flipping floppy disks in and out of your one disk drive.

AppleWorks can, however, be used with only one disk drive. If your computer system has only one disk drive, or for that matter if you are using a hard disk, you will have to adjust some of the instructions provided in this book. Apple-Works helps you by asking for another disk (or in the case of hard disks, for a directory name) if it cannot find what you're searching for on the disk or directory it has.

If you have a version of AppleWorks prior to 2.0, the disk drive number will appear on your screen as "Drive 1," for example. If you have release 2.0, the disk drive will be seen as "Disk 1." This book shows both in its screen images. They mean the same thing.

You will need a printer if you want to use AppleWorks

effectively. If you have an ImageWriter printer, you needn't do anything about making your printer work with Apple-Works, except to hook it up. AppleWorks assumes that you will be using an ImageWriter, and your program disk is already set up for this printer.

In addition to the ImageWriter 1 printer or ImageWriter 2 printer that AppleWorks automatically expects, AppleWorks can recognize and use a number of other printers that require only a few minor installation steps. If you have one of these, you will have to follow some very simple guidelines that are provided for you in Appendix A. These printers are the following: Apple Dot Matrix, Apple Daisy Wheel, Apple Silentype, Epson MX series, Epson MX/Graftrax+, Epson RX series, Epson FX series, Qume Sprint 5, Qume Sprint 11, and Apple Scribe.

Finally, you may have another printer altogether: Apple-Works refers to this as a *custom printer*. If this is the case, you can tell AppleWorks about the characteristics of this printer. Appendix A explains how.

AppleWorks is written for the ProDOS operating system. If you are using ProDOS on your computer, you won't have to think about the operating system at all as you use Apple-Works. If you have files that have been created with an earlier Apple II operating system, such as DOS 3.2 or DOS 3.3, you will have to convert them to ProDOS format. The programs for converting files to ProDOS are stored on the System Utilities disk on the Apple IIc. On the Apple IIe you must use CONVERT on the ProDOS Users disk. On the IIGS you will need to run the program SYSUTIL.SYSTEM in the subdirectory called SYS.UTIL on the System disk to convert the files. AppleWorks allows you to work with documents, lists, or spreadsheets that have not been created by Apple-Works under certain circumstances, but the file must have been formatted by ProDOS first. (In addition, the "outside" file must be an ASCII, DIF, or Quick File; *AppleWorks Made Easy* explains what these terms mean, and how files generated outside AppleWorks may be used within the program.

Finally, you need three blank disks to use while you're working with the examples in *AppleWorks Made Easy*. And, of course, you'll need the Startup and Program disk that contains the AppleWorks programs.

1

Introducing
AppleWorks

Chapter 1 discusses the three components of AppleWorks. First, though, we will briefly examine the concept and history of integration, since integration is what unites Apple-Works' components and constitutes one of the key advantages of the program. The second part of the chapter defines word processing, data base management, and spreadsheets, both generically and as productivity tools implemented by AppleWorks.

Integration

Integration is difficult to define because it is something of a moving target, changing as software technology advances. In addition, there are wide variations in integrated programs as well as in degrees of integration, as you will see. To get a sense of what integration means in AppleWorks, let's examine how the need for integrated software arose in microcomputers, what problems integration solves, and how AppleWorks compares.

Standalone, Single-Function Packages

The first packages developed for microcomputers appeared in the mid-1970s. They were single-function packages, designed to perform one function with no links to other packages. Among them were standalone spreadsheet packages (VisiCalc is an example), data base packages (for instance, dBase II), and word processing packages (such as WordStar).

Standalone packages, while solving many problems, presented users with two important limitations. First of all, each package had its own environment and it was not easy to move from one package to another. For example, moving from a spreadsheet package to one for word processing required loading separate programs, learning new commands, and having access to only one file at a time. Using these separate environments was comparable to traveling through different countries, each with its own language. Going from one country to another necessitates formally leaving one before entering the next, as well as learning a whole new language.

A second problem arose in extracting information from one package to use in another. The rules for how the data was held in a file in one program differed from the *data format* in another program, resulting in *data incompatibility*. Thus, in order to merge information from different packages into one unified document, the user was faced with the need to manually recopy information from one package into another. For example, if you were writing a business plan with a word processor and you wanted to support your narrative with budgets calculated in the spreadsheet, you had no way of combining the narrative and the budget into one clear and concise document without manually cutting and pasting or retyping the contents of the budget into the narrative.

These two limitations of standalone packages initiated the first efforts toward integrating microcomputer programs.

Enhancements to Standalone Packages

The main limitation of the standalone packages was data incompatibility, which prevented information from being shared between packages. Not only was it impossible to move data from a spreadsheet to a word processor, but even moving information between two spreadsheets could not be guaranteed. To achieve data compatibility, developers of microcomputer software began to use some of the techniques that had been in use for years by large computer software developers: standardization of data formats.

Data formats are simply algorithms that developers use to write information on storage media, such as disks. For example, a business letter may be stored using one of several different algorithms. Thereafter, the letter can be read by any package that can read the same algorithm. Software developers have banded together to establish several standard data formats that are commonly used in the industry. Two of the standard data formats are DIF (Data Interchange Format) and ASCII (American Standard Code for Information Interchange).

Even with the possibility of converting programs to standard formats, however, exchanging information between separate programs may not be easy since the user may still be forced to go through a slow, tedious process of converting the data files. With many programs, for instance, to move data from one package to another (such as the spreadsheet budget data to the word processing business plan), you must load the spreadsheet program, write the selected budget data onto a new file and save it, convert that file into a compatible standard data format, load the word processing program, read in the file, and then copy it into an existing word processing file.

Window packages are a way to pull these standalone packages under a common master program in order to make the physical task of transferring information easier. Windows simply allow you to divide the video screen into smaller segments. Each segment, or window, displays data that may be different parts of the same file or parts of different files. If your windows display different files, you can move and copy data from one window to another, thereby moving data between files.

While windows assist in achieving data compatibility, they are a limited means of achieving integration. Windows can work with only certain standalone software, and they still require that you learn the different commands and techniques used by each of the standalone packages.

Integrated Packages With Separate Environments

The level of integration that is typical of much integrated software occurs when the individual components have been designed together, even though each component maintains a separate operating environment and separate files. Because the separate components are designed together, the commands and the working environments are very similar, and learning the program is consequently easier. Since the program itself performs any conversion of data formats needed in order to move information between the components of the package, you need not bother with the conversion process. This permits you to create the spreadsheet, data base, and word processing files in different environments, but with similar commands, and to easily copy from and move information among them. A windowing feature within a package often gives you even greater ability to move data among the components.

Separate working environments with separate files still pose a limitation of not allowing more than one component to be used at any one time. In other words, you must leave one component before you can load the programs and files from another.

Table 1-1 summarizes the different standalone programs and the different degrees of integration that have been discussed.

Integrated Packages With a Shared Environment

The most recent integrated packages have a single work environment; that is, the software has only one environment, not one for each component. The components within the package may, in fact, be transparent. For example, you may not even be aware that you are working with the word processing component, but simply that you are writing a letter. With these most advanced integrated packages, access to each component is immediate:

Package Attribute	Data Compatibility	Common Design Structure	Ease of Moving Between Components	Immediate Access to All Components
Standalone package	No	No	No	No
Standalone package using standard data formats	Yes	No	No	No
Standalone package using windows	Yes	No	Yes	No
Integrated packages with separate environments	Yes	Yes	No	No
Separate environments with windows	Yes	Yes	Yes	No
Integrated packages with shared environments	Yes	Yes	Yes	Yes
AppleWorks	Yes	Yes	Yes	No

Table 1-1. Degrees of Integration

several kinds of information—for example, word processed text and spreadsheet calculations—can be simultaneously created within the same file. Working in this environment is very fast since all components are always available to you; you do not have to leave one component to work with another.

Integration in AppleWorks

Where does AppleWorks fall in this spectrum of integration? AppleWorks is an integrated package with separate environments and separate files for each component. It offers a commonly designed overall working environment that makes moving from one component to another easy and convenient. You can, however, use only one component at a time, and each component has separate files. Finally, AppleWorks does not have the type of window feature that allows you to view more than one file at a time.

Although you must create separate files for each component, data compatibility between the three is high. You can easily

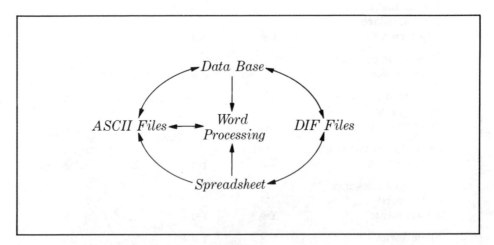

Figure 1-1. How components can be combined

move data between AppleWorks components using an automatic *cut and paste* feature to select portions of text, data base lists, or spreadsheets created in one component to be transferred to another component. To do this, you "cut" from a document one or more lines of text, or one or more items from a list or spreadsheet, placing them temporarily in a holding area until you "paste" these items or lines into the receiving text, list, or spreadsheet.

Figure 1-1 shows the directions that the cut and paste operations may take. For example, you may move data from the spreadsheet to the word processor, but if you were to move that data directly to the data base component, you would have to first convert the spreadsheet data to either of two standard data formats, ASCII or DIF. DIF is strongly recommended because with this format more characteristics of the spreadsheet data are actually moved than with the ASCII format. Thus, you must do less work to reformat the data once it has been converted to the data base. Since AppleWorks allows ASCII, DIF, and Quick Files (from Apple's separate data base product) to be accepted by one or more components, you can use standalone package files with AppleWorks (for example, files produced by VisiCalc, Word-Star, or Apple Writer).

One of AppleWorks' strongest features is its standardized command structure; spreadsheet, data base, and word processor use many of the same or similar commands. In addition, the appearance of the program is very similar across the three components. Commands are named with mnemonics in mind, making it easy to remember which key to press to invoke a particular command. Training time is greatly reduced since you are not learning three separate packages.

AppleWorks doesn't have the communications, graphics, and outlining components that are found in some packages. These are usually considered ancillary to the big three, which are the spreadsheet, data base, and word processor. AppleWorks has a *mail merge* capability for combining a name and address file with a form letter for direct mailings, as you will see in Chapter 9.

The Components of AppleWorks

Each of the three components in AppleWorks—word processor, data base, and spreadsheet—has a unique and important function. Let's first take a brief look at each from a generic standpoint in order to understand what it can do for you and how it fits into AppleWorks' total tool kit. You will learn about the details of each component and how to use them in upcoming chapters.

About Word Processing

A word processor replaces your typewriter: it provides an electronic way to create, store, revise, and print text. Just this one tool can double your productivity in writing and producing finished copy.

Examples of what you can do with word processing are plentiful. You can create letters, business plans, technical manuals, proposals, contracts, and invoices with the word processor, just as you would with a typewriter.

When you use a word processor, the text you type on a keyboard is stored in the computer's memory and displayed on the video screen. You may then compose and edit your document on the screen and print it when you are satisfied that it's exactly what you want.

With most word processors, one of the first surprises that you'll encounter when you initially enter text is a feature called *word wrap*. Word wrap allows you to forget about pressing a carriage return at the end of each line, as you would on a typewriter. You simply type and the software takes care of the linebreaks: words that extend beyond the right margin on one line are automatically wrapped around to the next line.

Word processors generally have two editing modes: *insert mode* and *overstrike mode*. Insert mode allows you to create new text by inserting it in between existing text so that the existing text is pushed to the right as new characters are entered. Overstrike mode allows you to simply type over the existing text, something like writing on a blackboard as you erase and rewrite words, except that the original text is automatically erased as you enter the new.

Revisions are much easier to make with a word processor because only the corrections are typed into the document being revised. The original unchanged text does not have to be retyped along with the corrections. The ability to enter a document, revise it again and again without rekeying the whole document, and then have it automatically printed in its final form is one of the biggest advantages of word processing and definitely one of the biggest productivity gains. And the final printed document is usually much more accurate because new typos have not been introduced in the unchanged text during retyping.

With a word processor, it is easy to move or copy text from one spot in a document to another or from one document to another. The surrounding text is automatically adjusted for the newly deleted or inserted text without having to retype any other text. For example, you can move a paragraph from page 1 to page 3 and AppleWorks will adjust the surrounding text to accommodate both the deleted paragraph on page 1 and the inserted paragraph on page 3.

Another valuable editing function that most word processors offer is the ability to search for any text and replace it with something else. You often have the choice of verifying each replacement before it is made, or of having all replacements done automatically by the software. For example, in Chapter 6 you will learn to type in text using an abbreviated company name and later to cause all occurrences of the shortened name to be automatically replaced with the actual company name.

Word processors allow you to set up rules to control the appearance of your documents as they will be printed. As Figure 1-2 shows, you can control the appearance of whole pages as well as of single letters and words. *Page formatting* allows you to establish the layout of a page: to adjust margins, tabs, spacing, page headers and footers, and other page attributes. *Character formatting* allows you to control the

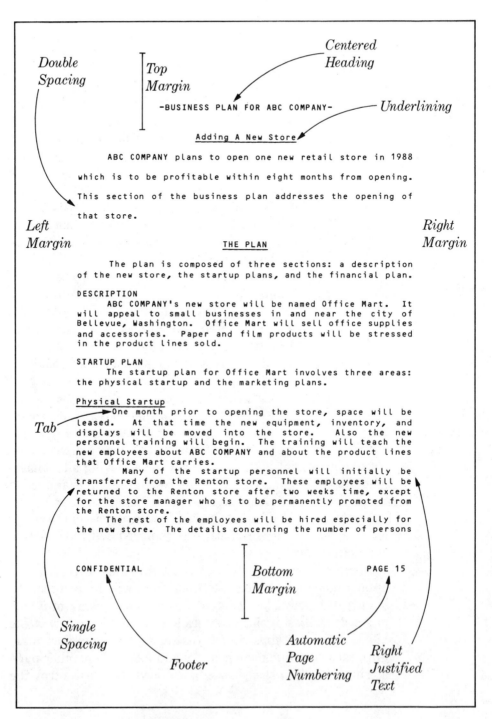

Figure 1-2. Page formatting features

appearance of particular characters. You can specify that boldface, underlining, subscripting, and superscripting should be associated with particular characters or words. In addition, you can format and print a page, review it, and then change the format and reprint it until the image is exactly what you want. To do this on a normal typewriter would just not be practical.

Using AppleWorks' Word Processor

AppleWorks provides many features to facilitate entering and editing text, formatting reports, and printing the final result.

Entering and editing text using AppleWorks' word processor is fast and convenient. You have both the insert and overstrike editing modes available to you, and you can switch between them easily. Two commands, called Move and Copy, allow you to move text within your document or between documents. AppleWorks' Replace command allows you to find all occurrences of a group of letters or words and to replace them with others. You may choose whether you want to change all occurrences automatically or to verify each occurrence before the replacement takes place.

Controlling the appearance of your text is easy with AppleWorks. At your request, AppleWorks presents you with a list of all the formatting options available. To control the appearance of the page or of particular words, you simply select the options you want. This saves you from memorizing complex commands and keystroke sequences.

In addition, AppleWorks allows you to preset many of the formatting options for a document: margins, tabs, single or double spacing, page numbering, or lines per page. In fact, AppleWorks itself automatically formats each new document according to a standard model. For example, the top margin is preset by AppleWorks to 0.0 inches and the bottom margin at 2.0 inches. These preset standards are known as *defaults*. You can choose between accepting the defaults that AppleWorks has established or setting up your own defaults for a document. If you have a group of documents that require the same formatting, you can set up a dummy document only for the purpose of defining the formatting and then copy it into each new document as you start it. This way you set up a standard format once and then use it again and again as appropriate.

In many word processors, particularly the older ones, the screen image will contain *control characters*, which are instructions to the printer specifying when to perform certain functions (for example, instructions that tell the printer to center a title or to underline a word), thus making it hard to see exactly what will be printed. In AppleWorks, you have the option of seeing the control characters on the screen, or not, as you wish. There are times when you want to see the control characters to correct a formatting error, but usually they just obscure your image and are confusing. Most of the time, the text on the screen will look very much like what you will see on paper. As a result, you can format your documents on the screen knowing that the printout will be almost the same.

In AppleWorks, page breaks are automatically calculated for you. You can move information around, delete paragraphs, and add lines of text freely, knowing that Apple-Works will take care of repaginating the text.

AppleWorks allows you to specify whether you want to print all of a document or only part of it. And you can print up to nine copies of a document, one copy right after the next.

Now that you have an overview of word processing, let's look at what a data base can do.

About Data Bases

A data base is for organizing, storing, and reporting lists of data. It acts as your electronic file cabinet. Common uses of a data base are to create data files for customer information,

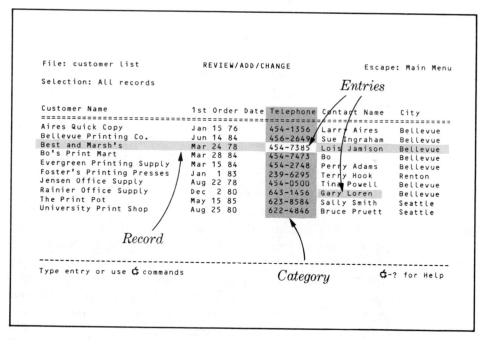

```
File: customer list            REVIEW/ADD/CHANGE              Escape: Main Menu

Selection: All records
                                                       Entries
Customer Name                1st Order Date  Telephone  Contact Name   City
=================================================================================
Aires Quick Copy              Jan 15 76      454-1356  Larry Aires     Bellevue
Bellevue Printing Co.         Jun 14 84      456-2649  Sue Ingraham    Bellevue
Best and Marsh's              Mar 24 78      454-7385  Lois Jamison    Bellevue
Bo's Print Mart               Mar 28 84      454-7473  Bo              Bellevue
Evergreen Printing Supply     Mar 15 84      454-2748  Perry Adams     Bellevue
Foster's Printing Presses     Jan  1 83      239-6295  Terry Hook      Renton
Jensen Office Supply          Aug 22 78      454-0500  Tina Powell     Bellevue
Rainier Office Supply         Dec  2 80      643-1456  Gary Loren      Bellevue
The Print Pot                 May 15 85      623-8584  Sally Smith     Seattle
University Print Shop         Aug 25 80      622-4846  Bruce Pruett    Seattle

                  Record
-----------------------------------------------------------------------------
Type entry or use Ꮹ commands              Category        Ꮹ-? for Help
```

Figure 1-3.   A typical data base screen

inventory items, accounts payable, accounts receivable, and so on. Almost any list or table of data can be stored in a data base file.

A data base is comprised of records, categories, entries, and characters. As shown in Figure 1-3, a *record* contains all information about a single data base unit. For instance, in a customer information file (CIF) all data about one customer would constitute one record. *Categories* (also known as *fields*) are the various types of data that a record may contain. For example, in the CIF the name, street address, city, state, and telephone number are all categories of data. Every record in the file contains similar categories of data.

The content of a particular record in a category is called an *entry*. Thus, looking at Figure 1-3, Aires Quick Copy is a name entry and "454-1356" is a telephone number entry. Finally, each entry is composed of *characters*, which may be letters, numbers, or special characters such as a dash or a period.

Most data bases offer organizational possibilities that just are not available with nonautomated lists. You can organize and reorganize the lists of data into any desired sequence by sorting them. For example, mailing lists can be sequenced either alphabetically by name, or numerically by ZIP code. You can select only certain records to see or print, so that not all records in the file are displayed, only the records you want. You can look at your data either as individual records or as lists of records—that means you can scan a list on the screen to identify a particular record and then zero in on it for more detail. You can also search the file for any records containing certain information and, when found, you can quickly view them on the screen.

Let's find out exactly what AppleWorks' data base is like.

Using AppleWorks' Data Base

AppleWorks' data base component gives you special capabilities in three areas: entering the data base, editing and maintaining the data base, and formatting and printing reports from the data base.

Entering data in AppleWorks is fast and convenient because of the flexibility you have in defining how your data will be entered. AppleWorks allows you to define and then change the layout of your input screen so that it more closely matches the document from which you will be entering data. This permits you to enter data faster and more easily, since your eyes can follow the input forms directly and not skip around looking for the next item to type in.

Another aid to efficient data entry is the easy way Apple-Works offers for moving through the data base. You move from one record to the next sequentially or skip through the file. For example, you can quickly move from the front of your file to the end, or anywhere in between.

To facilitate data entry, you can copy the contents of a category as it was entered on the last record. That way you don't have to continually retype repetitive information. Another feature allows you to copy groups of records that have similar contents so that you change only the data that differs in each record rather than all data. And you can preestablish values for those categories that are likely to have the same value, again saving you the task of typing repetitive information.

You can edit an AppleWorks data base with simple and easy commands that allow you to insert and delete records or categories of data and move and copy records from one spot to another. You can organize and reorganize the lists of data as you wish by sorting the lists alphabetically, numerically, or in descending or ascending sequence. You can select certain records to be displayed according to 12 different criteria.

One very efficient command within AppleWorks allows you to switch from looking at a list of items in a file (containing only some of the data actually stored about the items) to looking at all data available about only one item.

When it comes to designing and printing a final data base report, you have as much flexibility in this component as you do in the AppleWorks word processor. For example, you can format two types of reports: a labels-style report and a tables-style report, as illustrated in Figures 1-4 and 1-5. The labels-style report allows you to format and then print several lines of information about each record. For example, mailing labels are really a labels-style report. The tables-style report allows you to produce lists of information that look like tables, with one line per record and several columns of information for each line. You can also print only selected records in a file—for instance, only those names in a particular ZIP code range or an inventory of items above a certain dollar amount.

```
Aires Quick Copy
1345 South 8th
Bellevue WA 98004


Bellevue Printing Co.
456 East Bellevue Way
Bellevue WA 98005


Best and Marsh's
Department c
10476 NE 8th Street
Bellevue WA 98004


Bo's Print Mart
7264 Northrup Way South
Bellevue WA 98004


Evergreen Printing Supply
4769 NE 20th Street
Bellevue WA 98004


Foster's Printing Presses
83658 Pacific Hwy. South
Renton WA 98526


Jensen Office Supply
800 East 8th Street
Bellevue WA 98004


Rainier Office Supply
Suite 501
5327 148th Street
Bellevue WA 98004


The Print Pot
801 NW Adamson
Seattle WA 98134


University Print Shop
10056 Roosevelt Ave.
Seattle WA 98123
```

Figure 1-4. A labels-style data base report

```
File:    customer List                                         Page  1
Report: Telephone List                                   June 10, 1987
Customer Name         Telephone  Contact Name  City     State Prod 1st Order Date
--------------------  ---------  ------------  --------  ----- ---- --------------
Aires Quick Copy      454-1356   Larry Aires   Bellevue  WA    P    Jan 15 76
Bellevue Printing Co. 456-2649   Sue Ingraham  Bellevue  WA    P    Jun 14 84
Best and Marsh's      454-7385   Lois Jamison  Bellevue  WA    P    Mar 24 78
Bo's Print Mart       454-7473   Bo            Bellevue  WA    P    Mar 28 84
Evergreen Printing Su 454-2748   Perry Adams   Bellevue  WA    P    Mar 15 84
Foster's Printing Pre 239-6295   Terry Hook    Renton    WA    P    Jan  1 83
Jensen Office Supply  454-0500   Tina Powell   Bellevue  WA    P    Aug 22 78
Rainier Office Supply 643-1456   Gary Loren    Bellevue  WA    B    Dec  2 80
The Print Pot         623-8584   Sally Smith   Seattle   WA    P    May 15 85
University Print Shop 622-4846   Bruce Pruett  Seattle   WA    P    Aug 25 80
```

Figure 1-5. A tables-style data base report

AppleWorks can subtotal and then total categories of data. For example, you can calculate such totals as the value of inventory items, number of employees in a job class, or outstanding receivables. You can have up to three calculated categories where the contents are based on calculations performed on other categories. For instance, a "cost" category may be the product of the "price" times the "quantity" categories.

After you have formatted a report in AppleWorks, you can save it. By saving it, you can print the same report whenever you want it. You can also transfer the report and include it in a word processing document.

About Spreadsheets

Spreadsheets are used for accounting, budgeting, forecasting, or other numerical planning and modeling tasks. They essentially replace your calculator and multicolumn accounting paper for most purposes.

When you use a spreadsheet, it helps to visualize a series of rows and columns, since that's the way you enter the numbers. Figure 1-6 illustrates the vertical columns, designated by letters, and the horizontal rows, designated by numbers.

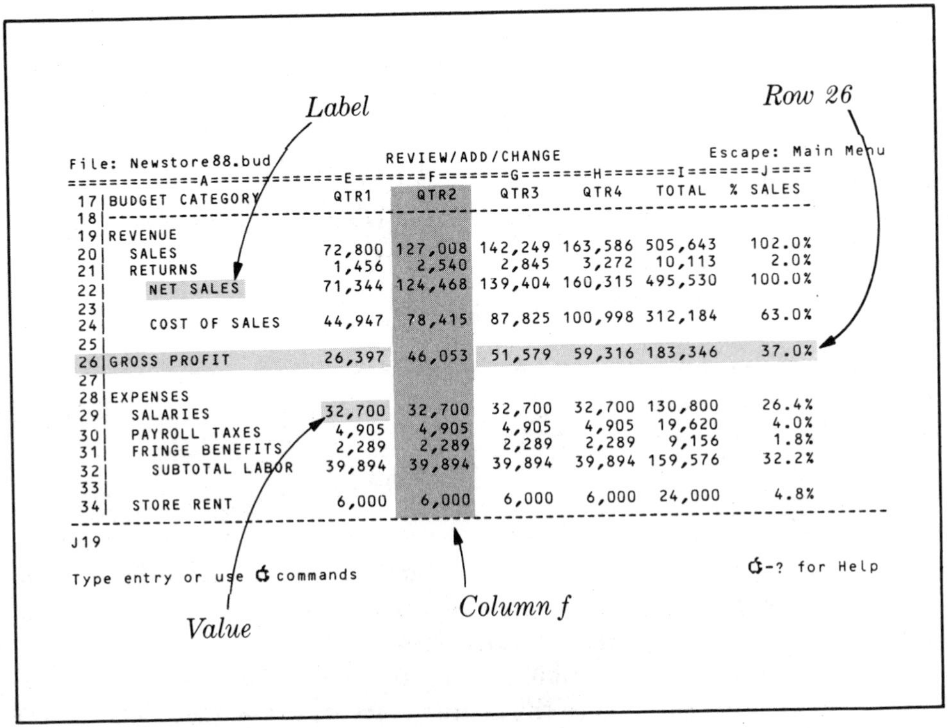

Figure 1-6.   A typical spreadsheet screen

Each intersection of a row and column is known as a *cell*. You refer to cells by the coordinates of column and row, such as B5 (column B, row 5) or AB20 (column AB, row 20). Each cell holds either values or words. If the content of a cell is a word (known as a *label*), it is most likely the name of a row or column. But it can also be the time of day, or the date, or another number not used in calculations, but for naming something. Values, on the other hand, can always be used in calculations and are usually not alphabetic entries, except that values may contain pointers to cells. Values can be simple numbers, formulas (arithmetic notations for calculating results), functions (preestablished formulas), or *pointers*, which indicate a value in the pointed-to cell which should be used in the cell containing the pointer.

One of the primary advantages of spreadsheets is the automatic recalculation of all the formulas and functions. You can vary critical figures in a plan and recalculate computed figures any number of times to determine what effect they have on related items. What happens to profits if the sales go up or down or if interest rates go up? Because calculations are done quickly, your response to changes in conditions can be swift and sure. The results are far more reliable, since the potential for human error has been reduced. If you make sure that the formulas and relationships are accurate, the spreadsheet will see to it that they are accurately executed.

Budgeting is an example of how a spreadsheet can be effectively used. For instance, if you are in retail, you can look at the impact of opening a new store in building your budget for the next year. You can play with the impact of the added costs against the increased revenues. You can evaluate how such plans as hiring additional employees affect this decision. With a spreadsheet model you can test many more variations than you could otherwise.

Using AppleWorks' Spreadsheet

AppleWorks' spreadsheet component provides many capabilities for you to use in building the spreadsheet, revising and editing it, and formatting and printing reports from it.

As with the data base, you can "program" the entry of data to be in a specific order, accommodating paper forms from which you are entering data. You can establish *default values* that are automatically filled in as you build a new spread-sheet. Consequently, you don't have to reestablish these values every time you bring up the spreadsheet to modify or print it.

You may be surprised at the wide variety of calculations that can be performed in AppleWorks' spreadsheet. You may establish your own equations or select preestablished functions such as SUM, AVERAGE, MAX, LESS THAN, GREATER THAN, or EQUAL. One rather complex function allows you to ask AppleWorks to consult a table in order to substitute a "real" value (such as a dollar amount) for a coded value (such as a product number) in a particular cell. In effect, AppleWorks looks up the value of the cell in the table and substitutes the corresponding value in the spreadsheet.

AppleWorks' spreadsheet component comes with a full range of editing features. You move or copy rows and columns, insert or delete them, sort the spreadsheet on selected rows, change the layout of the cells on the screen, and more. A recalculation feature allows you to revise numbers, values, or formulas in the spreadsheet and then recalculate the remaining values automatically. You can tell AppleWorks to recalculate the formulas and functions auto-matically each time you enter data into a cell, or to do so only at your command.

A *title feature*, found only in the spreadsheet component, allows you to freeze on the screen the names of your rows and columns while you scan all the rows and columns in the spreadsheet so that you don't lose sight of exactly where you are. And a *window feature* lets you view two parts of your spreadsheet at once. You can vary the numbers in one win-dow, recalculate the formulas, and see the results in another window. You'll have a chance to do this in Chapter 8.

Finally, AppleWorks provides a versatile reporting capa-bility for the spreadsheet. You can print the entire spread-sheet, or you can select a block of rows and columns, or only certain lines, to be printed. You can sort spreadsheets by rows based on the values contained in selected columns within the rows. If you calculate the value of several items, you can rank these items by sorting on the calculated value.

Chapter 2 takes a closer look at the AppleWorks environment. You will have an opportunity to try the program out
and experience some of the features just talked about.

2

The AppleWorks Environment

In Chapter 1 you saw that one of AppleWorks' greatest strengths is its unified design—the fact that its various components have been developed as one package, not as individual units. The similarities throughout the package are very obvious in the AppleWorks *environment*. By environment, what is meant is both how AppleWorks handles its resources (such as the computer's memory, disk, display, keyboard, and printer) and how the program appears to you, for example, as you enter commands, how the files are named and manipulated, what the screens look like, how you are informed about what is going on, and how you determine the layout of your printed report. The environment of the program is simply the work environment AppleWorks provides.

The first part of Chapter 2 orients you to AppleWorks by introducing some of the more important aspects of AppleWorks' environment. You will see how the computer's memory and disk are used together, how AppleWorks leads you through the components via menus, and how you use the "printer" to interface with the components and with packages other than AppleWorks. In the second part of the chapter, you will get some hands-on experience: you will bring up AppleWorks and learn to prepare your disks for use with AppleWorks. Finally, you'll create a letter to send to your customers announcing the opening of a new store. You'll save the letter on disk and then print it.

First let's take a look at how AppleWorks uses its memory and disk to store files.

How AppleWorks Uses Memory and Disk

Whenever you create something using one of AppleWorks' components, you create a *file*, which is simply the collection of pages in a word processor, or records in a data base, or rows and columns in a spreadsheet. Files created by AppleWorks can be thought of as regular file folders. For example, an AppleWorks file may hold a word processing letter or contract, a data base list or table, or a spreadsheet budget or forecasting model.

Any time you work with a file—to create, edit, or print it—you must first place it in the Apple's RAM (that is, random access memory). But the memory is temporary; its contents vanish when you turn off the computer. The disk, on the other hand, provides permanent storage. Once you write a file on disk it is saved, even after the power is turned off, until you direct AppleWorks to delete it or write over it with updated information, such as you would do when revising a document.

One of your most important tasks will be to save your documents to disk as you work with them and definitely when you've finished with them. Every time you want to save your file permanently, you must save it on disk. Otherwise, you will lose the file.

AppleWorks has established two special temporary memory areas for your convenience as you use the program. These two temporary memory areas are called the Desktop and the Clipboard.

The Desktop

Picture yourself working with a manual filing system. You are sitting at your desk. In your desk, or perhaps in a cabinet next to your desk, are drawers containing file folders. When you want to work on a project, you reach into a drawer and pull out a file folder, placing it on your desktop. You may have several folders on your desktop at one time.

AppleWorks uses these same simple concepts in referring to the way files are moved from disk to memory and back. When you read a file from disk ("pull it out of the file drawer"), you place it in a special place in memory known as your *Desktop*. Once a file is on the Desktop, it is available to you to be viewed and edited on your screen. You can have 12 files on your Desktop at one time, depending on the size of each file and the amount of memory you have in your computer. When you finish with one file and go on to another, you may either scan the folders on the Desktop, selecting the next one to work with, or you may retrieve another file from the disk and place it on your Desktop. As you finish with a file, you remove it from your Desktop, saving it on disk, or, in effect, putting it back in the file drawer.

The size of your Desktop depends upon how much memory you have in your computer. Consequently, the size of your files also depends upon the size of your Desktop. For example, if you have 128K of memory, your Desktop will hold one word processing file approximately 18 single-spaced pages long (at 65 lines per page) or more smaller files. However, if you add a memory expansion card, you can have larger word processing files on the Desktop.

The Clipboard

AppleWorks has another memory area called the *Clipboard*, which stores sections of files being transferred from one component to another. As with the Desktop, you can think of the function of the Clipboard in terms of how you worked with your paper files before computers. Before, as you thumbed through the file folders on your desktop, you might have seen an item that belonged in another file folder. You might have set the misplaced item aside on your clipboard, so that it wouldn't get lost, until you could transfer it to the other file folder. Later, when you opened the second file folder, you would have removed the item from the clipboard and inserted it into the newly opened file folder.

Similarly in AppleWorks, when you move items from one file to another, you temporarily store them on the Clipboard before you finally move them to the other file on the Desktop. There are two methods of getting text, data base lists, or spreadsheets onto the Clipboard. You can move or copy part of a document to the Clipboard using AppleWorks' "cut" feature, which allows you, in effect, to cut it out of the original document. Or you can "print" a report to the Clipboard rather than to the printer. In either case, you can then use the "paste" feature to move or copy the contents of the Clipboard to the file on the Desktop that you've chosen to place it in. The Clipboard holds up to 250 lines (about 5 word-processing pages or 250 data base records) at a time.

The information you put on the Clipboard will stay on it until you move it to another file, write something over it, or turn off the computer. Like the Desktop, the Clipboard is temporary storage; its contents vanish when the power is turned off.

Using Menus

AppleWorks uses a series of *menus* to guide you through the program. A menu is simply a list of options presented to you, not unlike a dinner menu in a restaurant. In AppleWorks this menu appears on a kind of index card. As you select an option, you might be shown a second menu, which is displayed as if you were pulling another index card out of a file. The new index card will be placed over the index card you started with, as shown here:

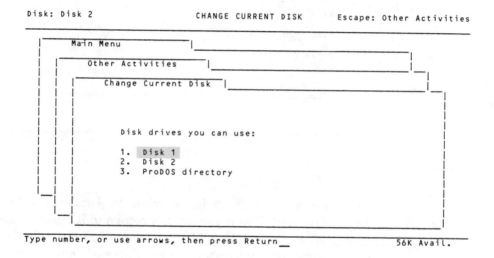

```
Disk: Disk 2              CHANGE CURRENT DISK       Escape: Other Activities
```

```
Disk drives you can use:

     1.  Disk 1
     2.  Disk 2
     3.  ProDOS directory
```

```
Type number, or use arrows, then press Return__          56K Avail.
```

In this way you are led through a series of menus, each menu allowing you to further define what you want, until the action you want has been performed.

The Main Menu and Other Activities Menu

AppleWorks begins its path of menus with the Main Menu, shown here:

```
Disk: Drive 1                         MAIN MENU
_____

  _____    _____
 |   Main Menu                 |  |                                |
 |                             |  |                                |
 |   1.  Add files to the Desktop                                  |
 |                                                                 |
 |   2.  Work with one of the files on the Desktop                 |
 |                                                                 |
 |   3.  Save Desktop files to disk                                |
 |                                                                 |
 |   4.  Remove files from the Desktop                             |
 |                                                                 |
 |   5.  Other Activities                                          |
 |                                                                 |
 |   6.  Quit                                                      |
 |                                                                 |
 |_____|


_____
Type number, or use arrows, then press Return _        Ĝ-? for Help
```

The Main Menu is the point of origin in AppleWorks: you always begin with it and you always return to it before leaving AppleWorks. The Main Menu presents you with six different *options*, or choices for action. Some of these options allow you to go further into AppleWorks to work with the word processor, spreadsheet, or data base; some allow you to manage the disk and printer resources. Notice that options 1, 2, 3, and 4 all work with the Desktop in some way. Option 6 allows you to leave AppleWorks. You use this option when you are finished with AppleWorks and want to do something else with your Apple computer.

Selecting option 5 will take you to the Other Activities menu, which looks like this:

```
Disk: Drive 1                  OTHER ACTIVITIES              Escape: Main Menu
_____
|     Main Menu                  |_____
|   |_____    |                                      |
|   |   Other Activities     |   |_____|_
|   |                                                                     |
|   |   1.  Change current disk drive or ProDOS prefix                    |
|   |                                                                     |
|   |   2.  List all files on the current disk drive                      |
|   |                                                                     |
|   |   3.  Create a subdirectory                                         |
|   |                                                                     |
|   |   4.  Delete files from disk                                        |
|   |                                                                     |
|   |   5.  Format a blank disk                                           |
|   |                                                                     |
|   |   6.  Select standard location of data disk                         |
|_  |                                                                     |
|   |   7.  Specify information about your printer(s)                     |
|                                                                         |
|_____|

Type number, or use arrows, then press Return _              56K Avail.
```

In the course of this book, you will explore most of the options listed in the Other Activities menu. For now, notice that all the options give you the ability to work directly with your disk or printer. You cannot change the contents of any of your files using the Other Activities menu; you can only work with the file as a whole unit.

Indicating Menu Choices

When AppleWorks presents you with a menu, you can select an option in two ways. You can type in the number of the option you want and then press RETURN. Or you can position the cursor by moving the UP and DOWN ARROW keys to the option you want and press RETURN. The RETURN key is a signal to AppleWorks that you have made your choice.

In this book, we will use the notations DOWN ARROW key, UP ARROW key, RIGHT ARROW key, and LEFT ARROW key to indicate the keys with the ↓, ↑, →, and ← symbols on them on your keyboard.

Highlighting is used to indicate the current choice in a menu. Highlighting is a feature that displays text on the screen using a reverse video image. For example, if your normal display is black letters on an amber background, highlighted text will appear in the reverse—amber letters on a black background. AppleWorks assumes you will choose certain options most often and will highlight them on each menu. You can either press RETURN to request the assumed option or move the cursor to another one. If you move the cursor down the menu to choose another option, the highlighting follows, emphasizing the option being pointed to.

Later on, highlighting will also be used to distinguish certain text so that you can work with it more easily. For example, if you are moving text from one spot to another, the words or letters to be moved will be highlighted for you. In this way you can easily tell if you've specified the correct text to be moved.

Printing

AppleWorks uses its printer in several ways that extend the normal definition of what printed output actually is. You can either print your text to the printer, producing a paper copy, or to disk, or to the Clipboard, producing an electronic copy. All three components allow you to print to a printer to get formatted reports and other hard copy output. Each component provides you with many formatting options that allow you to organize and arrange your document so that it is printed just as you choose. The exact formatting options differ within each component, but many options are identical. Much of the time you spend exploring AppleWorks' abilities will be in this area. You also can print the image of exactly what's on the screen on paper. The images of the screen shown in this book were produced in this way.

"Printing to" the disk is done in specific instances when you want to store a print image of a report on disk. You are temporarily saving your document until you can print it. You may choose to do this because your printer is busy or because you want to wait to print the report later on another Apple computer or printer.

Another reason you may wish to print to disk is to convert AppleWorks files from your spreadsheet or data base components to ASCII or DIF files. These ASCII and DIF files can then be used as input to programs other than AppleWorks or by other components within AppleWorks. For example, if you wish to transfer a data base file to the spreadsheet, you would first print the data base file to a DIF file on disk.

You print a report to the Clipboard, as mentioned earlier, for the special purpose of transferring data from the spreadsheet or data base to the word processing files.

Getting Started

You are now ready to begin working with AppleWorks. You will need the disk or disks containing AppleWorks and three blank disks that will be used to store the files you will create in this book. If you don't have any blank disks, get some now. You will not need the Sample Files diskette provided by Apple since none of those files will be used in this book.

Now you are going to start up AppleWorks, switch diskette assignments, and format the blank diskettes. These are preliminary tasks that you will need to perform often, if not every time you bring up AppleWorks.

Starting Up AppleWorks

Starting up (also called *booting*) AppleWorks is explained clearly in the *AppleWorks Tutorial*, so it will be reviewed only briefly here.

AppleWorks has two components; one for startup and another containing the main program. The Startup program is used only to boot AppleWorks. The main program is required whenever you're working with the system. Apple-Works comes in both 3 1/2-inch and 5 1/4-inch disk formats. One 3 1/2-inch disk contains the entire AppleWorks program. In the 5 1/4-inch disk format, programs may be stored on either side of a single disk or on two separate disks.

Before you go any further, you should make copies of the AppleWorks disks. Refer to *AppleWorks Tutorial* for directions on how to do this. When you've finished, put the original disks in a safe place and work with the copies. If something should happen to the copies, you'll always have your originals to return to. In the discussion that follows, we will assume that you have created a Startup disk and a separate Program disk.

After placing your copy of the Startup disk in disk drive 1, turn on the power for the video monitor, the printer, and the computer. (If your computer is already on, press the CON-TROL, OPEN-APPLE (⌘), and RESET keys simultaneously. On the IIGS, press the CONTROL, APPLE, and RESET keys. If you have an Apple IIc, you'll need to let go of the RESET key last.) You will hear the disk drive activate, and a light on disk drive 1 will light as the disk drive is being read. Booting takes about 10 seconds plus about 8 to 10 seconds if you are preloading the program on a memory expansion card.

Replace the Startup disk with the Program disk when you are prompted to do so by a message on the screen. Insert the

Program disk and press RETURN. When prompted, enter today's date and press RETURN. (If you have the optional system clock, the date will be automatically calculated and displayed for you. Otherwise, AppleWorks will remember the last date entered and display that. If the date displayed by AppleWorks is acceptable, simply press RETURN.) If you make an error in entering the date, press ESC before you press RETURN, and you will be given another opportunity to enter the date.

After the date is accepted, the Main Menu will be displayed.

A Closer Look at the Main Menu

The Main Menu screen has many elements on it that you will find on screens throughout AppleWorks. These elements are pointed out on an Apple IIe screen in Figure 2-1. For example, in the upper left corner of the screen the *assigned disk drive* number (and/or the slot number, depending on the model of your computer) appears, indicating where AppleWorks goes to find and store files. When you boot up, AppleWorks automatically makes drive 1 the assigned drive.

Moving toward the middle at the top of the screen, you see the *name of the screen*, the Main Menu. Every screen in AppleWorks, whether or not it is a menu, has a name that describes its function.

The Main Menu offers you six *options* displayed within the borders of the "index card." When you Add files to the Desktop, you are instructing the computer either to read a file from disk into the computer's temporary memory, the Desktop, or to create a new file and place that on the Desktop as well. If your file is already on the Desktop, you would select the second option, Work with one of the files on the Desktop. In that case, you would be shown an index of all files in memory or on the Desktop. The third option allows you to Save Desktop files to disk permanently. With this option, all of the changes you have made to a file during an AppleWorks session will be permanently saved. If you have too many files on your Desktop and need to clear some space in your memory, you must select the fourth option, Remove files from the Desktop. This allows you to clear memory space for other files either by saving the files on the Desktop on the disk and then removing them from the Desktop, or by throwing away the files without first saving them. It's your choice whether to save the Desktop files first or not. Option 5, Other Activities, allows you to change the default disk drive, format a disk, and perform other activities. To leave the Main Menu and AppleWorks, you select option 6, Quit.

Another way that you are asked to communicate with the computer is through prompts. At the bottom of the screen, beneath the dashed line, is the *prompt line. Prompts* are messages that appear on the screen asking you to enter information or instructions. For example, you are prompted with a

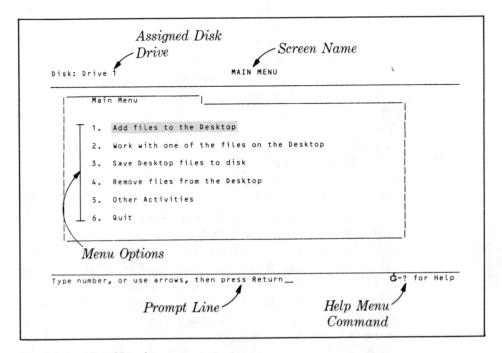

Figure 2-1. Main Menu layout

message to enter new file names. Another prompt requests the date when you boot AppleWorks. The prompt on the Main Menu asks you to enter on the prompt line the number of the option you want from the menu or to move the cursor to it using the arrow keys. You'll do this in a minute.

On the bottom right the command for getting help from the Help menu instructions is displayed. To get help, you press the key with an open apple graphic on it (to the left of the spacebar) and the question mark key simultaneously. In our text we use the letters OA (for OPEN-APPLE) instead of the Apple symbol (🍎) to refer to this key. In the screen illustrations, the OPEN-APPLE is shown as an @ sign. Now let's look at the Help menu.

Getting Help

Press the OA key and the ? key (question mark) simultaneously to scan the Help screen. Unless you have an expanded memory card, you will hear the computer accessing the disk for the Help screen. The computer must do this occasionally when a desired item is not in memory. AppleWorks pauses in the meantime. Simply wait until the Help screen appears and then continue.

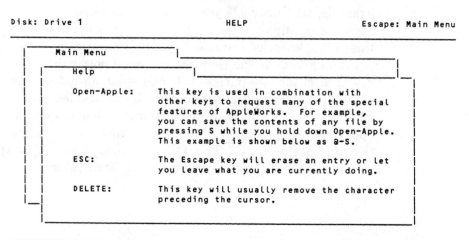

```
Disk: Drive 1                    HELP              Escape: Main Menu
_____
|    _____|_____
|   | Main Menu          |                                |
|   |   _____|_____|__
|   |  | Help               |                                 |
|   |  |                    |                                 |
|   |  | Open-Apple:    This key is used in combination with  |
|   |  |                other keys to request many of the special
|   |  |                features of AppleWorks.  For example, |
|   |  |                you can save the contents of any file by
|   |  |                pressing S while you hold down Open-Apple.
|   |  |                This example is shown below as @-S.    |
|   |  |                                                      |
|   |  | ESC:           The Escape key will erase an entry or let
|   |  |                you leave what you are currently doing.|
|   |  |                                                      |
|   |  | DELETE:        This key will usually remove the character
|   |__|                preceding the cursor.                 |
|      |                                                      |
|      |_____|
_____
Use arrows to see remainder of Help _              56K Avail.
```

Press the DOWN ARROW key to look at all of the commands presented. This Help screen is unique to the Main Menu. Each component of AppleWorks (that is, the word processor, data base, and spreadsheet) has its own Help screen.

Look at the first instruction listed on the menu: the Open-Apple instruction. On either side of the spacebar are two important keys: the OPEN-APPLE (OA) key to the left of the spacebar and the CLOSED-APPLE key to the right. (On the IIGS keyboard these keys are called APPLE and OPTIONS respectively.) These keys are used in conjunction with other keys in key combinations; that is, you hold down the OA key while you press one or two other keys. The combination of keys informs AppleWorks that a command is being entered rather than a number or letter. For example, if you press the OPEN-APPLE key and the S key together, AppleWorks knows that you are directing it to Save a file. Without the OPEN-APPLE key, AppleWorks would assume you were entering the letter s.

Both the OPEN-APPLE and CLOSED-APPLE keys perform exactly the same function in AppleWorks. They may be used interchangeably and so are *both* referred to as the OA key in this book (and in the Apple documentation). When you are to use an OPEN-APPLE key combination, a hyphen will be placed between the OA key and the other key you are to press. For example, OA-? instructs you to press either one of the OPEN-APPLE keys plus the question mark key. As you now know, this is AppleWorks' command for the Help menu.

Turning back to the Help screen, you'll notice that the ESC key is used for two purposes. It can erase an entry, such as today's date, which you just entered. It can also let you cancel an action you're currently performing. For example, in the upper right-hand corner of the screen, you'll see the message "Escape: Main Menu." This tells you that if you press the ESC key, you will be returned to the Main Menu screen.

Thus, the ESC key is your handy "out" key. You can use it to halt commands you want to abort—for example, a command to delete a block of text—or to return to a previous screen without invoking more options or commands. Keep an eye on the Escape route message. You'll use ESC often to help you move around in AppleWorks and to cancel operations you're finished with.

At this point, you needn't concern yourself with the other commands listed on this Help menu. They'll be used later in the course of practicing with AppleWorks.

In the lower right-hand corner of the Help screen, there is another new message that you'll see often. This message tells you that you now have "56K" (approximately 56,000 characters) of space available to you on the Desktop. (Depending on the amount of memory that your computer has, this number may vary from those in this book.) As you create files or retrieve files to put on the Desktop, this number will decrease. You will need to watch this figure as you create your files since your files are restricted to this size. The Desktop space may fill, in which case you'll have to remove some files from the Desktop in order to continue working with a file.

Now press ESC to return to the Main Menu.

Changing the Assigned Disk Drive

AppleWorks automatically "assigns" a disk drive that is used for retrieving and storing new data files. When you first start up AppleWorks, drive 1 is the assigned disk drive (and at the moment contains the Program disk with the Apple-Works software). If you don't change the assigned disk drive, you will either have to store data files on the Program disk, or constantly exchange the data disk for the Program disk.

To avoid these awkward procedures, change the disk assignment to drive 2. That tells AppleWorks that you want to dedicate drive 1 to programs and drive 2 to data.

From the starting point in the Main Menu, you should go to the Other Activities menu in order to change the disk assignment. To select the option from the menu, you will move the highlighting pointer directly to the option you want and press RETURN.

Follow these steps to change the assigned disk drive:

1. Select option 5, Other Activities, by pressing the DOWN ARROW key until the Other Activities option is highlighted, and then press RETURN.

The Other Activities menu will be displayed, like this:

```
Disk: Drive 1                    OTHER ACTIVITIES                Escape: Main Menu
_____
  |‾‾‾‾‾‾‾‾‾‾‾‾‾‾‾‾‾‾‾‾‾‾‾‾‾|_____
  |     Main Menu          |                                                     |
  |  |‾‾‾‾‾‾‾‾‾‾‾‾‾‾‾‾‾‾‾‾‾‾‾|_____|
  |  |   Other Activities  |_____|_
  |  |                                                                          |
  |  |  1.  Change current disk drive or ProDOS prefix                          |
  |  |                                                                          |
  |  |  2.  List all files on the current disk drive                            |
  |  |                                                                          |
  |  |  3.  Create a subdirectory                                               |
  |  |                                                                          |
  |  |  4.  Delete files from disk                                              |
  |  |                                                                          |
  |  |  5.  Format a blank disk                                                 |
  |  |                                                                          |
  |__|  6.  Select standard location of data disk                              |
  |                                                                            |
  |     7.  Specify information about your printer(s)                          |
  |_____|
_____
Type number, or use arrows, then press Return _                       56K Avail.
```

The first option, Change current disk drive or ProDOS prefix, is already highlighted since AppleWorks assumes that this is the option you'll usually want.

2. Press RETURN to select this first option.

The Change Current Disk menu is now displayed:

```
Disk: Disk 1              CHANGE CURRENT DISK        Escape: Other Activities
_____
  |-------Main Menu--------|_____|
  | |-----Other Activities----|_____|_
  | | |----Change Current Disk--|_____|_
  | | |                                                              | |
  | | |                                                              | |
  | | |    Disk drives you can use:                                  | |
  | | |                                                              | |
  | | |    1.  Disk 1                                                | |
  | | |    2.  Disk 2                                                | |
  | | |    3.  ProDOS directory                                      | |
  | |_|                                                              | |
  |_|  |                                                             |_|
    |__|_____|
_____
Type number, or use arrows, then press Return __          56K Avail.
```

You have three options to select from. Disk 1, which is highlighted, is currently the assigned disk drive; this is the one you want to change. Option 3 would give you an opportunity to change the ProDOS pathname if you are using directories. (Users with a hard disk will want to use directories to help organize their disks into smaller segments. Most floppy disks don't require directories, since they hold fewer files and the files can be effectively organized disk by disk.) You want to select the second option, Disk 2.

3. Press the DOWN ARROW key to highlight Disk 2 and press RETURN.

The Other Activities menu will be redisplayed. You can see that the disk drive assignment has been changed by the message in the upper left-hand corner of the screen. This new assignment will remain in effect until you change it, or until you reboot AppleWorks.

Now you need to prepare some blank disks for use in AppleWorks.

Formatting Blank Disks

In order for AppleWorks to be able to use new disks, they must be formatted. Formatting disks simply prepares the disks for use. If any old data resides on the disk, formatting erases it. If the disk has never been used, formatting prepares it to receive data by building the framework for a directory and other required functions. Exactly what happens during formatting is not important to know; the important thing is that formatting erases a disk and prepares it for use by AppleWorks. All disks must be formatted before you can use them.

From the Other Activities menu, you will select the fifth option, and this time you will select the option from the menu by typing the option number directly.

You will be formatting three disks to use in the practice sessions in this book. To format the disks, follow these steps:

1. Type 5 for the fifth option, Format a blank disk, and press RETURN.

The Disk formatter screen will be displayed:

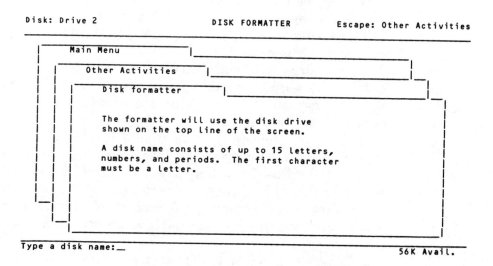

```
Disk: Drive 2                 DISK FORMATTER          Escape: Other Activities
_____
   |   Main Menu               |_____
   |   |   Other Activities        |_____
   |   |   |   Disk formatter           |_____
   |   |   |                                                                    |
   |   |   |       The formatter will use the disk drive                        |
   |   |   |       shown on the top line of the screen.                         |
   |   |   |                                                                    |
   |   |   |       A disk name consists of up to 15 letters,                    |
   |   |   |       numbers, and periods.  The first character                   |
   |   |   |       must be a letter.                                            |
   |   |   |                                                                    |
   |   |   |                                                                    |
   |   |_ |                                                                     |
   |      |                                                                     |
   |      |_                                                                    |
   |        |_____|
_____
Type a disk name:__                                              56K Avail.
```

It tells you that drive 2 will be used to do the formatting. It also advises you on how to enter a name for the disk—that is, to use up to 15 letters, numbers, and periods, with the first character always a letter. The name will be used to identify this disk from others.

2. Enter **AppleWorks1** with no spaces between the letters and the number, and then press RETURN.

3. Place your blank disk into drive 2.

4. Press the spacebar to signal the formatting to begin.

You will see a screen cautioning you that the present contents of your disk will be destroyed by formatting. If the disk has already been formatted using ProDOS, the volume name will be displayed. If this is the disk you want to use, type **YES** and press RETURN; otherwise, press RETURN and insert another disk into drive 2.

The disk drive light will turn on as the disk is being formatted. The word "Formatting" will appear on the screen. When the formatting is completed, the words "Successfully formatted" will appear.

At this point, remove the disk from drive 2 and label it "AppleWorks1." Then press the spacebar so that you can return to the Disk formatter screen to insert, name, and format another disk. Format two more disks, and name them **AppleWorks2** and **AppleWorks3**, respectively. Don't forget to label each one with its name after it has been formatted.

5. Press ESC to return to the Other Activities menu when you are finished formatting both disks.

6. Press ESC again to return to the Main Menu screen.

You can insert the disk labeled AppleWorks1 into drive 2 and put the other two disks away for now. AppleWorks1 will be used to store the file you'll be creating next.

Creating a Word Processing File

Now you are ready to create a file. On the Main Menu, option 1, Add files to the Desktop, is what you want. Actually, this option is the one you will use whether the file is new or old.

That is, when you add a file to the Desktop, you can either retrieve an existing file from the disk, or create a new file.

Since Add files to the Desktop is the choice on the menu that AppleWorks assumes you will usually select, it is highlighted; the highlighting indicates that the option is preselected for you. Thus, you can select the option by simply pressing RETURN. If the correct option were not highlighted, you would, of course, select the one you wanted by either moving the cursor to it or typing the option number and pressing RETURN.

1. From the Main Menu select option 1, Add files to the Desktop, by pressing RETURN.

Having selected this option, you will be shown the Add Files menu:

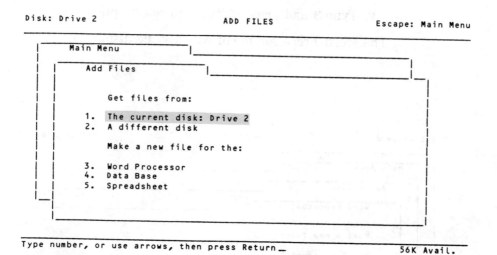

```
Disk: Drive 2                  ADD FILES              Escape: Main Menu
_____
  |-----------------------------|_____
  |   Main Menu                 |                                |
  |  |-----------------------------|_____|
  |  |   Add Files                 |                             | |
  |  |                                                           | |
  |  |      Get files from:                                      | |
  |  |                                                           | |
  |  |   1.  The current disk: Drive 2                           | |
  |  |   2.  A different disk                                    | |
  |  |                                                           | |
  |  |      Make a new file for the:                             | |
  |  |                                                           | |
  |  |   3.  Word Processor                                      | |
  |  |   4.  Data Base                                           | |
  |  |   5.  Spreadsheet                                         | |
  |__|                                                           | |
     |                                                           | |
     |_____| |
      |_____|
_____
Type number, or use arrows, then press Return _          56K Avail.
```

When you specified that you wanted to add files to the Desktop, you didn't tell AppleWorks whether you wanted to add a new file or an existing one. The Add Files menu is where you clarify your need. The Add Files menu allows you to accomplish three tasks: (1) get an existing file from your currently assigned disk, (2) change your currently assigned disk if it isn't where your desired file is, and (3) create a new file for one of the components.

You'll notice that you could have changed the disk assignment on this screen rather than using the Other Activities menu. But it was more efficient to use the Other Activities screen since you also needed to format the blank disks from that screen. (This is a good example of how AppleWorks has provided alternative ways of performing tasks for your convenience.)

Since you want to create a new word processing file, option 3 is the choice to select.

2. Type **3** and press RETURN to select option number 3.

The Word Processor menu will now be displayed:

```
Disk: Drive 2                    WORD PROCESSOR              Escape: Add Files
_____
 |‾‾‾‾‾‾‾‾‾‾‾‾‾‾‾‾‾‾‾‾‾‾‾‾‾|_____
 | |  Main Menu          ||                                              |
 | |‾‾‾‾‾‾‾‾‾‾‾‾‾‾‾‾‾‾‾‾‾‾‾|_____ |
 | | |  Add Files         ||                                            |_|
 | | |‾‾‾‾‾‾‾‾‾‾‾‾‾‾‾‾‾‾‾‾‾‾‾|_____ |
 | | | |  Word Processor     ||                                          |_|
 | | | |                     |                                            |
 | | | |  Make a new file:   |                                            |
 | | | |                     |                                            |
 | | | |  1.  From scratch   |                                            |
 | | | |                     |                                            |
 | | | |  2.  From a text (ASCII) file                                   |
 | | | |                                                                 |
 |_| | |                                                                 |
   |_| |                                                                 |
     |_|_____ |
_____
Type number, or use arrows, then press Return_           56K Avail.
```

The Word Processor menu presents two options: you can create a file from scratch or you can use an existing ASCII file. You would use the ASCII file if you were tranferring information from a package other than AppleWorks (from AppleWriter, for example).

Since you want to create a file from scratch, not edit an existing ASCII file, you'll want to select option 1, From scratch.

3. Press RETURN to accept the highlighted option.

You must now name this new file. Filenames can be 15 characters long. They can contain both letters and numbers, but must begin with a letter, and they can contain either upper- or lowercase letters, numbers, periods, and spaces (but not special characters such as ?-@#$%△,). Let's first enter a name incorrectly to see what AppleWorks will do, and then enter the filename correctly.

4. In response to the prompt, Type a name for this new file, enter the name, **First-file**, and then press RETURN (the dash in the name is incorrect).

Appleworks beeps when you make an error it can detect. For example, it beeps when you type in the wrong instruction during a command or when you type in a filename with characters other than letters, numbers, and periods. Don't be alarmed when AppleWorks beeps. It's AppleWorks' way of telling you to keep alert. Now let's enter the correct name.

5. Enter the name **Opening.ltr** and press RETURN.

You will be shown the Review/Add/Change screen.

The Review/Add/Change Screen

Before you actually enter the file's contents, let's look at the screen itself, as shown in Figure 2-2. It is different from the others in that it is mostly blank. This is so you can enter text as you please. It is like a blank sheet of paper, waiting for you to type on it.

On the top line, you'll see the name of the file you're working on, which in this case is Opening.ltr. In the center, the name of the screen, Review/ Add/Change, indicates that this is the screen where you can create, edit, and correct new documents or revise existing documents as you wish. In the upper right-hand corner, you'll see the name of the screen that you will return to if you press the ESC key. As mentioned earlier, the ESC key cancels whatever you're doing and returns you to an earlier task or screen—in this case, to the Main Menu screen.

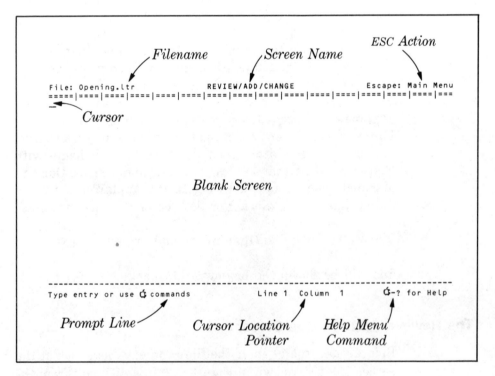

Figure 2-2.   Review/Add/Change screen

At the bottom of the screen, beneath the dashed line, is the prompt line. Like the prompt line on the Main Menu screen, the prompt line here is where you'll receive messages from the program and respond by entering commands.

Also shown on this line are the current line and column numbers. These show you exactly where your cursor is. Experiment with the cursor keys now. Press the LEFT and RIGHT ARROW keys, noticing how the column numbers change. Then press the DOWN and UP ARROW keys, noticing the line numbers. In Chapter 3 you will use these numbers to help you line up columns in a letter.

Getting Help From Within the Word Processor

On the lower right-hand side of the screen are the Help menu directions. Press OA-? to see the word processing Help screen. This Help menu, unlike the Main Menu's Help menu, lists all commands available to you in the word processing component. Each of the components has a unique Help menu that can be used whenever you've forgotten which command to use. The document on the screen will not go away; it will reappear immediately after you've pressed the ESC key.

You should now be looking at the list of word processing commands:

```
File: Opening.ltr                      HELP            Escape: Review/Add/Change
=====|====|====|====|====|====|====|====|====|====|====|====|====|====|===
                       a-C    Copy text (includes cut and paste)

                       a-D    Delete text

                       a-F    Find occurrences of....

                       a-K    Calculate page numbers

                       a-M    Move text (includes cut and paste)

                       a-N    Change name of file

                       a-O    Options for print formatting

                       a-P    Print

                       a-R    Replace occurrences of....

                       a-T    Set and clear tab stops
-------------------------------------------------------------------------
Use arrows to see remainder of Help_                        56K Avail.
```

(Recall that the OPEN-APPLE symbol on the screen appears as an @ sign in this text.) Use the UP ARROW and DOWN ARROW keys to view all the commands. When you've done this, press ESC to return to the Review/Add/Change screen.

Entering Your Text

Now let's enter the text of your file. Suppose that your company, ABC Company, is opening a new store and you want to send a short announcement to your customers. Figure 2-3 shows the letter you will be writing.

Notice that although you'll be entering the customer name and address as you type this letter now, in Chapter 9 you'll learn how to merge a separate name and address file with this letter so that you don't have to type the individual names and addresses for each letter.

If you make a typing error, press the DELETE key and then type the correct letters. You'll learn some very efficient ways to correct errors in the next chapter.

Use the RETURN key to create blank lines and to end paragraphs. You will need to use the RETURN key, for example, to generate blank lines to space the text down from the top of the page. (Later you'll learn how to create the top margins using the formatting features of AppleWorks.) All paragraphs and single-phrase lines should terminate with a RETURN to indicate that a new paragraph is desired or that the following text should start on a new line.

```
Aires Quick Copy
1345 South 8th
Bellevue, WA  98004

Dear Larry Aires,

ABC COMPANY is pleased to announce the opening of a new
retail outlet, the Office Mart.  It will be located in the
Evergreen Northwest Shopping Mall, in Bellevue, Washington.

The grand opening will be on February 4, 1988 and you are
invited to attend.  We will be showing off our new line of
paper products.  Wine and cheese will be served and there
will be a drawing for a door prize.  Be sure to attend!

Sincerely,


Your Name
```

Figure 2-3. Opening.ltr text to be entered

1. Enter five blank lines by pressing RETURN five times.

2. Enter the customer's name and address, ending each line with a RETURN as you would on a typewriter.

3. Separate the address from the greeting by pressing RETURN to create a blank line.

4. Enter the greeting and end it with a RETURN.

5. Separate the greeting from the body of the letter by pressing RETURN to create another blank line.

As you begin entering the body, you will notice one of the most productive characteristics of a word processor: *word wrap*. Word wrap automatically moves words to the next line when the end of the line is encountered, without your pressing the RETURN key. For example, notice how this happens with the words "retail" and "Evergreen" on the first two lines. As you type in the text, AppleWorks notices where the end of the line is, calculates that there is not enough room for what's being typed, and moves the words to the next line, as shown in Figure 2-4.

Remember, however, that you must press the RETURN at the end of a paragraph.

6. Enter the body of the letter.
7. Enter the closing of the letter and fill in your own name.

Now that you've typed your first letter, be sure to save it before printing it.

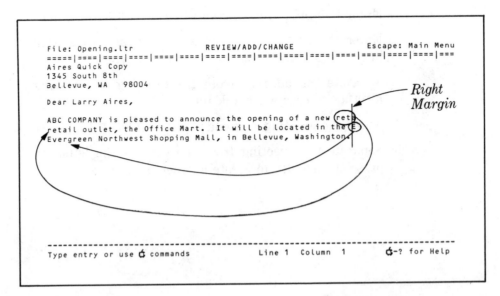

Figure 2-4. Example of word wrap

Saving Your File

Periodically you must save your text in order to protect your work against loss. It may be lost for several reasons, from electrical power outages or fluctuations to your own errors. At this point Opening.ltr only exists on the computer Desktop—that is, in its temporary memory. You must save it on disk so that it is permanently stored.

When you save Opening.ltr (or any other file), you are copying the contents of what is on the Desktop onto a disk. Whether you save the file or not, the copy of Opening.ltr that is on the Desktop will disappear: you'll either remove it from the Desktop or turn off the power. But the copy on the disk is permanent. Later you'll be able to remove the disk from drive 2 and store it for future use.

AppleWorks provides two ways to save your files. One method is a "quick save" by means of which you save the file but remain in the editing environment so that you can continue with your work. The other method of saving takes longer and you must leave the editing environment to do it, but it has more options. Chapter 3 will explore this more complex saving procedure and its options. Now let's do a quick save on your Opening.ltr.

Press OA-S for Save. You will be shown a temporary screen displaying a message that the file is being saved. After a few seconds, when your document has been saved onto the disk, you will be returned to your original editing place. (You can "undo" the save by pressing ESC before the save operation has been completed.)

Now you are ready to print the letter.

Printing Your File

Prior to printing a file with AppleWorks, you must tell AppleWorks about your printer. This process is called *installing your printer*. If your printer is not installed, refer to Appendix A for instructions on how to set up your printer to respond to AppleWorks. Once the printer is installed, you only have to turn it on, insert paper and a ribbon, and give AppleWorks the Print command.

Printing a file in AppleWorks is very easy. Your file must be on the Desktop, which Opening.ltr is. After that, you simply follow these steps to print your file:

1. Press OA-P to invoke the Print command.

The Print menu will be displayed, with questions listed at the bottom of the screen:

```
File: Opening.ltr              PRINT MENU           Escape: Review/Add/Change
=====|====|====|====|====|====|====|====|====|====|====|====|====|====|====|===
Aires Quick Copy
1345 South 8th
Bellevue, WA  98004

Dear Larry Aires,

ABC COMPANY is pleased to announce the opening of a new
retail outlet, the Office Mart.  It will be located in the
Evergreen Northwest Shopping Mall, in Bellevue, Washington.

The grand opening will be on February 4, 1988 and you are
invited to attend.  We will be showing off our new line of
paper products.  Wine and cheese will be served and there
will be a drawing for a door prize.  Be sure to attend!

Sincerely,


Your Name
--------------------------------------------------------------------------------
Print from? Beginning  This page  Cursor
```

The Print menu asks you how much of your document you want to print. You will be asked whether you want to print the entire document from the Beginning, from the top of This page to the end of the document, or from the Cursor position to the end of the document. You want to print the document from the Beginning, which is the highlighted option.

2. Press RETURN to print the whole file from the beginning.

You will then be shown a second Print menu, which gives you the option of printing to a named printer or to disk. The screen looks like this (it may list different printers):

```
File: Opening.ltr                    PRINT MENU            Escape: Review/Add/Change
=====|====|====|====|====|====|====|====|====|====|====|====|====|====|====|===




                 Where do you want to print the file?

                 1.    ImageWriter

                 2.    Qume 5

                 3.    A text (ASCII) file on disk




------------------------------------------------------------------------------
Type number, or use arrows, then press Return                        56K Avail.
```

If you choose the disk file, you will create a print file on disk that you can use with programs other than AppleWorks. In this case any special formatting that you have done will be removed, except for the RETURN characters. AppleWorks assumes you will want the printer, which, in this case, you do.

3. Press RETURN to indicate that you want the file printed on the printer.

Finally, you will be given a chance to enter the number of copies (up to nine) that you may wish to print. AppleWorks guesses that you will normally want one copy.

4. Press RETURN and the printer will begin printing.

You can halt the printer in two ways. By pressing ESC you cancel printing and return to the Review/Add/Change screen. Or you can cause the printer to pause and then continue by pressing the SPACEBAR to stop and start the printing.

In this chapter you explored some of the features making up AppleWorks' environment: its use of memory and disk storage, the way AppleWorks uses menus to lead you through the many functions you can perform, and the way you can use the printer to produce various types of electronic and printed copies. You also got a taste of the word processing component when you created a letter and printed it. In Chapter 3 you are going to continue learning about word processing. Specifically, you will learn how to edit and manipulate your text so that you can work with more complex and lengthy documents.

3

Working
With the Word
Processor

You learned in Chapter 2 that it's easy to create a simple document with AppleWorks. In Chapter 3 you will produce a more complex letter that will be of special interest to readers who write business letters or use form letters. The letter contains several intentional errors to demonstrate the editing features, such as inserting and deleting text, and correcting mistyped characters, that AppleWorks provides. As you enter the document, you will also practice formatting it, with such formatting options as setting margins, centering a title, and entering a table. Finally, you will save the letter permanently on a disk and print it.

In a second exercise, having made a copy of the first document under a new and different name, you will turn it into a form letter and then save and print it.

Setting Up a New File: A Quick Review

Your first step is to bring up AppleWorks as you learned to do in Chapter 2. Follow these familiar steps to do it. If you have questions, return to Chapter 2 and review the detailed procedure for bringing up AppleWorks and creating a new file.

1. First, using the Startup disk, boot AppleWorks, replacing the Startup disk with the Program disk when requested to do so.
2. Enter today's date when prompted for it.
3. From the Main Menu select option 1, Add files to the Desktop, by simply pressing RETURN .
4. Insert the Appleworks1 data disk into disk drive 2.

This will be used as the storage disk for your letter. When you reach the Add Files menu, check which disk drive is the assigned drive by looking at the upper left-hand corner of the screen. If it is drive 1 and you have two disk drives, change the assigned drive to drive 2 in this way:

5. Position the cursor on the second option, A different disk, and press RETURN.
6. Select drive 2 by positioning the cursor on option 2 and pressing RETURN.

Now you're back at the Add Files menu, ready to perform the task of creating a new file for word processing. To do this:

7. Select option 3, Make a new file for the: 3. Word Processor, by typing **3** and pressing RETURN.
8. On the Word Processor menu, press RETURN to accept the highlighted option to create a file From scratch.
9. In response to the prompt, Type a name for this new file, enter the name, **Advant.ltr.**

The name tells you that the file is a letter (ltr) and that it is addressed to your customer, the Advant Printing Company.

10.Press RETURN to get the Review/Add/Change screen.

Entering the Letter

The letter is composed of five parts: the title; the name, address, and greeting; the main text; a small table; and the closing. Each of these parts will give you an opportunity to work with different features of AppleWorks' word processor. But first you must perform some formatting in order to set the margins and center the title.

Setting Margins and Centering the Title

The first job in composing the Order Acknowledgment letter is to set margins for the letter and to center the title. This will give you the chance to work with AppleWorks' formatting capabilities.

Setting printer options. As you will recall from Chapter 1, formatting tells the printer how to print various page and character attributes of the text. Since formatting features are really instructions to the printer, AppleWorks calls them printer options. Let's take a look at these options:

1. Press OA-O for printer options.

You will see a half screen of options, as displayed in Figure 3-1.

The Printer Options menu lists the formatting options in four columns. Each option is identified by a two-character code; for example, "PW" represents "Platen Width." To change an option, you simply enter the code for the option and then answer any prompts, such as the number of inches for the platen width. Some of the options don't have additional prompts, such as the option for centering (CN). This option is simply an on/off switch: the line is centered, or it is not.

The highlighted strip across the top of the menu (in the center of the screen) reveals certain information about the

```
   File: Advant.ltr                PRINTER OPTIONS        Escape: Review/Add/Change
   =====|====|====|====|====|====|====|====|====|====|====|====|====|====|====|===




        PW=8.0  LM=1.0  RM=1.0  CI=10  UJ  PL=11.0  TM=0.0  BM=2.0  LI=6  SS
   Option: _               UJ: Unjustified     GB: Group Begin       BE: Boldface End
                           CN: Centered         GE: Group End         +B: Superscript Beg
   PW: Platen Width        PL: Paper Length     HE: Page Header       +E: Superscript End
   LM: Left Margin         TM: Top Margin       FO: Page Footer       -B: Subscript Begin
   RM: Right Margin        BM: Bottom Margin    SK: Skip Lines        -E: Subscript End
   CI: Chars per Inch      LI: Lines per Inch   PN: Page Number       UB: Underline Begin
   P1: Proportional-1      SS: Single Space     PE: Pause Each page   UE: Underline End
   P2: Proportional-2      DS: Double Space     PH: Pause Here        PP: Print Page No.
   IN: Indent              TS: Triple Space     SM: Set a Marker      EK: Enter Keyboard
   JU: Justified           NP: New Page         BB: Boldface Begin    MM: Mail Merge
```

Figure 3-1. Printer Options menu

printer options. Some options have preset values and this strip displays their values. For example, the platen width (PW) is preset to 8.0 inches, the right margin (RM) to 1.0 inch, the characters per inch (CI) to 10 characters per inch, and so on.

The printer options you will be entering will remain in effect until they are changed to something else. Some options only last for a sentence or a paragraph. You'll learn about these and the rest of the important printer options in Chapter 6.

When you're writing text, you will call up the Printer Options menu several times. Formatting is not an activity you normally perform just once per document; rather, you do it as you see the need for formatting. For example, right now you want to set margins and center a title in order to see how the formatting affects the text on the screen as it is entered. You could format the text later, but then you wouldn't be able to see how the text looks as it is entered.

Now let's look at the settings for the top and bottom margins, TM=0.0 and BM=2.0, which you can see in the highlighted strip. These margins are not acceptable for the business letter we will be writing; you need to change both margins to 1 inch. (The other margin settings are fine for now.)

2. Enter **TM** for Top Margin, and press RETURN.

3. In response to the message "Inches," enter **1** and press RETURN.

```
File: Advant.ltr                PRINTER OPTIONS       Escape: Review/Add/Change
=====|=====|=====|=====|=====|=====|=====|=====|=====|=====|=====|=====|=====|=====|=====|===
---------Top Margin: 1.0 inches
```

```
     PW=8.0  LM=1.0   RM=1.0  CI=10  UJ  PL=11.0  TM=1.0  BM=2.0  LI=6  SS
Option: _                 UJ: Unjustified       GB: Group Begin      BE: Boldface End
                          CN: Centered          GE: Group End        +B: Superscript Beg
PW: Platen Width          PL: Paper Length       HE: Page Header      +E: Superscript End
LM: Left Margin           TM: Top Margin         FO: Page Footer      -B: Subscript Begin
RM: Right Margin          BM: Bottom Margin      SK: Skip Lines       -E: Subscript End
CI: Chars per Inch        LI: Lines per Inch     PN: Page Number      UB: Underline Begin
P1: Proportional-1        SS: Single Space       PE: Pause Each page  UE: Underline End
P2: Proportional-2        DS: Double Space       PH: Pause Here       PP: Print Page No.
IN: Indent                TS: Triple Space       SM: Set a Marker     EK: Enter Keyboard
JU: Justified             NP: New Page           BB: Boldface Begin   MM: Mail Merge
```

You'll see two indications of the changed option: the highlighted strip on the screen will show the change for the top margin setting, and on the top of your screen, you can see a message "----Top Margin: 1.0 inches."

4. Enter **BM** for the Bottom Margin, and press RETURN.

5. In response to the message "Inches," enter **1** and press RETURN.

Again notice the changed margin setting both on the top of the screen and in the highlighted strip on the Printer Options menu.

Before leaving the Printer Options menu, center the title. The Centered option must be used differently from the options for setting margins. Once you have specified that you want to center text, the Centered option remains in effect until you turn it off; the option centers *all* lines, whether or not they are titles, since AppleWorks can't distinguish a line of text from a title unless you tell it.

Consequently, you must first select the Centered option, then type in the text to be centered, and finally turn off the Centered option.

Follow these steps:

6. Type the option code listed on the menu for centering text, **CN**, and press RETURN.

You'll see the same two indications of your change: beneath the filename, Advant.ltr, you see "----Centered." Also on the top line of the Printer Options menu, the Centered code, **CN**, will appear as shown here:

```
File: Advant.ltr              PRINTER OPTIONS        Escape: Review/Add/Change
=====|====|====|====|====|====|====|====|====|====|====|====|====|====|====|===
--------Top Margin:  1.0 inches
--------Bottom Margin:  1.0 inches
--------Centered
```

```
    PW=8.0  LM=1.0  RM=1.0  CI=10  CN  PL=11.0  TM=1.0  BM=1.0  LI=6  SS
Option:_                 UJ: Unjustified      GB: Group Begin      BE: Boldface End
                         CN: Centered         GE: Group End        +B: Superscript Beg
PW: Platen Width         PL: Paper Length     HE: Page Header      +E: Superscript End
LM: Left Margin          TM: Top Margin       FO: Page Footer      -B: Subscript Begin
RM: Right Margin         BM: Bottom Margin    SK: Skip Lines       -E: Subscript End
CI: Chars per Inch       LI: Lines per Inch   PN: Page Number      UB: Underline Begin
P1: Proportional-1       SS: Single Space     PE: Pause Each page  UE: Underline End
P2: Proportional-2       DS: Double Space     PH: Pause Here       PP: Print Page No.
IN: Indent               TS: Triple Space     SM: Set a Marker     EK: Enter Keyboard
JU: Justified            NP: New Page         BB: Boldface Begin   MM: Mail Merge
```

Now you must leave the Printer Options menu and enter the title.

7. Press ESC to leave the Printer Options menu.

The "----Centered" message and the Printer Options menu will disappear. (You'll learn later how to make the message reappear at will.) Now continue with the title.

8. Press the CAPS LOCK key and type in the words **ORDER ACKNOLEDGMENT** (deliberately misspelling it) and then press RETURN.

The title will be centered between the preset right and left margins of the text, like this:

```
File: Advant.ltr              REVIEW/ADD/CHANGE           Escape: Main Menu
=====|====|====|====|====|====|====|====|====|====|====|====|====|====|===
                    ORDER ACKNOLEDGMENT
---
```

```
------------------------------------------------------------------------
Type entry or use ⌂ commands            Line 5  Column  1        ⌂-? for Help
```

You must now disable the Centered option so that the next lines entered will not also be centered. To disable it, you must return to the Printer Options menu and select another option.

In addition to centering a line, you have two other choices for formatting lines on the page. One is to align the right-hand edge of the text, or to *justify* it (to "justify" text in AppleWorks means to "right-justify" it). The second is to *unjustify* text, or print the text with ragged right margins. You can only specify one of these formatting options at a time. Figure 3-2 shows examples of centered, justified, and unjustified text.

Follow these steps to instruct AppleWorks to cancel the Centered option and allow the next lines to be ragged, or unjustified, which is the option you want for the name, address, and greeting of the letter:

9. Press OA-O to get the Printer Options menu.

10. Enter **UJ** for Unjustified, and press RETURN.

You'll see both the "----Unjustified" message appear and that the code UJ has replaced the CN in the highlighted strip of the Printer Options menu.

11. Press ESC to return to the Review/Add/Change screen.

The "----Unjustified" message and the Printer Options menu will disappear, leaving you with a blank screen. The formatting options are still in effect, though, until you change them.

```
                    This paragraph is Centered.
        Each line that ends with a RETURN will be centered.
                   It is used for poetry and verse
                      and titles and headings.


This paragraph is Unjustified.  That is, the right margins
are ragged, not evenly spaced.  This is the normal format
that you will probably use in your writing.  It is the
default that AppleWorks assigns to each document.


This paragraph is Justified.   The characters on the line
will be spaced so that the right margins are even.  It is
achieved by varying the spacing between words.  This method
of printing presents a more formal appearance of your
document.   You must have a printer that supports
justification before it will work correctly.
```

Figure 3-2. Examples of centered, justified, and unjustified text

Displaying formatting characters. Up to this point you have seen the formatting characters and messages appear intermittently as you select printer options. They disappear when you leave the Printer Options menu. For example, although you cannot see formatting messages such as the "----Unjustified" message, you know they are still in effect. You'll want to see these formatting messages occasionally as you edit, since the image on the screen may not be formatted as you want it to be. To let you see what is controlling the formatting before you make any changes, AppleWorks provides a quick and convenient way for you to check. You simply press OA-Z, for Zoom, and the formatting characters will be displayed.

Press OA-Z now and watch the formatting messages and the RETURN character (the gray block) appear in your text like this:

```
File: Advant.ltr              REVIEW/ADD/CHANGE              Escape: Main Menu
=====|====|====|====|====|====|====|====|====|====|====|====|====|====|===
--------Top Margin:  1.0 inches
--------Bottom Margin:  1.0 inches
--------Centered
                    ORDER ACKNOLEDGMENT
--------Unjustified
▓
```

```
---------------------------------------------------------------------------
Type entry or use ⌕ commands         Line 6  Column  1        ⌕-? for Help
```

Press the OA-Z command a few times, watching how the formatting messages and the RETURN characters appear and disappear. Leave the formatting characters not showing; they tend to be confusing at this point. You'll use them later in the editing session.

Now enter the name, address, and greeting.

Entering the Name, Address, and Greeting

The name and address are entered in much the same way as you would enter them on a typewriter. That is, you type in the name or address and end the line with a RETURN. The RETURN is used to create blank lines and to force the next words entered to begin on a new line.

The following steps will lead you through the entry of the text shown in Figure 3-3. Type the letter as it is. Deliberate errors have been underlined.

```
                    ORDER ACKNOLEDGMENT

Advant Printing Company
100 South Eighth Street
Bellevue, WA  98004

Dear Mr. Johnsonn:

This is to acknowledge that we have receeved your order as
descrobed below.  We can deliver your order by June 7.  We
understand that you are anticippating an additional order.
If you are able to confirm it by the first of Jun, we will
be able to include it with this shipmint.

Your order is as follows:

      Item Qty  Units          Description              Price
      -----------------------------------------------------
        1    5  1000      #10 sub 24 circa 83 Laid EPS  27.53
                         Nantucket Gray
        2    5  Ream      Classic Laid Bond 8 1/2x11     7.46
                         Hearthstone
        3    5  Ream      NCR Bond CF 8 1/2x11           5.31

Thank you for your order.  We are always glad for your
business as you are one of our favorites!

Sincerely Yours,


Your name
```

Figure 3-3. Order Acknowledgment letter with errors

Do not correct them at this point; you will do that later. If you make additional errors, do not bother about them now. You can also correct them later.

1. Release the CAPS LOCK key and press RETURN once to enter a blank line after the title.

2. Type the customer's name and address, ending each line with a RETURN.

3. Press the RETURN to create a blank line after the address.

4. Enter the greeting (note the misspelled name) and press RETURN.

The screen should now look like the following illustration.

```
File: Advant.ltr           REVIEW/ADD/CHANGE          Escape: Main Menu
=====|====|====|====|====|====|====|====|====|====|====|====|====|===
                    ORDER ACKNOLEDGMENT
Advant Printing Company
100 South Eighth Street
Bellevue, WA  98004

Dear Mr. Johnsonn:

___



Type entry or use Ġ commands        Line 12  Column  1       Ġ-? for Help
```

5. Add an additional blank line by pressing RETURN once again.

Entering the Main Text

Entering the body of the letter is handled slightly differently from entering the name and address. This is because of the word wrap feature you saw in Chapter 2. Word wrap, as you remember, automatically moves words to the next line when the end of the line is encountered without your pressing the RETURN key.

Now type in the first paragraph of the letter as shown here, but this time *do not* press the RETURN key at the end of the line. You will see how the words "descrobed" and "understand" on the first two lines are wrapped around to the next lines. Don't forget to enter the underlined errors, and don't worry about any other errors that you may make. End the paragraph with two RETURNs: one to end the paragraph and one for the blank line.

Next, type in the short sentence, "Your order is as follows:", and press RETURN twice. (Again, one RETURN is to terminate the sentence and the other is to create a blank line.) Your screen should now look like the following illustration.

```
File: Advant.ltr               REVIEW/ADD/CHANGE             Escape: Main Menu
=====|====|====|====|====|====|====|====|====|====|====|====|====|====|===
                    ORDER ACKNOWLEDGMENT

Advant Printing Company
100 South Eighth Street
Bellevue, WA  98004

Dear Mr. Johnsonn:

This to acknowledge that we have receeved your order as
descrobed below.  We can deliver your order by June 7.  We
understand that you are anticippating an additional order.
If you are able to confirm it by the first of Jun, we will
be able to include it with this shipmint.

Your order is as follows:

---


-------------------------------------------------------------------------
Type entry or use Ć commands              Line 19  Column 26        Ć-? for Help
```

Setting Up a Small Table

The next part of your letter is a small table itemizing the details of the order. Later, you will learn how to create a table in the data base or spreadsheet components of AppleWorks and copy it into your word processing text. But for simple tables, you can use the word processor.

First, you'll need to set the right margin slightly wider than the rest of the text in order to set up columns for the order information. After setting the margin, you'll enter the column headings and then the actual order detail. You'll create the columns as you would on a typewriter, by pressing the TAB key. The TAB is preset to advance the cursor five spaces at a time. You can change the TAB settings, but for now use them as set. If you should make an error, correct it using the DELETE key, which deletes the character to the left of the cursor. After the error is deleted, type the text correctly. Proceed as follows:

1. Press OA-O for Options.

2. Enter **RM** for Right Margin and press RETURN.

3. Enter .5 inches and press RETURN.

4. Press ESC to leave the Printer Options menu.

Now that your margin is wider, you can enter the column headings.

5. Press TAB, and enter **Item**.

6. Press TAB, and enter **Qty**.

7. Press TAB, and enter **Units**.

8. Press TAB twice, and enter **Description**.

9. Press TAB three times, and enter **Price**.

10. Press RETURN, ending the heading line.

11. Press TAB, type a hyphen (-), and hold it down until the column number is 66 (watch the column number in the bottom middle of the screen).

12. Press RETURN, ending the dotted separator line.

You now have your column headings established, so that you can type the order detail. As you type the detail, be careful not to enter too many tabs or spaces; if you do, the line will wrap around. If you accidentally do cause the line to wrap around, just press the DELETE key until the incorrect spacing is erased, and reenter the line correctly. To enter the detail, follow these steps:

13. Press TAB, and enter **1** for the item number.

14. Press TAB, and enter **5** for the quantity.

15. Press TAB, and enter **1000** for the units.

16. Press TAB twice, and enter **#10 sub 24 circa 83 Laid EPS** for the description.

17. Press TAB, and enter **27.53** for the price.

18. Press RETURN to end the first line for item 1.

This is how your screen should now look:

```
File: Advant.ltr                REVIEW/ADD/CHANGE              Escape: Main Menu
=====|====|====|====|====|====|====|====|====|====|====|====|====|====|====|===
This to acknowledge that we have receeved your order as
descrobed below.  We can deliver your order by June 7.  We
understand that you are anticippating an additional order.
If you are able to confirm it by the first of Jun, we will
be able to include it with this shipmint.

Your order is as follows:

   Item Qty  Units        Description            Price
   --------------------------------------------------------
    1   5    1000     #10 sub 24 circa 83 Laid EPS  27.53
 ─




   ----------------------------------------------------------------------
Type entry or use Ć commands            Line 32  Column 1        Ć-? for Help
```

19. Press TAB five times, and enter **Nantucket Gray** to continue the description for item 1.

20. Press RETURN to signal the end of data entry for the first item.

Continue with items 2 and 3 in the same way. When entering the price information, enter a leading space in front of the dollar figure so that the decimal points will be aligned.

When you are done with the items, your screen will look like this:

```
File: Advant.ltr              REVIEW/ADD/CHANGE              Escape: Main Menu
=====|====|====|====|====|====|====|====|====|====|====|====|====|====|===
This is to acknowledge that we have receeved your order as
descrobed below.  We can deliver your order by June 7.  We
understand that you are anticippating an additional order.
If you are able to confirm it by the first of Jun, we will
be able to include it with this shipmint.

Your order is as follows:

    Item Qty  Units          Description             Price
    -----------------------------------------------------
     1    5   1000      #10 sub 24 circa 83 Laid EPS  27.53
                        Nantucket Gray
     2    5   Ream      Classic Laid Bond 8 1/2x11     7.46
                        Hearthstone
     3    5   Ream      NCR Bond CF 8 1/2x11           5.31
    _



------------------------------------------------------------------------
Type entry or use Ô commands         Line 29  Column  1      Ô-? for Help
```

Finishing the Letter

To complete the letter, press RETURN, type the last sentence, press RETURN twice, and enter the closing, like this:

```
File: Advant.ltr              REVIEW/ADD/CHANGE              Escape: Main Menu
=====|====|====|====|====|====|====|====|====|====|====|====|====|====|===
be able to include it with this shipmint.

Your order is as follows:

    Item Qty  Units          Description             Price
    ----------------------------------------------------
     1    5   1000      #10 sub 24 circa 83 Laid EPS  27.53
                        Nantucket Gray
     2    5   Ream      Classic Laid Bond 8 1/2x11     7.46
                        Hearthstone
     3    5   Ream      NCR Bond CF 8 1/2x11           5.31
Thank you for your order.  We are always glad for your business
as you are one of our favorites!

Sincerely yours,


Your Name _


------------------------------------------------------------------------
Type entry or use Ô commands         Line 36  Column  1      Ô-? for Help
```

Enter your own name as the sender of the letter.

You have just completed entering the letter and are now ready to edit it.

Editing the Letter

You edit a document when you revise or change it. In editing your letter, you will use many new commands. Not only will you learn how to correct errors, but you will also learn how to move the cursor through your text more efficiently.

Moving the Cursor Quickly

Until now the LEFT and RIGHT ARROW keys have been moved one character at a time, and the UP and DOWN ARROW keys one line at a time. This is effective enough, but slow. There are faster methods of moving the cursor.

Move the cursor to the first word in the first paragraph. To move quickly across a line, from the left to right margins and back, you can use the OA-RIGHT ARROW and OA-LEFT ARROW key combinations. These move the cursor across the line by *words* rather than by *characters*. Try these commands now, alternating between margins. If you hold the keys down, the cursor will fly over the line. Continue experimenting with the OA-LEFT ARROW and OA-RIGHT ARROW commands until you are comfortable using them.

To move the cursor quickly to the top and bottom of the screen, you can use the OA-UP ARROW and OA-DOWN ARROW key combinations. Try these as well, sending the cursor to the top and bottom of the screen.

An efficient method of "thumbing" through your text is to use the OA-1 through OA-9 keys. The OA-1 command sends your cursor to the beginning of your document; the OA-9, to the end. The OA-2 through OA-8 commands position your cursor relative distances (20% to 80%) through the document. For example, pressing OA-5 positions the cursor halfway into the document. Experiment with this command. Press OA-1 for the beginning of your document, OA-9 for the end, and OA-5 for halfway.

Inserting and Overstriking

Two ways that errors or typos can be corrected in your text are by *inserting* additional text, or by *overstriking* erroneous text. These two editing modes give you flexibility in how you revise a document. So far, you have been operating in the insert mode since this is the mode that AppleWorks starts with. You can tell that you are in insert mode because the cursor is a blinking underline in this mode.

The overstrike mode is easily obtained by pressing OA-E for Edit. Do this now. See how the cursor changes to a solid rectangle rather than an underline.

Press the OA-E again and see how you return to the insert mode. The OA-E command acts as a switch to transfer you quickly from insert mode to overstrike and back.

As you would expect, inserting causes new characters to be inserted in between existing ones. Overstriking, on the other hand, replaces existing characters by causing them to be typed over. Both methods are very useful for certain situations. You use inserting to add new characters, as when you've left out a letter in a word. You use overstriking when you've typed the wrong letters.

Now use these two editing modes to correct some of the mistakes you deliberately entered. As you correct these errors, you will want to switch back and forth between the modes. When you've omitted a letter or word, the most convenient mode is insert. But when you've typed the wrong letter or word, the overstrike mode is just what you want.

The first error to correct is in the title. There is a missing "W" in "ACKNOLEDGMENT." Follow these steps to correct it:

1. In the title, position your cursor on the letter "L" to the right of where the letter "W" is to be inserted.

2. Check that your cursor is a blinking underline, ensuring that you are in the insert mode. (If you are not, press OA-E.)

3. Then press SHIFT and enter **W** to correct the title.

```
File: Advant.ltr            REVIEW/ADD/CHANGE         Escape: Main Menu
=====|====|====|====|====|====|====|====|====|====|====|====|====|====|====|===
                       ORDER ACKNOWLEDGMENT

Advant Printing Company
100 South Eighth Street
Bellevue, WA  98004

Dear Mr. Johnsonn:

This to acknowledge that we have receeved your order as
descrobed below.  We can deliver your order by June 7.  We
understand that you are anticippating an additional order.
If you are able to confirm it by the first of Jun, we will
be able to include it with this shipmint.

Your order is as follows:

   Item Qty  Units          Description        Price
   ---------------------------------------------------
    1    5   1000      #10 sub 24 circa 83 Laid EPS  27.53
                       Nantucket Gray
-------------------------------------------------------------------------
Type entry or use ⌂ commands          Line 4   Column  1      ⌂-? for Help
```

Although the next error is in the name "Johnsonn," you can skip that for now and correct other errors. In the first sentence of the first paragraph, position your cursor on the misspelled word, "receeved." You will want to replace the second "e" with an "i."

4. Place your cursor under the second "e."

5. Press OA-E to get into overstrike mode.

Note the cursor has changed to a solid rectangle.

```
File: Advant.ltr            REVIEW/ADD/CHANGE         Escape: Main Menu
=====|====|====|====|====|====|====|====|====|====|====|====|====|====|====|===
                       ORDER ACKNOWLEDGMENT

Advant Printing Company
100 South Eighth Street
Bellevue, WA  98004

Dear Mr. Johnsonn:

This to acknowledge that we have receeved your order as
descrobed below.  We can deliver your order by June 7.  We
understand that you are anticippating an additional order.
If you are able to confirm it by the first of Jun, we will
be able to include it with this shipmint.

Your order is as follows:

   Item Qty  Units          Description        Price
   ---------------------------------------------------
    1    5   1000      #10 sub 24 circa 83 Laid EPS  27.53
                       Nantucket Gray
-------------------------------------------------------------------------
Type entry or use ⌂ commands          Line 13  Column 38      ⌂-? for Help
```

6. Enter **i** and see how the offending "e" is replaced with the correct "i."

The next error to be corrected is the misspelled word "descrobed." You are already in the correct mode to overstrike.

7. Place your cursor over the "o" and enter **i** to correct the spelling to "described."

Finally, move your cursor to the last sentence. The "e" in "June" is missing.

8. Press OA-E to return to the insert mode.

9. Position your cursor where the missing letter is to be inserted, over the comma following "Jun," like this:

```
File: Advant.ltr              REVIEW/ADD/CHANGE              Escape: Main Menu
=====|====|====|====|====|====|====|====|====|====|====|====|====|====|====|===
                      ORDER ACKNOWLEDGMENT
Advant Printing Company
100 South Eighth Street
Bellevue, WA  98004

Dear Mr. Johnsonn:

This to acknowledge that we have received your order as
described below.  We can deliver your order by June 7.  We
understand that you are anticippating an additional order.
If you are able to confirm it by the first of Jun, we will
be able to include it with this shipmint.

Your order is as follows:

    Item Qty  Units        Description           Price
    ----------------------------------------------------------
     1   5    1000      #10 sub 24 circa 83 Laid EPS  27.53
                        Nantucket Gray
--------------------------------------------------------------------
Type entry or use Ú commands          Line 16   Column 50     Ú-? for Help
```

10. And then type **e.**

Deleting

In your Order Acknowledgment letter, there are other errors that need to be corrected for which the insert and overstrike modes are not well suited. You must be able to delete characters, words, and sentences as you wish.

AppleWorks allows you to delete in two ways: by deleting single characters and by deleting whole blocks.

Character deletes.   The first way is a simple and fast *character delete* using the DELETE key. You probably have already used this key earlier in entering either Opening.ltr or the order information in the Order Acknowledgment letter. The DELETE key deletes one character to the immediate left of the cursor. Use it now to delete one of the "n"s in the name "Johnsonn."

1. Position your cursor over the last "n" and press the DELETE key.

Notice how the first "n" is deleted. Now find the misspelled word in the second sentence, "anticippating."

2. Position your cursor on the second "p" to delete the first one, and press the DELETE key.

See how the first "p" is deleted and the other letters move to fill in the gap.

Find the misspelled word, "shipmint"—the last word in the first paragraph. You could correct this using the overstrike mode; instead you will delete the "i" and insert an "e" to demonstrate the flexibility of having two editing techniques. By correcting the error in this manner, you avoid having to switch editing modes.

3. Position your cursor over the "n" and press DELETE.

4. Look for the blinking underline cursor to be sure you are in insert mode, and press OA-E if you're not.

5. Type e.

Your text should now look like the following illustration.

```
File: Advant.ltr              REVIEW/ADD/CHANGE            Escape: Main Menu
=====|====|====|====|====|====|====|====|====|====|====|====|====|====|====|===
                          ORDER ACKNOWLEDGMENT

Advant Printing Company
100 South Eighth Street
Bellevue, WA  98004

Dear Mr. Johnson:

This to acknowledge that we have received your order as
described below.  We can deliver your order by June 7.  We
understand that you are anticipating an additional order.
If you are able to confirm it by the first of June, we will
be able to include it with this shipment.

Your order is as follows:

     Item Qty  Units         Description            Price
     ------------------------------------------------------
      1    5   1000      #10 sub 24 circa 83 Laid EPS  27.53
                        Nantucket Gray
--------------------------------------------------------------------------
Type entry or use ⌂ commands          Line 17   Column 39       ⌂-? for Help
```

Block deletes.   You will also want to delete whole words, phrases, paragraphs, and even pages as you create text. The second method of deleting, block deletes, allows you to delete such larger blocks of text. AppleWorks provides you with an excellent way to do this.

Suppose that you change your mind about ending the letter with the sentence, "We are always glad for your business as you are one of our favorites!" Instead you would like to say, "We appreciate your business and hope to continue serving you in the future."

To delete the first phrase, follow these steps:

1. Position your cursor on the first character you want deleted, the "W" in "We."

2. Press the command OA-D for Delete.

A message will be displayed instructing you to move the cursor to highlight the block of text to be deleted.

3. Move your cursor so that it is positioned on the last character you want deleted, the "!".

Notice that using the DOWN ARROW key first is faster than using the RIGHT ARROW key to move through the two lines of text. The text to be deleted will be highlighted. Notice that the RETURN characters also appear on the Delete Text screen.

```
File: Advant.ltr                  DELETE TEXT           Escape: Review/Add/Change
=====|====|====|====|====|====|====|====|====|====|====|====|====|====|===
described below.  We can deliver your order by June 7.  We
understand that you are anticipating an additional order.
If you are able to confirm it by the first of June, we will
be able to include it with this shipment.※
※
Your order is as follows:※
※
--------Right Margin:  0.5 inches
    Item Qty  Units            Description             Price ※
    ------------------------------------------------------------ ※
      1    5   1000      #10 sub 24 circa 83 Laid EPS  27.53※
                         Nantucket Gray※
      2    5   Ream      Classic Laid Bond 8 1/2x11     7.46※
                         Hearthstone※
      3    5   Ream      NCR Bond CF 8 1/2x11           5.31※
Thank you for your order.  We are always glad for your business
as you are one of our favorites! ※
※
Sincerely yours,※
--------------------------------------------------------------------------
Use cursor moves to highlight block, then press Return _          56K Avail.
```

4. Press RETURN and the delete will be accomplished.

If you change your mind and wish to cancel the delete, press ESC instead of RETURN, and the delete will not occur.

You can delete whole pages, or even the contents of an entire document, by first positioning the cursor at the top of the page or document, pressing OA-D, and then blocking what you wish to delete by using OA-DOWN ARROW or OA-9 to move the cursor to the end of the screen or document.

At this point you can insert the text you *do* want with these steps:

5. If you are not in the insert mode (with a blinking underline cursor), press OA-E.

6. Type the following sentence: **We appreciate your business and hope to continue serving you in the future.**

7. End the sentence with a RETURN.

```
File: Advant.ltr              REVIEW/ADD/CHANGE              Escape: Main Menu
=====|====|====|====|====|====|====|====|====|====|====|====|====|====|====|===
described below.  We can deliver your order by June 7.  We
understand that you are anticipating an additional order.
If you are able to confirm it by the first of June, we will
be able to include it with this shipment.

Your order is as follows:

   Item Qty  Units          Description              Price
   --------------------------------------------------------------
    1    5   1000      #10 sub 24 circa 83 Laid EPS  27.53
                       Nantucket Gray
    2    5   Ream      Classic Laid Bond 8 1/2x11     7.46
                       Hearthstone
    3    5   Ream      NCR Bond CF 8 1/2x11           5.31
Thank you for your order.
We appreciate your business and hope to continue serving you in
the future.

Sincerely yours,
--------------------------------------------------------------------
Type entry or use ⌂ commands          Line 33  Column  1      ⌂-? for Help
```

You will notice that your text is incorrectly spaced. But it's difficult to see why. Now is a good opportunity to use the Zoom command to see the formatting characters. Perhaps you can find out why the sentences are spaced incorrectly.

8. Press OA-Z for Zoom.

You can see the gray rectangles that represent the RETURN characters. You'll see that one of the RETURN characters is improperly located between the first sentence and the new one. This resulted from the Delete command, which moved the RETURN character to the left of the deleted text. Delete the misplaced RETURN.

9. Place the cursor on the "W" in "We."

10. Press DELETE twice.

The erroneous RETURN character will be deleted.

11. Press OA-Z again to view the text without formatting characters.

Now you can insert, overstrike, or delete as you wish. You can view your document with and without formatting characters as you need to. Using these tools, go back through your text and correct any of your own errors. When you are finished correcting all remaining errors, you should save your document before moving on.

Saving and Duplicating Text

As explained in Chapter 2, you'll want to save your files by periodically copying them to disk. This preserves them so that if the copy of the file on the Desktop is accidentally destroyed, you'll have another copy.

In Chapter 2 you also learned that there are two ways to save files. One is a "quick save" that leaves you in the editing mode, and the other is a more complex save that gives you several options, such as renaming your file. Chapter 2 used the quick save (by pressing OA-S, for Save) to save Opening.ltr. Now you'll use the second method of saving and learn about some of the options you have when you save a file in this way.

You would normally choose this second method of saving a document when you are finished editing and want to go on to some other task. You are going to use this second method to perform two save operations. First, you'll leave the editing screen and save Advant.ltr to disk, performing a simple straightforward save. Then you will save the file a second time, this time giving it a different name. In this way, you'll save two copies of the letter on disk, but with different names. Later the renamed copy will be modified into a standard form letter.

Saving the Letter

Let's save the Order Acknowledgment letter to Advant Printing Company now.

1. Press ESC to return to the Main Menu.

2. Move the cursor down to option 3, Save Desktop files to disk, and press RETURN.

The Save Files screen will display the names of the files that you might want to save on the Desktop. In this instance, only one file is on the Desktop.

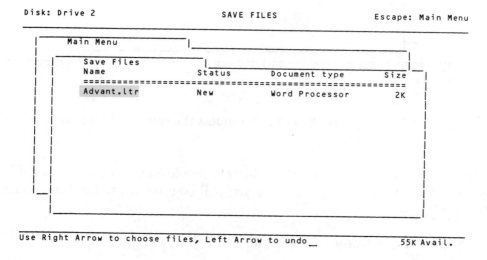

```
Disk: Drive 2                    SAVE FILES              Escape: Main Menu
_____

  |  Main Menu              |  _____
  |                         |                                         |
  |  |  Save Files          |  __                                     |
  |  |  Name              Status      Document type        Size  |    |
  |  |  ==========================================================    |
  |  |  Advant.ltr        New         Word Processor         2K  |    |
  |  |                                                              |  |
  |  |                                                              |  |
  |  |                                                              |  |
  |  |                                                              |  |
  |  |                                                              |  |
  |  |_                                                             |  |
  |  |                                                              |  |
  |  |_____| |
  |_____|
_____
Use Right Arrow to choose files, Left Arrow to undo_          55K Avail.
```

3. Select the Advant.ltr file to save by pressing RETURN.

The Filename screen gives you a choice of saving the file on the currently assigned disk (displayed at the upper left-hand corner of the screen) or of changing to another disk (or directory, if you have a hard disk).

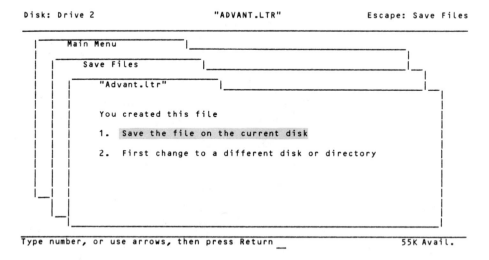

```
Disk: Drive 2                    "ADVANT.LTR"              Escape: Save Files
_____
  |‾‾Main Menu‾‾‾‾‾‾‾‾‾‾‾‾‾|_____
  |  |                    |                                        |
  |  |‾‾Save Files‾‾‾‾‾‾‾|_____|_
  |  |  |              |                                          |  |
  |  |  |‾‾"Advant.ltr"‾‾‾‾|_____|_
  |  |  |  |               |                                         | |
  |  |  |  You created this file                                     | |
  |  |  |                                                            | |
  |  |  |  1.  Save the file on the current disk                     | |
  |  |  |                                                            | |
  |  |  |  2.  First change to a different disk or directory         | |
  |  |  |                                                            | |
  |  |  |                                                            | |
  |  |_|                                                            | |
  |  |                                                              | |
  |_ |                                                              | |
     |_____| |
_____
Type number, or use arrows, then press Return __                   55K Avail.
```

4. Press RETURN to request the same disk (the one in drive 2).

You will now be told that AppleWorks is saving your file. After a few seconds, you will be returned to the Main Menu.

Renaming a Copy of Your File

Now let's create a duplicate of Advant.ltr and rename it. You will later modify this copy to be a standard form letter used for all customer orders. Follow these steps:

1. Type **3** and press RETURN to select option 3, Save Desktop files to disk.

2. When the menu of files on the Desktop is presented, press RETURN to select Advant.ltr.

You will be told that you've made "NO changes" to the file since it's just been saved.

```
Disk: Drive 2                    "ADVANT.LTR"              Escape: Save Files
_____
  |    Main Menu               |_____
  |  |                         |                                         |_
  |  |   Save Files           |_____|_
  |  |  |                     |                                             |_
  |  |  |   "Advant.ltr"     |_____|
  |  |  |                                                                    |
  |  |  |   You made NO changes to this file                                 |
  |  |  |                                                                    |
  |  |  |   1.  Save the file on the current disk                            |
  |  |  |                                                                    |
  |  |  |   2.  First change to a different disk or directory                |
  |  |  |                                                                    |
  |  |  |                                                                    |
  |  |_|                                                                     |
  |  |                                                                       |
  |_ |                                                                       |
  |__|_____|
_____
Type number, or use arrows, then press Return__          55K Avail.
```

3. Again press RETURN to select the current disk (Disk 2) to save the copy of the letter.

The Filename screen now informs you that a file of the same name exists on disk (the one you just saved). The screen looks like this:

```
Disk: Disk 2                     "ADVANT.LTR"              Escape: Save Files
_____
  |    Main Menu               |_____
  |  |                         |                                         |_
  |  |   Save Files           |_____|_
  |  |  |                     |                                             |_
  |  |  |   "Advant.ltr"     |_____|
  |  |  |                                                                    |
  |  |  |   This file already exists on Disk 2                               |
  |  |  |                                                                    |
  |  |  |   1.  Let the new information replace the old.                     |
  |  |  |                                                                    |
  |  |  |   2.  Save with a different name.                                  |
  |  |  |                                                                    |
  |  |  |                                                                    |
  |  |_|                                                                     |
  |  |                                                                       |
  |_ |                                                                       |
  |__|_____|
_____
Type number, or use arrows, then press Return__          55K Avail.
```

You are asked whether you want to replace that file or to save the file under a new name. You want to create a second file with a different name, so

4. Move the cursor down to option 2 and press RETURN.

The screen now asks you for the new name of the file. The old name is displayed for your information.

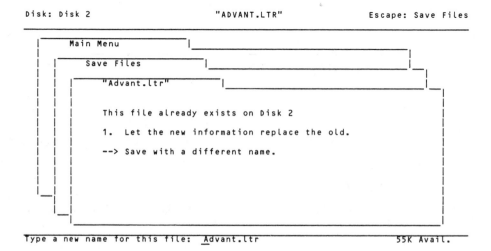

```
Disk: Disk 2                        "ADVANT.LTR"              Escape: Save Files
_____
 |--------------------------|_____
 | |   Main Menu            |                                              |
 | |------------------------|_____| |
 | | |  Save Files          |                                          |_  |
 | | |----------------------|_____| | |
 | | | |  "Advant.ltr"      |                                        |_| | |
 | | | |--------------------|_____| | | |
 | | | |                                                            | | | |
 | | | |  This file already exists on Disk 2                        | | | |
 | | | |  1.  Let the new information replace the old.               | | | |
 | | | |  --> Save with a different name.                           | | | |
 | | | |                                                            | | | |
 | | |_|                                                            | | | |
 | |_|                                                              | | |
 |_|                                                                |_| |
 | |_____| |
 |_____|
Type a new name for this file:  Advant.ltr                          55K Avail.
```

Notice whether you are in insert or overstrike mode. If you are in insert mode, your new letters will be inserted to the left of the old. You will need to position the cursor to the right of the old characters and press DELETE in order to delete the old letters. A better method is to press OA-E and overstrike the old name.

5. Enter **OrderAck.form** as the new name and press RETURN.

The file will be saved after a few seconds and you will be returned to the Main Menu. You now have two identical files, one named OrderAck.form and the other named Advant.ltr. You will retrieve the Advant.ltr file from disk and print it. Later you will come back to OrderAck.form.

Retrieving Your File From Disk

In order for you to edit your file *or* print it, you must first put it on the Desktop and view it on the Review/Add/Change screen. Your file may already be on the Desktop, in which case you can quickly bring it up on the Review/Add/Change screen using a *quick index*, as you'll do in a moment. But if your file is on disk, you must ask AppleWorks to get it from the disk and put it on the Desktop for you.

Because Advant.ltr is no longer on the Desktop (Apple-Works removed it when the file was renamed), it must be retrieved from disk. That is, you must ask AppleWorks to add it to the Desktop so that you can view it on the Review/Add/Change screen. Follow these steps to retrieve the file.

1. From the Main Menu select option 1, Add files to the Desktop, by pressing RETURN since that is the option already highlighted by AppleWorks.

2. From the Add Files menu, select the first option (which is Get files from: 1. The Current disk: Disk 2) by again pressing RETURN.

The filenames will be displayed alphabetically, like this:

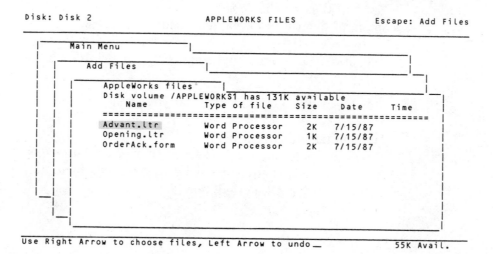

3. Since Advant.ltr is already highlighted, just press RETURN.

The file will then be displayed on the Review/Add/Change screen, as you wanted.

Printing Your Text

Now that the letter is on the Review/Add/Change screen, you can print it. Since you've already printed a file in Chapter 2, only a quick review of the steps will be given here. Of course, one of the first things you must do is make sure that your printer is plugged in, turned on, has adequate paper, and a ribbon in place. If you have problems with your printer, refer to Appendix A, to the printer's manual, or to the AppleWorks *Reference Manual*.

1. Press the command for printing—OA-P for Print.

2. Press RETURN to print the document from the Beginning, which is highlighted.

You will then be shown the Print menu, which gives you the option of printing to a named printer or to disk.

3. Move your cursor to the name of your printer, and press RETURN.

4. Press RETURN to verify that you want one copy.

The printer will begin printing.

Now go back and get the second copy of the letter (Order-Ack.form) and modify it to be a standard form for all customer order acknowledgments.

Retrieving Files From the Desktop

Before you can modify OrderAck.form, you need to view it on the Review/Add/Change screen. Earlier you learned to retrieve Advant.ltr from the disk and put it on the Desktop in order to print it. But a copy of OrderAck.form already exists on the Desktop: it was put there when you renamed Advant.ltr, creating the copy. So now you want to retrieve a file that is already on the Desktop and view it on the Review/Add/Change screen.

To do this, you will use the *quick index* method that was referred to earlier. (The AppleWorks documentation calls this the "quick change" feature.) Basically the quick index is a menu that quickly displays all the files currently on the Desktop and allows you to choose the one you want to edit.

Follow these two easy steps to retrieve OrderAck.form using the quick index method.

1. Press OA-Q for Quick Index.

An index of the files will be displayed:

```
File: Advant.ltr              REVIEW/ADD/CHANGE            Escape: Main Menu
=====|====|====|====|====|====|====|====|====|====|====|====|====|====|====|===
                    ORDER ACKNOWLEDGMENT

Advant Printing Company
100 South Eighth Street
Bellevue, WA  98004

Dear Mr. Johnson:

This to acknowledge that  |       Desktop Index       |
described below.  We can  |---------------------------|   We
understand that you are a | 1.   OrderAck.form     WP |   r.
If you are able to confir | 2.   Advant.ltr        WP |   will
be able to include it wit |_____|

Your order is as follows:

     Item Qty  Units          Description          Price
     -------------------------------------------------------------
      1   5    1000     #10 sub 24 circa 83 Laid EPS  27.53
                        Nantucket Gray
-------------------------------------------------------------------------
Type number, or use arrows, then press Return[]              54K Avail.
```

2. Position the cursor over the name of the file you want (OrderAck.form), and press RETURN.

The file will be displayed on the Review/Add/Change screen, as desired.

Creating a Form Letter

Now you can alter the copy of the Advant Printing Company letter to use as a standard form for all customer orders. It should end up looking like Figure 3-4.

Modifying the Address and Greeting

First you'll need to replace the customer's name and address with blanks that can be filled in at the time a new customer's order comes in. To do this, first delete the customer's name and address, replacing them with blank lines and a reminder of what is to be typed in later. Follow these steps:

1. Using OA-2 to get to the top of the document quickly, place the cursor on the first letter of the name, the "A" in "Advant."

2. Press OA-D for Delete and move the cursor to the last character to be deleted by pressing the DOWN ARROW key three times.

3. Press RETURN to complete the delete operation.

4. Make sure that you're in the insert mode, so that you won't overwrite the greeting, and then enter the description (**Name and Address**), and press RETURN four times, once to end the line and three times for blank lines.

Notice that as you enter the text, the greeting line will appear to be pushed aside.

```
File: OrderAck.form              REVIEW/ADD/CHANGE             Escape: Main Menu
=====|====|====|====|====|====|====|====|====|====|====|====|====|====|====|===
                             ORDER ACKNOWLEDGMENT
(Name and Address)


Dear Mr. Johnson:

This to acknowledge that we have received your order as
described below.  We can deliver your order by June 7.  We
understand that you are anticipating an additional order.
If you are able to confirm it by the first of June, we will
be able to include it with this shipment.

Your order is as follows:

    Item Qty  Units        Description          Price
    --------------------------------------------------------
     1   5    1000      #10 sub 24 circa 83 Laid EPS  27.53
                        Nantucket Gray
--------------------------------------------------------------------------------
Type entry or use ⌘ commands            Line 11   Column  1      ⌘-? for Help
```

```
                         ORDER ACKNOWLEDGMENT
     (Name and Address)


     Dear (Title and Name):

     This to acknowledge that we have received your order as
     described below.  We can deliver your order by (Date).

     Your order is as follows:

         Item Qty  Units        Description          Price
         --------------------------------------------------------




     Thank you for your order.  We appreciate your business and hope
     to continue serving you in the future.

     Sincerely yours,


     Your Name
```

Figure 3-4. Order Acknowledgment form letter

Now you need to replace the name, "Mr. Johnson," with spaces and the words **(Title and Name)**.

5. Position the cursor over the "M" in "Mr."

6. Press OA-E for overstrike mode.

7. Enter **(Title and** , leaving a space after "and."

8. Press OA-E for insert mode so you won't overwrite the colon.

9. Enter **Name)**.

```
File: OrderAck.form           REVIEW/ADD/CHANGE           Escape: Main Menu
=====|====|====|====|====|====|====|====|====|====|====|====|====|====|====|===
                   ORDER ACKNOWLEDGMENT

(Name and Address)


Dear (Title and Name):_

This to acknowledge that we have received your order as
described below.  We can deliver your order by June 7.   We
understand that you are anticipating an additional order.
If you are able to confirm it by the first of June, we will
be able to include it with this shipment.

Your order is as follows:

    Item Qty  Units         Description              Price
    -----------------------------------------------------------
    1    5    1000      #10 sub 24 circa 83 Laid EPS  27.53
                        Nantucket Gray
    -----------------------------------------------------------
Type entry or use ⌂ commands              Line 11   Column 22      ⌂-? for Help
```

Modifying the Body of the Letter

The body of the letter has two areas that need to be changed—the date of delivery and the order detail. Since the date of delivery will vary for each order, you'll need to replace it with **(Date)**. Follow these steps:

1. Press OA-E for overstrike mode and position the cursor over the "J" in "June" in the second sentence.

2. Type **(Date)** so that it exactly replaces "June 7."

Next you want to delete the two sentences unique to Advant Paper Company's order, "We understand that you are antici- pating..." through to the end of the paragraph. These sen- tences only apply to Advant Printing Company and are not appropriate for a form letter. To delete them,

3. Place your cursor over the beginning "W" in the third sentence.

4. Press OA-D to invoke the Delete command.

5. Move your cursor to the last character of the sentence, the period following the word "shipment." The screen will show the RETURN characters and will look like this:

```
File: OrderAck.form              DELETE TEXT          Escape: Review/Add/Change
=====|====|====|====|====|====|====|====|====|====|====|====|====|====|====|===
--------Top Margin:  1.0 inches
--------Bottom Margin:  1.0 inches
--------Centered
                    ORDER ACKNOWLEDGMENT▒
--------Unjustified
▒
(Name and Address)▒
▒
▒
▒
Dear (Title and Name):▒
▒
This to acknowledge that we have received your order as
described below.  We can deliver your order by (Date).  We
understand that you are anticipating an additional order.
If you are able to confirm it by the first of June, we will
be able to include it with this shipment. ▒
▒
Your order is as follows:▒
▒
-------------------------------------------------------------------------------
Use cursor moves to highlight block, then press Return□          53K Avail.
```

6. Press RETURN to delete the two sentences.

Of course, the items ordered will vary from one order to another. You must delete the current order detail, keeping the column headings so that you can fill in the blank lines correctly lined up. To do this,

7. Position the cursor on the left margin of the first line of item 1 in the order list (line 21 and column 1).

8. Press OA-D.

9. In response to the message, press the DOWN ARROW key five times and the LEFT ARROW key once, until all lines of the order are highlighted.

```
File: OrderAck.form            DELETE TEXT         Escape: Review/Add/Change
=====|====|====|====|====|====|====|====|====|====|====|====|====|====|===
(Name and Address)▓
▓
▓
▓
Dear (Title and Name):▓
▓
This to acknowledge that we have received your order as
described below. We can deliver your order by (Date).
▓
Your order is as follows:▓
▓
--------Right Margin:  0.5 inches
     Item Qty  Units          Description              Price▓
     ------------------------------------------------------------▓
       1    5   1000      #10 sub 24 circa 83 Laid EPS  27.53
                          Nantucket Gray
       2    5   Ream      Classic Laid Bond 8 1/2x11     7.46
                          Hearthstone
       3    5   Ream      NCR Bond CF 8 1/2x11           5.31▓
▓
-----------------------------------------------------------------------
Use cursor moves to highlight block, then press Return▯        54K Avail.
```

10. Press RETURN once to complete the delete, and then five more times for blank lines.

The letter with only the framework of the order list looks like this:

```
File: OrderAck.form            REVIEW/ADD/CHANGE              Escape: Main Menu
=====|====|====|====|====|====|====|====|====|====|====|====|====|====|====|===
(Name and Address)



Dear (Title and Name):

This to acknowledge that we have received your order as
described below.  We can deliver your order by (Date).

Your order is as follows:

--------Right Margin:  0.5 inches
    Item Qty  Units           Description            Price
    ----------------------------------------------------------------



[]
-------------------------------------------------------------------------------
Type entry or use Ğ commands          Line 6  Column  1        Ğ-? for Help
```

The next time you wish to use the form letter, you can simply fill in the new customer name and order.

Saving and Printing the New File

Now you must save the file again, and then print it. Since you are not changing the name and will want to remain on the Review/Add/Change screen in order to print your file, you should perform a quick save.

1. Press OA-S for Save.

The screen will display a message that the file is being saved. When the save is completed, you can print the file and see what your new letter looks like on paper.

2. Press OA-P for Print.

3. Press RETURN to select the highlighted option, Beginning, indicating that you want the whole document printed.

4. Press RETURN again to select the highlighted first option, naming the printer as the destination of the printout.

5. Press RETURN to tell AppleWorks that you indeed want to print as AppleWorks has assumed.

The letter should now be printing. Return to the Main Menu by pressing ESC.

This completes your first full practice session with the AppleWorks word processor. You can now leave AppleWorks and turn off the computer. Or you can continue to another chapter.

If you choose to leave AppleWorks, select option 6, Quit, by moving the cursor down and pressing RETURN. Respond to the question, "Do you really want to do this?" by moving the cursor to Yes and pressing RETURN. For each file you will be told that you've made changes to the files, and you will be given three options on how to dispose of them. First, you can save the files again. The second option saves them on a different disk (or directory, if you have a hard disk). And the third option ignores the changes you've made. Since you have just saved your files, you can ignore the warnings that you should save your Desktop files by choosing option 3, Throw out the changes to the file. This simply discards the files from the Desktop without saving them again. Then you'll be asked to verify your choice. You'll go through this sequence twice — once for OrderAck.form, and then for Advant.ltr. When the screen displays the ProDOS prompt, "ENTER PREFIX (PRESS RETURN TO ACCEPT)," you can turn off the computer, monitor, and printer.

If you want to continue, you have two more choices. Chapter 4 explains the basic functions that you will use in the data base module. If you want to continue with word processing, turn to Chapter 6, which explains more advanced word processing procedures.

4

Building a Data Base

The data base component of AppleWorks serves as an organizer. As a filing system it's similar to the revolving cardfile you may keep on your desk, but much superior to it. This automated filing system allows you to set up your files, add information to them, and revise the information. You can sort the information into any sequence you want and select specific items to view so that only a subset of the whole file is displayed. Finally, you can store the information on disk and print all or only parts of it in reports formatted to your specifications.

In this chapter you will learn how to build a data base in AppleWorks. You will create a file on the Desktop, define the data base's data categories, and enter the data. You will learn how to insert and delete categories and records and how to edit their contents, getting help from the program as you need it. You also will learn how to scan the data base file, looking at the records one at a time or as line items on a list of records. You will learn how to modify the layout of the screen so that you can see the data in each record that you want and in the sequence that you want. Finally, you will learn how to format a data base report and print it.

Getting Started

Building a data base consists of three steps. First, you decide what list or table you want to put on a data base. Next, you define the type of information that will be contained in your data base; that is, you tell AppleWorks what data items you will be entering for each record. Third, you enter the data. That's really all there is to it.

We have simplified your first step, which is deciding what lists or tables you want to include in your data base. In this chapter you will build a Customer Information File (CIF), which is used to generate telephone lists and name and address labels. The categories into which this information will be organized have already been developed for you.

Reviewing the Elements of a Data Base

Each name and address entry is called a record, as shown in Figure 4-1. You can think of a record as one card in a cardfile. The CIF file you will build has only ten records to start with, but others can be added.

The records consist of several data *categories:* for example, customer name and telephone number are both categories. You can see five categories on the sample screen in Figure 4-1. AppleWorks provides two special categories for your convenience. If a category contains the word "date" or "time" within it, AppleWorks will automatically convert the entries under those categories into standard date and time format. For an example of this format, look at the category called 1ST ORDER DATE in Figure 4-1.

When you refer to a specific piece of data in a category within one record, you are referring to an *entry.* Each entry consists of characters—letters, numbers, or punctuation.

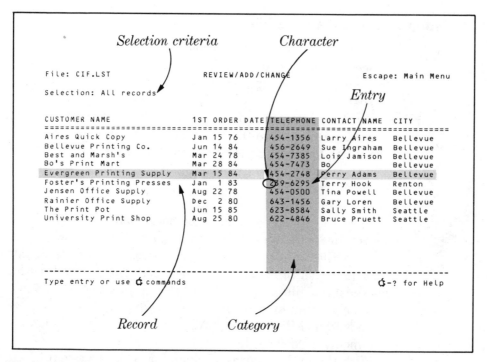

Figure 4-1. Elements of a data base

The data base has *selection criteria* connected to it. In Figure 4-1, for example, Selection: All records indicates that all records in the CIF data base can be viewed on the screen. You might wish to change that to select only certain records.

Finally, if you were building a data base from scratch in actual practice, you would enter the data you need from lists or tables containing the information. These are called *source documents.* The data for our customer information file might come from a typical order slip that is filled out when a customer submits an order. If the customer is new, you will enter the information on the slip into the Customer Information File for the first time.

Creating a New Data Base File

At this time you should start AppleWorks following the procedure described in Chapter 2. If AppleWorks is already loaded in your computer, press ESC until the Main Menu appears.

Creating a data base file is very similar to creating a word processing file. From the Main Menu, you first want to select the option for adding files—namely, Add files to the Desktop. You then want to change the assigned disk drive from drive 1 to drive 2 as you did in Chapters 2 and 3, if it is not already correctly assigned.

Once the assigned drive has been changed, you should insert the AppleWorks1 disk that you used for the word processing files into disk drive 2. Here you will use the same disk for word processing and data base files, as well as for spreadsheet files, although in actual practice you would probably want to dedicate a whole disk to the Customer Information File or to put this file on the same disk with commonly used form letters.

With the preliminaries of changing disk drives out of the way, you should be back at the Add Files menu. At this point, you want to

1. Type 4 and press RETURN to select Make a new file for the: Data Base.

You will be shown the Data Base menu, from which you must select the source of the new file. You have four options: to create a file from scratch, from an ASCII text file, from a Quick File, or from a DIF file. Right now you want to create a file from scratch.

2. Press RETURN to select the default option, Make a new file called From scratch.

You would use the other options if you were using a file from another software system or from another AppleWorks component to create your new data base file.

Now a RIGHT ARROW will point to the option you selected, and you will be asked to enter a filename.

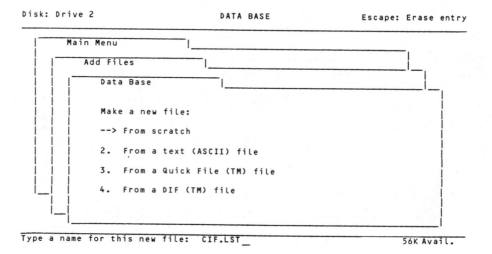

```
Disk: Drive 2                    DATA BASE              Escape: Erase entry
_____

  | Main Menu                |_____
  |  | Add Files              |_____  |
  |  |  | Data Base             |_____  | |
  |  |  |                                                              | | |
  |  |  | Make a new file:                                             | |
  |  |  |                                                              | |
  |  |  | --> From scratch                                             | |
  |  |  |                                                              | |
  |  |  | 2.  From a text (ASCII) file                                 | |
  |  |  |                                                              | |
  |  |  | 3.  From a Quick File (TM) file                              | |
  |  |  |                                                              | |
  |_ |  | 4.  From a DIF (TM) file                                     | |
     |_ |                                                              | |
        |_____|
_____
Type a name for this new file:  CIF.LST_                      56K Avail.
```

3. On the prompt line, enter the filename **CIF.LST** and press RETURN.

Remember that the name you enter can be 15 characters or less and that it can contain upper- or lowercase letters, numbers, periods, and spaces, although it must begin with a letter.

The Change Name/Category screen will then be displayed.

Setting Up Categories

The Change Name/Category screen is used to define your data base categories—to give them names. The screen has several important parts, as shown here:

```
File: CIF.LST              CHANGE NAME/CATEGORY      Escape: Review/Add/Change



Category names
==============================================================================
Category 1
_                                        |
                                         | Options:
                                         |
                                         | Change category name
                                         | Up arrow   Go to filename
                                         | Down arrow Go to next category
                                         | a-I        Insert new category
                                         |
                                         |
                                         |
                                         |
                                         |
--------------------------------------------------------------------------------
Type entry or use d commands                                      56K Avail.
```

At the top and bottom borders of the screen AppleWorks lists the information it usually lists: the name of the file you are working on (CIF.LST in this case), the name of the current screen (Change Name/Category), the screen you would escape to by pressing ESC (Review/Add/Change in this case), and the amount of memory you may still use on the Desktop (56K on our screen—yours may differ).

Notice that the screen is divided into two areas. The left is where category names are defined. In a moment you will be entering category names on this side of the screen, at the place where the cursor is blinking—under the "C" in Category 1. The right side of the Change Name/Category is a kind of menu, listing the options you have for using this screen, that is, the tools available to you with this Change Name/Category screen.

The first option in the menu explains that you can change the category name you see on the left-hand side of the screen. AppleWorks assumes that you are going to name your categories in sequential order and indicates this with the placeholder Category 1. The cursor rests on the name Category 1, waiting for you to approve it by pressing RETURN, or to change it by entering your own category name on top of it. The next category name you enter will be entered below it.

The second item on the Change Name/Category menu tells you that you can use the UP ARROW to go to the filename. You might wish to use the UP ARROW if you wanted to change the filename or if you wished to move up the screen to a previously entered category name: that is, to go backward through the names you've entered. Conversely, the DOWN ARROW, which is third in the Options portion of the screen, allows you to go to the next category name down—for example, to what would be Category 2. Finally, the OA-I command (for Insert) will allow you to insert a new category name amidst others that have been previously entered. Notice that the OPEN-APPLE key is represented by the at sign (@) in our depiction of the menu. Menu screens throughout this chapter will show the @ sign when you are to press the OA key in conjunction with another key.

Entering Category Names

Your customer information data base will have 11 categories. The names can contain up to 20 characters. Here is a list of the category names and what they mean:

- CUSTOMER NUMBER: a unique, sequential number assigned to each customer. (You will overwrite Category 1.)

- CUSTOMER NAME: the individual or company name.

- STREET: the street address or P.O. box number.

- CITY: the customer's city name.

- STATE: a two-letter abbreviation for the state.

- ZIP CODE: a five-digit ZIP code.

- TELEPHONE: the telephone number.

- CONTACT NAME: the name of the customer's primary contact.

- CREDIT LIMIT: the credit limit granted to the customer.

- PRODUCT TYPE: a one-character code identifying the primary product line that the customer purchases.

- 1ST ORDER DATE: the date that the customer first ordered from your company.

Follow these steps to change the category names, remembering that if you strike an incorrect letter you can erase it using the DELETE key. Be sure the CAPS LOCK key is down since the category names will be entered in all capital letters.

1. To type over the current category name of Category 1, press OA-E to switch from insert mode to overstrike mode.

Remember from Chapter 3 that you can tell what mode you are in by the appearance of the cursor: in overstrike mode the cursor is a blinking block; in insert mode the cursor is a blinking underline. Now when you type, your letters will be displayed over the existing letters.

2. Enter the first category name, **CUSTOMER NUMBER**, and press RETURN.

3. Enter the rest of the category names, and after entering each name, press RETURN.

If you've made any errors, use the UP and DOWN ARROW keys to move the cursor to the incorrect category and simply type over it. This is what your screen should look like when you've entered all the names:

```
File: CIF.LST              CHANGE NAME/CATEGORY     Escape: Review/Add/Change


Category names
=========================================================================
CUSTOMER NUMBER                       |
CUSTOMER NAME                         | Options:
STREET                                |
CITY                                  | Type category name
STATE                                 | Up arrow   Go to previous category
ZIP CODE                              |
TELEPHONE                             |
CONTACT NAME                          |
CREDIT LIMIT                          |
PRODUCT TYPE                          |
1ST ORDER DATE                        |
☐                                     |
                                      |
                                      |
------------------------------------------------------------------------
Type entry or use  commands                              56K Avail.
```

Deleting and Inserting Categories

As you look over the categories, you'll notice that there is only one street address. Let's suppose that in some instances you wish to enter more than one street address for a customer. In order to add a second address, you will want to add the category STREET 2. But adding STREET 2 will make the existing category name, STREET, too unspecific. The solution, of course, is to replace STREET with STREET 1.

Enact these changes to the list of categories now. To do so, you will need to delete STREET and insert STREET 1 and STREET 2. Follow these steps:

1. Move the cursor to the STREET category name.

2. Press OA-D to delete the entry.

3. Press OA-I for Insert. A new entry position will open up, like this:

```
File: CIF.LST              CHANGE NAME/CATEGORY      Escape: Review/Add/Change



Category names
===================================================================================
CUSTOMER NUMBER              |
CUSTOMER NAME                | Options:
▣                            |
CITY                         | Change category name
STATE                        | Up arrow   Go to previous category
ZIP CODE                     | Down arrow Go to next category
TELEPHONE                    | ⌐-I        Insert new category
CONTACT NAME                 | ⌐-D        Delete this category
CREDIT LIMIT                 |
PRODUCT TYPE                 |
1ST ORDER DATE               |
                             |
                             |
                             |
-----------------------------------------------------------------------------------
Type entry or use ⌂ commands                                        56K Avail.
```

4. Type in the category name, **STREET 1**, and press RETURN.

5. Press OA-I to insert the second category name.

6. Type in the name, **STREET 2**, and press RETURN.

7. Press ESC when you are sure you have entered the new category names correctly.

AppleWorks will inform you that no data exists for this file and that you will be automatically put in the insert mode if you press the spacebar. Do this and your screen will display the new category names on the Insert New Records screen.

```
File: CIF.LST                INSERT NEW RECORDS      Escape: Review/Add/Change


Record 1 of 1
==================================================================================
CUSTOMER NUMBER: ⊟
CUSTOMER NAME: -
STREET 1: -
STREET 2: -
CITY: -
STATE: -
ZIP CODE: -
TELEPHONE: -
CONTACT NAME: -
CREDIT LIMIT: -
PRODUCT TYPE: -
1ST ORDER DATE: -



----------------------------------------------------------------------------------
Type entry or use ⌂ commands                                        56K Avail.
```

You are now ready to enter the actual data.

Entering the Data

The data you will enter is shown in Figure 4-2. You'll notice that there are only ten customers and hence ten records in this file. In an actual business you will probably have many more, but ten records is enough for our sample data base.

In entering the data you will learn how to establish standards, to insert and delete records, and to scroll back and forth through your file as you enter the data.

Before entering the data, you can save yourself some typing by using one of the AppleWorks data base's special features: setting and changing standard values.

Setting and Changing Standard Values

If you scan the list in Figure 4-2 you will see several entries that are the same. For example, most of the customers are from Bellevue, WA 98004. Most of the customers also purchase the product type P. And the credit limit for new customers is $1000. For these entries, you can establish a standard value; that is, a default value that you can override if you choose, but that you won't have to type in when the data to be entered is the same as this standard value. Follow these steps to set standard values:

1. Press OA-V for Value.

You will be shown the Set Standard Values screen:

```
File: CIF.LST              SET STANDARD VALUES    Escape: Insert New Records


Record
================================================================================
CUSTOMER NUMBER: ☐
CUSTOMER NAME: -
STREET 1: -
STREET 2: -
CITY: -
STATE: -
ZIP CODE: -
TELEPHONE: -
CONTACT NAME: -
CREDIT LIMIT: -
PRODUCT TYPE: -
1ST ORDER DATE: -



--------------------------------------------------------------------------------
Type standard category values                                       56K Avail.
```

```
                                              Page   1

File:   CIF.LST
Report: Customer List

CUST: 1   Aires Quick Copy           CONTACT NAME: Larry Aires
          1345 South 8th             CREDIT LIMIT: 5000
                                     PRODUCT TYPE: P
          Bellevue WA 98004          1ST ORDER DATE: Jan 15 76
          TELEPHONE: 454-1356

CUST: 2   Rainier Office Supply      CONTACT NAME: Gary Loren
          Suite 5C                   CREDIT LIMIT: 3000
          5327 148th Street          PRODUCT TYPE: B
          Bellevue WA 98004          1ST ORDER DATE: Dec  2 80
          TELEPHONE:  643-1456

CUST: 3   Bellevue Printing Co.      CONTACT NAME: Sue Ingraham
          456 East Bellevue Way      CREDIT LIMIT: 2000
                                     PRODUCT TYPE: P
          Bellevue WA 98005          1ST ORDER DATE: Jun 14 84
          TELEPHONE: 456-2649

CUST: 4   Evergreen Printing Supply  CONTACT NAME: Perry Adams
          4769 NE 20th Street        CREDIT LIMIT: 2000
                                     PRODUCT TYPE: P
          Bellevue WA 98004          1ST ORDER DATE: Mar 15 84
          TELEPHONE: 454-2748

CUST: 5   Jensen Office Supply       CONTACT NAME: Tina Powell
          800 East 8th Street        CREDIT LIMIT: 4000
                                     PRODUCT TYPE: P
          Bellevue WA 98004          1ST ORDER DATE: Aug 22 78
          TELEPHONE: 454-0500

CUST: 6   University Print Shop      CONTACT NAME: Bruce Pruett
          10056 Roosevelt Ave.       CREDIT LIMIT: 10000
                                     PRODUCT TYPE: P
          Seattle WA 98123           1ST ORDER DATE: Aug 25 80
          TELEPHONE: 622-4846

CUST: 7   Fred's Department Store    CONTACT NAME: Kelly Johnson
          3745 Wayne Ave.            CREDIT LIMIT: 2000
                                     PRODUCT TYPE: P
          Renton WA 98526            1ST ORDER DATE: APR 12 79
          TELEPHONE:  239-8750

CUST: 8   Bo's Print Mart            CONTACT NAME: Bo
          7264 Northrup Way South    CREDIT LIMIT: 2000
                                     PRODUCT TYPE: P
          Bellevue WA 98004          1ST ORDER DATE: Mar 28 84
          TELEPHONE: 454-7473

CUST: 9   Foster's Printing Presses  CONTACT NAME: Terry Hook
          83658 Pacific Hwy. South   CREDIT LIMIT: 3000
                                     PRODUCT TYPE: P
          Renton WA 98526            1ST ORDER DATE: Jan  1 83
          TELEPHONE: 239-6295

CUST: 10  Best's                     CONTACT NAME: Lois Jamison
          Department C               CREDIT LIMIT: 6000
          10476 NE 8th Street        PRODUCT TYPE: P
          Bellevue WA 98004          1ST ORDER DATE: Mar 24 78
          TELEPHONE: 454-7385
```

Figure 4-2.   Customer list to be entered

Since the information will contain both upper- and lowercase letters, release the CAPS LOCK key. To set the values you must move your cursor to the categories containing standard values and enter the values, as follows:

2. Move your cursor to the CITY category by pressing RETURN four times.

3. Enter **Bellevue** and press RETURN to move to the next category.

4. Enter the STATE abbreviation **WA** and press RETURN to move to the next category.

5. Enter the ZIP CODE **98004** and press RETURN to move to the next category.

6. Press RETURN two times to position the cursor on CREDIT LIMIT.

7. Enter **1000** and press RETURN to move to the next category.

8. Enter the PRODUCT TYPE **P** and press RETURN.

The Set Standard Values screen now shows the five standard values established:

```
File: CIF.LST              SET STANDARD VALUES    Escape: Insert New Records


Record
================================================================================
CUSTOMER NUMBER: -
CUSTOMER NAME: -
STREET 1: -
STREET 2: -
CITY: Bellevue
STATE: WA
ZIP CODE: 98004
TELEPHONE: -
CONTACT NAME: -
CREDIT LIMIT: 1000
PRODUCT TYPE: P
1ST ORDER DATE: ▉



-------------------------------------------------------------------------------
Type standard category values                                       56K Avail.
```

9. Press ESC to stop entering standard values and return to the insert screen.

The first record that you've created in the process of setting up standard values now shows the standard values you've set. Suppose that, upon reflection, you decide that the credit limit of $1000 is unrealistic: you have actually been starting new customers with a $2000 limit. In order to make the standard values more up-to-date, change the default to $2000 by following these steps:

1. Press OA-V to return to the Set Standard Values screen.

2. Position your cursor on CREDIT LIMIT.

3. Press CONTROL-Y to delete the current contents of the category. (You could also either press OA-Y or position your cursor at the end of the category and press DELETE four times.)

4. Type in **2000** and press RETURN.

5. Press ESC to return to the Insert Screen.

It's important to note that the change in the standard value only affects all future records—that is, records that have not already been created and for which a standard value has not been entered. In this case, Record 1, since no data has been entered and the second record has not been created, will be affected by the change; normally you would have to return to previous records created to manually change the standard value for the CREDIT LIMIT. The reason why standard values cannot be altered retroactively is that AppleWorks has no way of knowing which entries obtained their contents as a result of standard values and which entries were deliberately altered from the standard value. You might, for all Apple-Works knows, have gone back expressly to enter 1000 as the value for the CREDIT LIMIT. If the program changed standard values retroactively, you would have no control.

Now your standard values have been set. The values you

typed in will be automatically established for all records you enter. You can change these values whenever they differ from the standard, but you will be spared the effort of retyping them whenever the data to be entered is the same as the default established. Thus it is always to your advantage to set standard values before you enter data if there are significant repetitions in your data.

Inserting the Data

Now you are ready to enter the data listed in Figure 4-2 into the data base.

As you enter the data, the default values will be entered automatically into each record. If the default is correct, press RETURN to pass on to the next entry. If the entry for this record is different, type over the default with the correct entry. You can enter up to 76 characters in each category. If you make a mistake, you can blank out letters using the spacebar or DELETE. You should make sure, however, that the letters that you want in the entry are in fact there before you go to the next category. After each entry has been entered, press RETURN to signal that it is complete. You can use the cursor arrow keys to move between categories if you need to.

If you have no data for a category—for example, nothing to list for Street 2—skip it by pressing RETURN.

Follow these steps to enter the first record:

1. Position your cursor on the first category, CUSTOMER NUMBER.

2. Type **1** for the CUSTOMER NUMBER and press RETURN.

3. Type **Aires Quick Copy** and press RETURN.

4. Type **1345 South 8th** and press RETURN.

5. Press RETURN to skip STREET 2.

6. Press RETURN to accept the standard value for CITY.

7. Press RETURN to accept the default value for STATE.

8. Press RETURN to accept the default for ZIP CODE.

9. Type **454-1356** for the TELEPHONE NUMBER and press RETURN.

10. Type **Larry Aires** for the PRIMARY CONTACT name and press RETURN.

11. Type **5000** for the CREDIT LIMIT and press RETURN.

12. Press RETURN to accept the PRODUCT TYPE.

13. Type **1/15/76** for 1ST ORDER DATE and press RETURN.

A new blank record, Record 2 of 2, will be displayed for you to fill in the contents for the next record. But for one more look at Record 1 of 2,

14. Press the UP ARROW to return to the first record.

Notice that AppleWorks has converted the date format in 1ST ORDER DATE from 1/15/76 to Jan 15 76, the program's automatic standard format for dates.

```
File: CIF.LST                  INSERT NEW RECORDS      Escape: Review/Add/Change


Record 1 of 2
===============================================================================
CUSTOMER NUMBER: 1
CUSTOMER NAME: Aires Quick Copy
STREET 1: 1345 South 8th
STREET 2: -
CITY: Bellevue
STATE: WA
ZIP CODE: 98004
TELEPHONE: 454-1356
CONTACT NAME: Larry Aires
CREDIT LIMIT: 5000
PRODUCT TYPE: P
1ST ORDER DATE: []Jan 15 76



---------------------------------------------------------------------
Type entry or use Ú commands                                56K Avail.
```

15. Press the DOWN ARROW once to return to the blank record layout, for Record 2 of 2.

Now enter the rest of the data as shown in Figure 4-2. When you have finished entering all your records, you will be looking at a blank entry form for Record 11 of 11. At this point press ESC. A listing of all the entries you have made will be displayed for you:

```
File: CIF.LST                REVIEW/ADD/CHANGE            Escape: Main Menu

Selection: All records


CUSTOMER NUMBER CUSTOMER NAME   STREET 1         STREET 2         CITY
================================================================================
 1              Aires Quick Cop 1345 South 8th   -                Bellevue
 2              Rainier Office  Suite 5c         5327 148th Stre  Bellevue
 3              Bellevue Printi 456 East Bellev   -               Bellevue
 4              Evergreen Print 4769 NE 20th St   -               Bellevue
 5              Jensen Office S 800 East 8th St   -               Bellevue
 6              University Prin 10056 Roosevelt   -               Seattle
 7              Fred's Departme 3745 Wayne Ave.   -               Renton
 8              Bo's Print Mart 7264 Northrup W   -               Bellevue
 9              Foster's Printi 83658 Pacific H   -               Renton
10              Best's          Department C     10476 NE 8th St  Bellevue



--------------------------------------------------------------------------------
Type entry or use ⌂ commands                              ⌂-? for Help
```

With all the data entered, our next step is to learn how to get around in the data base file.

Scanning the File

AppleWorks gives you some very convenient ways to scan through your data base. When you were entering the data, you were looking at your data base record by record on the Insert New Record screen. This is called *single-record layout*. In single-record layout you can see all data entries made on any one record. The other data base layout used in Apple-Works is the *multiple-record layout*, which allows you to see some data on all the records in a list format. Multiple-record layout is the layout currently on your screen.

Zooming In and Out

To switch from viewing the multiple- to the single-record layout, again press OA-Z for Zoom. (You may remember this command from the word processing component. In that case, the zoom feature allowed you to switch between seeing and not seeing control characters embedded in your text.) To switch back from single- to multiple-record layout, press OA-Z again; now you will see a list of your records. As you can see, the OA-Z command works as a toggle.

Look at the multiple-record layout more closely now. You will notice that the screen is not wide enough for you to see all of the categories. What is more, you cannot see all the data for some categories, like CUSTOMER NAME. AppleWorks has in fact shortened some of the categories so that more categories can be seen on the screen. The data is still intact in the data base; it is just not displayed on the screen. To see another example of this space-saving truncation, move your cursor to the seventh record by pressing the DOWN ARROW key. The customer name for this entry is cut off: "Fred's Departme." Now press OA-Z to see the single-record layout for that particular record. The name is still there.

The zoom feature makes it easy to scan a list of records in multiple-record layout and then zoom in on the record you want to see in more detail. Practice zooming between the different layouts until you are comfortable with the OA-Z command.

Moving the Cursor

AppleWorks provides several commands for getting around within your data base. Some are common to both the multiple- and single-record layouts, and others are unique to one or the other.

The following exercises introduce you to ways of moving the cursor that are common to both single- and multiple-record layouts. While in the multiple-record layout, move your cursor to the first record by pressing the UP ARROW. Then press OA-Z to change to single-record layout on the first record, that of Aires Quick Copy.

One task you'll want to do in either record layout is to move through an entry so that you can edit the information it contains. To try this, first move the cursor to the CUSTOMER NAME entry and then through the name using the RIGHT ARROW. Use the LEFT ARROW to reverse the direction.

To skip from one entry to another, you can use either the TAB or the UP and DOWN ARROW keys, as you wish. Press TAB now to move across from entry to entry. Press OA-TAB to reverse the direction. Then try using the UP and DOWN ARROW keys to do the same thing. Repeat both techniques until you are comfortable using them.

From Chapter 3, you'll remember the commands OA-1 through OA-9, which allow you to thumb through the file at ten percent intervals. To see how these commands work in the data base, first press OA-1 to place the cursor on the first record of the file. Now press OA-9 to reach the last record of the file. Finally, press OA-5 to go halfway through the file (that is, to Record 5, since you have 10 records in the file).

Experiment with all these commands until you feel you are able to use them in the data base file. All the common commands just discussed work identically in the multiple-record layout. The OA-1 through OA-9 commands are particularly valuable when you are viewing many records within multiple-record layout. Try this now.

Moving the cursor within single-record layout.   The following exercises are unique to the single-record layout. Position the cursor on the first record of the file by pressing OA-1. Press OA-Z for the single-record layout. Now to display the next record in the file, press OA in conjunction with the DOWN ARROW. You will be moved from the first to the second record. Continue to do this three more times and see how you are advanced through the file one record at a time.

To display the previous record, press OA-UP ARROW. Do this now and see how you are returned to previous records in a file. If you do it four times, you will return to the first record.

To move the cursor to the next entry, you can use the RETURN as well as the TAB or the DOWN ARROW keys. Try using RETURN now. Notice that you cannot go backwards with the RETURN key.

Moving the cursor within multiple-record layout. Multiple-record layout also has some unique commands that affect the cursor. Position yourself now on the first record of the file by pressing OA-1, and then press OA-Z to switch from the single- to the multiple-record layout.

In multiple-record layout, the RETURN key can be used in two ways: to go from record to record, or to go from entry to entry. You alter the direction of the RETURN according to what you are doing. For example, if you are updating all entries of a single category it would be most convenient for the cursor to move down, from one record to the next. If you are updating unrelated categories in various records, however, the cursor movement to the right is probably most helpful to you.

Press RETURN and see how the cursor moves from record to record, unlike the cursor in single-record layout, which moves from entry to entry when you press RETURN. To change this so that the cursor moves from entry to entry, press OA-L for Layout. After a short wait you will be shown a menu of layout options which you don't want at this time. Press ESC and a second menu will appear at the top of your screen.

```
File: CIF.LST                CHANGE RECORD LAYOUT      Escape: Review/Add/Change


================================================================================
                     What direction should the cursor
                     go when you press Return?

                        1.  Down (standard)
                        2.  Right


--------------------------------------------------------------------------------

CUSTOMER NUMBER  CUSTOMER NAME   STREET 1         STREET 2          CITY
---------------  ---------------  ---------------  ---------------  ---------------
1                Aires Quick Cop 1345 South 8th                     Bellevue
2                Rainier Office  Suite 5c         5327 148th Stre  Bellevue
3                Bellevue Printi 456 East Bellev                   Bellevue

-------------------------------------------------------------- More --->
Type number, or use arrows, then press Return                  55K Avail.
```

This menu explains how to change the behavior of the RETURN for multiple-record layout. Move the cursor to the second option, Right, which is the direction you want the cursor to move in when you press RETURN. When you press RETURN to select the Right option, you will be returned to the multiple-record layout screen. Now press RETURN to see that the direction of the cursor has in fact changed: it moves to the right instead of moving down to the next record.

The OA-UP and DOWN ARROW keys can be used to quickly move to the top and bottom of the screen from wherever you are. Position the cursor on the STREET 1 category of the sixth record (10056 Roosevelt). Do this now and then press the OA-DOWN ARROW key combination to move the cursor to the bottom of the screen, but within the same category. Press OA-UP ARROW to get to the top of the screen. Now move the cursor to another category and use the OA-UP and DOWN ARROW keys.

Although there are not enough records in this file to really test this, you can move the cursor from the top of one screen to the top of the next screen using the OA-UP ARROW, and to the bottom of the next screen using the OA-DOWN ARROW. In this way you can move through the file one screen at a time.

Now let's move on and use some of these new skills to edit the file.

Editing the File

Just like your desktop cardfile, data base files must be edited if they are to stay updated and useful. AppleWorks provides much flexibility in its editing features.

Inserting vs. Overstriking

To edit a data base file, you must be able to both insert new data into an existing category and type over existing data. To alternate between the insert and overstrike modes, you simply press OA-E for Edit, just as you did in AppleWorks' word processor. When you are in insert mode, the cursor appears as a blinking underline. When you are in overstrike mode, it is a blinking block. Press OA-E a couple of times now and see how the cursor changes.

Now let's use inserting and overstriking to correct errors in the CIF file.

Suppose, for example, that you've noticed that in Record 10 the customer name is incorrect. It should be Best and Marsh's, rather than just Best's. Follow these steps to correct the name:

1. Press OA-Z to place yourself in multiple-record layout if you are not already there.

2. Position your cursor on the record for Best's.

3. Press OA-TAB until the cursor is on the customer name, Best's.

4. Position your cursor on the apostrophe in "Best's." You are going to insert the letters **and Marsh** in front of the "'s," effectively sliding the "'s" over to the end of the word "Marsh."

5. Press OA-E to change to the insert mode (the cursor should be a blinking underline).

6. Press the spacebar and type in the words **and Marsh**. Press RETURN.

The name is now correct even though the ending "s" in "Marsh's" has disappeared from the multiple-record layout screen. Now press OA-Z to see the record in single-record layout and to assure yourself that all of the name is still in the data base. Press OA-Z to return to multiple-record layout, and then press OA-1 to get to the first record.

Now suppose that you have also noticed that the suite number for Rainier Office Supply in incorrect. It should be number 501, not 5C. Edit this time by overstriking.

1. Move the cursor down to the Rainier Office Supply record by pressing the DOWN ARROW once.

2. Your cursor is already on the STREET 1 category, so just move it over the "C" in "5C" using the RIGHT ARROW.

3. Press OA-E to switch to overstrike mode.

4. Type **01** over the "C" and press RETURN.

Deleting and Inserting Records

Finally, suppose that you discover that the record for Fred's Department Store is completely wrong—that in fact you removed that customer from your files months ago. You want to delete the record and replace it with a brand new customer from whom you have just taken an order. Follow these steps:

1. Remaining in the multiple-record layout, move the cursor to Fred's Department Store.

2. Press OA-D for Delete. The record will be highlighted.

At this point you could select more records to be deleted if you wanted by moving the cursor up or down the screen with the UP and DOWN ARROWS.

3. Press RETURN and the entire record for Fred's Department Store will be deleted.

You can insert the new customer record wherever the cursor is, so we'll simply replace the record just deleted with the new one.

4. Press OA-I for Insert to display the Insert New Records screen, complete with the preestablished standard values.

5. Enter the new customer information as shown here:

```
Record 7 of 10
=============================================================================
CUSTOMER NUMBER: 7
CUSTOMER NAME: The Print Pot
STREET 1: 801 NW Adamson
STREET 2: -
CITY: Seattle
STATE: WA
ZIP CODE: 98134
TELEPHONE: 623-8584
CONTACT NAME: Sally Smith
CREDIT LIMIT: 2000
PRODUCT TYPE: P
1ST ORDER DATE: 6/15/85 ☐



------------------------------------------------------------------------
Type entry or use ⌘ commands                              55K Avail.
```

After you press RETURN for the last category, 1ST ORDER DATE, a blank screen will be displayed. Press ESC and you will be returned to the multiple-record layout screen.

Now that you have practiced the major editing techniques, let's look at some other aspects of editing the data base.

Shortening a Category

As you have seen, AppleWorks truncates some categories, with the result that not all the data stored in the data base can be seen on the screen. At the same time, other categories may seem to be too long, taking too much room on the screen. You can, however, adjust the screen format so that the data is displayed more efficiently. For example, if you look at your data base in multiple-record layout, you'll notice that while the contents of the CUSTOMER NAME category are truncated, the heading CUSTOMER NUMBER is longer than the contents of that category, the single customer numbers, actually warrant. You can make more efficient use of the space on the screen by shortening this category in two ways: shortening the category name and condensing the column width of the category.

First, shorten the category name by actually changing it. If you change the name by simply truncating it, the original name will remain as the official name in the file, although the truncated name will appear on the screen.

To change the category name you must return to the Change Name/Category screen. Follow these steps to alter the category name CUSTOMER NUMBER:

1. Press OA-N, for Name, and the Change Name/Category screen will be displayed:

```
File: CIF.LST              CHANGE NAME/CATEGORY     Escape: Review/Add/Change



Category names
===========================================================================
CUSTOMER NUMBER          |
CUSTOMER NAME            | Options:
STREET 1                 |
STREET 2                 | Change filename
CITY                     | Return    Go to first category
STATE                    |
ZIP CODE                 |
TELEPHONE                |
CONTACT NAME             |
CREDIT LIMIT             |
PRODUCT TYPE             |
1ST ORDER DATE           |
                         |
                         |
                         |
-----------------------------------------------------------------------------
Type filename:  ▓IF.LST                                           55K Avail.
```

At this point you can change the name of the file (from CIF.LST) by keying in another name. But you want to change the category name, not the filename.

2. Press RETURN to place the cursor on the first category name, CUSTOMER NUMBER.

3. Press CONTROL-Y to delete the contents of the entry so that the new category name can be entered.

4. Type in the new name **CUST** and then press RETURN.

5. Press ESC to return to the Review/Add/Change screen.

As you can see, although you have shortened the category name, the column is still too wide. Follow these steps to compress the column:

1. Press OA-L for Layout.

A menu of options will be displayed:

```
File: CIF.LST                  CHANGE RECORD LAYOUT    Escape: Review/Add/Change



===============================================================================
              --> or <--   Move cursor
               >  a  <     Switch category positions
              --> a <--    Change column width
              a-D          Delete this category
              a-I          Insert a previously deleted category

-------------------------------------------------------------------------------
CUST                CUSTOMER NAME   STREET 1         STREET 2          CITY
----------------    ------------    ------------    ---------------    ----------
1                   Aires Quick Cop 1345 South 8th                     Bellevue
2                   Rainier Office  Suite 501       5327 148th Stre    Bellevue
3                   Bellevue Printi 456 East Bellev                    Bellevue

----------------------------------------------------------------- More --->
Use options shown above to change record layout              55K Avail.
```

Since your cursor is already on the CUST category, you do
not have to move it farther.

2. Select and activate the Change Column Width option by
pressing OA-LEFT ARROW 11 times.

The displayed data will be shortened and you can now see
the entire address, except for ZIP CODE, on the screen, like
this:

```
File: CIF.LST                CHANGE RECORD LAYOUT      Escape: Review/Add/Change



================================================================================
                 --> or <--   Move cursor
                   >  a  <     Switch category positions
                 --> a  <--    Change column width
                 a-D           Delete this category
                 a-I           Insert a previously deleted category

       -------------------------------------------------------------------
CUST CUSTOMER NAME   STREET 1         STREET 2        CITY         STATE
|--- ---------------  ---------------  ---------------  ------------  ----------
1    Aires Quick Cop 1345 South 8th                    Bellevue     WA
2    Rainier Office  Suite 501        5327 148th Stre Bellevue     WA
3    Bellevue Printi 456 East Bellev                   Bellevue     WA
       ------------------------------------------------------------- More --->
Use options shown above to change record layout                     55K Avail.
```

3. Press ESC twice to return to the Review/Add/Change
screen.

You can use these procedures to change column names and
widths whenever you wish to customize your screen for maximum visual efficiency.

Arranging the File

AppleWorks allows you to sort or arrange files in four different ways: (1) alphabetically in ascending sequence (A-Z); (2) alphabetically in descending sequence (Z-A); (3) numerically in ascending sequence (0-9); and (4) numerically in descending sequence (9-0). You can also sort by time or date, if your category names have been set up properly.

The CIF.LST file is now in the order in which the data was entered. Although it is currently arranged numerically by CUSTOMER NUMBER, since that is the order in which we entered it, the file might be more useful if it were arranged in order of CUSTOMER NAME. Accomplishing this task is very simple and fast.

1. Move the cursor on the multiple-record layout to the CUSTOMER NAME category (it doesn't matter which record).

2. Press OA-A for Arrange. A menu of sort options will be displayed.

```
File: CIF.LST              ARRANGE (SORT)        Escape: Review/Add/Change
Selection: All records


===============================================================================
                    This file will be arranged on
                    this category: CUSTOMER NAME

                    Arrangement order:

                        1.  From A to Z
                        2.  From Z to A
                        3.  From 0 to 9
                        4.  From 9 to 0




-------------------------------------------------------------------------------
Type number, or use arrows, then press Return                    55K Avail.
```

3. Press RETURN to select the highlighted first option, From A to Z.

After a short wait the records will be rearranged for you in alphabetic sequence by customer name like this:

```
File: CIF.LST                  REVIEW/ADD/CHANGE                 Escape: Main Menu

Selection: All records


CUST CUSTOMER NAME    STREET 1        STREET 2        CITY           STATE
==========================================================================
1     Aires Quick Cop 1345 South 8th  -               Bellevue       WA
3     Bellevue Printi 456 East Bellev -               Bellevue       WA
10    Best and Marsh' Department C    10476 NE 8th St Bellevue       WA
8     Bo's Print Mart 7264 Northrup W -               Bellevue       WA
4     Evergreen Print 4769 NE 20th St -               Bellevue       WA
9     Foster's Printi 83658 Pacific H -               Renton         WA
5     Jensen Office S 800 East 8th St -               Bellevue       WA
2     Rainier Office  Suite 501       5327 148th Stre Bellevue       WA
7     The Print Pot   801 NW Adamson  -               Seattle        WA
6     University Prin 10056 Roosevelt -               Seattle        WA




------------------------------------------------------------------------------
Type entry or use ⌕ commands                              ⌕-? for Help
```

If you want to produce a list that is ordered or sequenced by several different categories, you must sort each category separately, starting with the most minor one. For example, to obtain a list of all customers alphabetically within each ZIP code, you would sort first by name alphabetically, and then by ZIP code numerically.

Saving the File

At this point you need to save the file. You have entered data, edited it, and rearranged it. You should periodically save the file, even if you're not completely finished working with it.

Although the danger of losing data is slight, faulty electrical power, human error, and other factors can bring about such minor disasters. For this reason, saving your files periodically is important.

Press OA-S for Save, as you did for the word processing files, and within a few seconds the data base file will be saved.

Printing a Report

Printing a report of the data base is slightly more complex than printing a word processed document. You must first design the report as you want it and name it. AppleWorks gives you the capability to format and print two basic types of reports. As you saw in Chapter 1, one type of report is in the form of a list, containing one line per record. This type of report is called *tables-style*. The other basic form of report is *labels-style*, where the data from each record can occupy more than one line, as it does on mailing labels. In this chapter you will print a simple tables-style report. Chapter 7 will discuss designing both kinds of reports in greater detail.

Deciding What to Print

Choosing which categories you want to see in a report is the first step in formatting it. To choose wisely you need to determine exactly how the report will be used. To create a simple telephone list that can be used by anyone, you might want to exclude any confidential information, such as the credit limit. Thus, for purposes of the report, the following categories would be acceptable:

- CUSTOMER NAME

- TELEPHONE NUMBER

- CONTACT NAME

- CITY

- STATE

- PRODUCT TYPE

- 1ST ORDER DATE

Formatting the Report

Formatting a report consists of eliminating unwanted categories and then arranging the remaining categories in the order in which you want them to be printed. These formats are then saved and become a part of the data file, although as you will see in a moment they exist quite separately from the file. You can establish up to eight different report formats for each data base. For now you will learn to design and print just one report, the Telephone List.

Follow these steps to format a tables-style report.

1. From the multiple-record layout of the CIF.LST, press OA-P (for Print) to display the Report menu:

```
File: CIF.LST                        REPORT MENU          Escape: Review/Add/Change
Report: None



===============================================================================



          1.  Get a report format
          2.  Create a new "tables" format
          3.  Create a new "Labels" format
          4.  Duplicate an existing format
          5.  Erase a format




-------------------------------------------------------------------------------
Type number, or use arrows, then press Return □                    55K Avail.
```

This menu allows you to select whether you want to (1) get an existing report format to print (none exists right now); (2) create a new tables-style format (the default when no formats exist); (3) create a new labels-style format; (4) make a copy of an existing report format; or (5) delete an existing format that you no longer want.

2. Since the second option, Create a new "tables" format, is what we want and is also highlighted, press RETURN to select it.

3. When prompted, enter the report name, **CIF Telephone List**, and press RETURN.

The Report Format screen will be displayed.

```
File: CIF.LST                   REPORT FORMAT              Escape: Report Menu
Report: CIF Telephone List
Selection: All records




================================================================================
--> or <--   Move cursor                    a-J   Right justify this category
  >  a  <    Switch category positions      a-K   Define a calculated category
--> a  <--   Change column width            a-N   Change report name and/or title
a-A  Arrange (sort) on this category        a-O   Printer options
a-D  Delete this category                   a-P   Print the report
a-G  Add/remove group totals                a-R   Change record selection rules
a-I  Insert a prev. deleted category        a-T   Add/remove category totals
--------------------------------------------------------------------------------

CUST         CUSTOMER NAM STREET 1     STREET 2     CITY       STATE      Z
A----------- -B---------- -C---------- -D---------- -E-------- -F--------- -
1            Aires Quick  1345 South 8              Bellevue   WA         9
3            Bellevue Pri 456 East Bel              Bellevue   WA         9
10           Best and Mar Department C 10476 NE 8th Bellevue   WA         9

---------------------------------------------------------------- More --->
Use options shown above to change report format                  55K Avail.
```

Take a look at the screen. In the upper left-hand corner you can see that the filename, CIF.LST, is identified, as well as the report name, CIF Telephone List. You see from the Selection that no special criteria have been applied; all records will be displayed in the report. In the right-hand corner, you see that pressing the ESC key will return to the Report menu.

Immediately beneath the double line is the menu of formatting options, for changing the format of a report. Chapter 7 will investigate most of these in more detail. For now you will be using only five commands: Move the cursor, Switch category positions, Change column width, Delete this category, and Print the report.

On the bottom of the screen is a display of three records. Above them are the category names, such as CUSTOMER NAM (NAME is truncated), and beneath the names are alphabetic designations for each of the categories. For example, CUST is A, CUSTOMER NAME is B, and so on. The column designators serve several functions. First, they provide a reference point for you as you switch category positions. And second, the column designators allow you to perform arithmetic calculations involving categories, as you'll see in Chapter 7.

Deleting unwanted categories. Now delete the categories you don't want in the report: namely, the CUST, STREET 1, STREET 2, ZIP CODE, and CREDIT LIMIT categories. These categories will remain in the data base, of course; they will simply not be printed in the report.

To delete these unneeded categories, you will first move the cursor to the unwanted categories and then press the OA-D command. Follow these steps:

1. Since the cursor is already on CUST, press OA-D. The category will be removed.

2. Pressing the RIGHT ARROW key once, move the cursor to STREET 1. Now press OA-D.

3. Since the cursor is now on STREET 2, simply press OA-D again to delete the STREET 2 category.

4. Press the RIGHT ARROW key twice to move the cursor to ZIP CODE and press OA-D.

5. Press the RIGHT ARROW key twice to move the cursor to

CREDIT LIMIT and press OA-D.

If you accidentally delete the wrong category, you can easily restore it by pressing OA-I for Insert. A list of all of the deleted categories will be displayed for you to select the one to be restored. Then by pressing ESC you can return to the Report Format screen.

You have now deleted the unwanted categories and your screen looks like this:

```
File: CIF.LST                    REPORT FORMAT              Escape: Report Menu
Report: CIF Telephone List
Selection: All records



================================================================================
--> or <--  Move cursor                     @-J  Right justify this category
  >  @   <    Switch category positions      @-K  Define a calculated category
--> @  <--  Change column width              @-N  Change report name and/or title
@-A  Arrange (sort) on this category         @-O  Printer options
@-D  Delete this category                    @-P  Print the report
@-G  Add/remove group totals                 @-R  Change record selection rules
@-I  Insert a prev. deleted category         @-T  Add/remove category totals
--------------------------------------------------------------------------------

CUSTOMER NAM CITY         STATE       TELEPHONE    CONTACT NAME PRODUCT TYPE 1
-A---------- -B---------- -C--------- -D---------- -E---------- ⊟F---------- -
Aires Quick  Bellevue     WA          454-1356     Larry Aires  P           J
Bellevue Pri Bellevue     WA          456-2649     Sue Ingraham P           J
Best and Mar Bellevue     WA          454-7385     Lois Jamison P           M

------------------------------------------------------------------- More --->
Use options shown above to change report format                    55K Avail.
```

Now you must rearrange the categories on the page.

Changing the category positions.   The categories are not in the position that you want them. You want them in the following order: CUSTOMER NAME, TELEPHONE, CONTACT NAME, CITY, STATE, PRODUCT TYPE, and 1ST ORDER DATE. To produce this arrangement of categories you simply have to move TELEPHONE and CONTACT NAME next to CUSTOMER NAME. To switch the positions of categories, you use the OA key in conjunction with the LESS THAN (<) and GREATER THAN (>) keys. Follow these steps:

1. Using the LEFT ARROW, move the cursor to the TELE-PHONE category.

2. Press OA-< (LESS THAN key without SHIFT) two times to move the TELEPHONE category left, so that it is positioned next to CUSTOMER NAME.

3. Using the RIGHT ARROW, move the cursor to CONTACT NAME.

4. Move the CONTACT NAME category next to TELEPHONE by pressing OA-< two times.

The categories are now in the correct order:

```
File: CIF.LST                  REPORT FORMAT              Escape: Report Menu
Report: CIF Telephone List
Selection: All records


================================================================================
--> or <--   Move cursor                    a-J  Right justify this category
  >   a   <   Switch category positions     a-K  Define a calculated category
--> a  <--   Change column width            a-N  Change report name and/or title
a-A   Arrange (sort) on this category       a-O  Printer options
a-D   Delete this category                  a-P  Print the report
a-G   Add/remove group totals               a-R  Change record selection rules
a-I   Insert a prev. deleted category       a-T  Add/remove category totals
--------------------------------------------------------------------------------
CUSTOMER NAM TELEPHONE     CONTACT NAME CITY        STATE       PRODUCT TYPE 1
-A---------- -B----------  ▯C---------- -D--------- -E--------- -F---------- -
Aires Quick  454-1356      Larry Aires  Bellevue    WA          P            J
Bellevue Pri 456-2649      Sue Ingraham Bellevue    WA          P            J
Best and Mar 454-7385      Lois Jamison Bellevue    WA          P            M

------------------------------------------------------------------ More --->
Use options shown above to change report format                 55K Avail.
```

Altering the column width.   In the last few screens, the contents of the CUSTOMER NAME category have been truncated to create more room on the screen. But for this report you do not want this category to be truncated. Let's lengthen the column width.

1. Move your cursor to CUSTOMER NAME.

2. Press OA-RIGHT ARROW ten times.

You will see the names fill in from the data base contents, as follows.

```
File: CIF.LST                    REPORT FORMAT              Escape: Report Menu
Report: CIF Telephone List
Selection: All records



=================================================================================
--> or <--   Move cursor                    @-J   Right justify this category
 >   @   <   Switch category positions       @-K   Define a calculated category
--> @ <--    Change column width             @-N   Change report name and/or title
@-A  Arrange (sort) on this category         @-O   Printer options
@-D  Delete this category                    @-P   Print the report
@-G  Add/remove group totals                 @-R   Change record selection rules
@-I  Insert a prev. deleted category         @-T   Add/remove category totals
---------------------------------------------------------------------------------

CUSTOMER NAME              TELEPHONE      CONTACT NAME CITY          STATE        PROD
▯A-------------------- -B---------- -C---------- -D---------- -E---------- -F--
Aires Quick Copy           454-1356       Larry Aires  Bellevue      WA           P
Bellevue Printing Co.      456-2649       Sue Ingraham Bellevue      WA           P
Best and Marsh's           454-7385       Lois Jamison Bellevue      WA           P

--------------------------------------------------------------------- More --->
Use options shown above to change report format                   55K Avail.
```

At this point if you move the cursor back and forth across the whole record using the RIGHT and LEFT ARROWS, another problem with column width emerges: some of the columns are too wide for all the information to fit on one screen, and therefore the screen will not print on an 8 1/2 by 11-inch piece of paper, which is what you need in order to print your report. For this reason, you need to shorten the column width of categories. The categories that seem too long are STATE and PRODUCT TYPE. If that still isn't enough, a few characters can be squeezed out of CITY.

3. Move your cursor to STATE and press OA-LEFT ARROW seven times to reduce the column width to five positions.

4. Move your cursor to PRODUCT TYPE and press OA-LEFT ARROW eight times.

The column title will be truncated to PROD, which is acceptable.

If you move your cursor back to CUSTOMER NAME using the LEFT ARROW, you can see that the screen is still too wide for all the data to appear at once. The 1ST ORDER DATE column is cut off. To fix this,

5. Move your cursor to CITY and press OA-LEFT ARROW three times.

All information needed now fits on one screen.

```
File: CIF.LST                  REPORT FORMAT              Escape: Report Menu
Report: CIF Telephone List
Selection: All records



===============================================================================
--> or <--   Move cursor                    @-J   Right justify this category
 >  @  <     Switch category positions      @-K   Define a calculated category
--> @ <--    Change column width             @-N   Change report name and/or title
@-A   Arrange (sort) on this category        @-O   Printer options
@-D   Delete this category                   @-P   Print the report
@-G   Add/remove group totals                @-R   Change record selection rules
@-I   Insert a prev. deleted category        @-T   Add/remove category totals
-------------------------------------------------------------------------------

CUSTOMER NAME            TELEPHONE    CONTACT NAME CITY        STATE PROD 1ST ORDER
-A--------------------- -B---------- -C---------- [d-------- -E--- -F-- -G------
Aires Quick Copy         454-1356     Larry Aires  Bellevue    WA    P    Jan 15 76
Bellevue Printing Co.    456-2649     Sue Ingraham Bellevue    WA    P    Jun 14 84
Best and Marsh's         454-7385     Lois Jamison Bellevue    WA    P    Mar 24 78

------------------------------------------------------------------ More --->
Use options shown above to change report format                  55K Avail.
```

Printing to the Screen and the Printer

The report now is ready to print. Check that your printer is turned on and has both paper and ribbon correctly mounted. Press OA-P for Print. The Print the Report menu will be displayed:

```
File: CIF.LST                    PRINT THE REPORT           Escape: Report Format
Report: CIF Telephone List
Selection: All records


================================================================================
                     Where do you want to print the report?

                     1.  ImageWriter
                     2.  Qume 5
                     3.  The screen
                     4.  The clipboard (for the Word Processor)
                     5.  The clipboard (for Mail Merge)
                     6.  A text (ASCII) file on disk
                     7.  A DIF (TM) file on disk




--------------------------------------------------------------------------------
Type number, or use arrows, then press Return__            55K Avail.
```

You have several options. First, you will be able to choose which printer, out of the three you may have defined, you want. The other options on this menu allow you to print to the screen, to the Clipboard (for either word processing or mail merge), or to a type of file on disk, such as ASCII or DIF.

If you want to test your report before committing it to paper, you would choose to print on the screen. This is especially handy in the data base because when you reformat a report, you can't see it as a whole; the Report Format screen only allows you to see three lines of the report at a time. By sending the finished report to the screen as you'll do in a moment, however, you can see what you're going to get before you go to the trouble of printing it.

Printing to the Clipboard allows you to move your data base file directly to a word processing document. You'll also do that in a later chapter.

Finally, you would want to print your report to an ASCII or DIF file on disk if you were going to use your data base report in a program other than AppleWorks. And by using the DIF file, you can send a data base report to the Apple-Works spreadsheet component.

Now let's test our report on the screen.

Printing to the screen.   Printing to the screen allows you to take a quick look at your report before printing it on paper. Follow these steps:

1. Move your cursor to option 3, The screen (this may be option 2 for you), and press RETURN. You will be shown this screen:

```
File: CIF.LST                   PRINT THE REPORT              Escape: Report Format
Report: CIF Telephone List
Selection: All records



==============================================================================


            While the printer is running
            you can use these keys:

            Escape        to stop printing and
                          return to report format

            Space Bar     to pause
                          to continue printing



-------------------------------------------------------------------------------
Type report date or press Return: __                          55K Avail.
```

The screen explains how to stop the printer temporarily or permanently, and also asks you to type in a date if you want. Since this is just a screen print, the date is unimportant.

2. Press RETURN to print the report on the screen.

```
File:   CIF.LST                                          Page  1
Report: CIF Telephone List
CUSTOMER NAME          TELEPHONE     CONTACT NAME CITY      STATE PROD 1ST ORDER
---------------------- ------------- ------------ --------- ----- ---- ---------
Aires Quick Copy       454-1356      Larry Aires  Bellevue  WA    P    Jan 15 76
Bellevue Printing Co.  456-2649      Sue Ingraham Bellevue  WA    P    Jun 14 84
Best and Marsh's       454-7385      Lois Jamison Bellevue  WA    P    Mar 24 78
Bo's Print Mart        454-7473      Bo           Bellevue  WA    P    Mar 28 84
Evergreen Printing Sup 454-2748      Perry Adams  Bellevue  WA    P    Mar 15 84
Foster's Printing Pres 239-6295      Terry Hook   Renton    WA    P    Jan  1 83
Jensen Office Supply   454-0500      Tina Powell  Bellevue  WA    P    Aug 22 78
Rainier Office Supply  643-1456      Gary Loren   Bellevue  WA    B    Dec  2 80
The Print Pot          623-8584      Sally Smith  Seattle   WA    P    Jun 15 85
University Print Shop   622-4846      Bruce Pruett Seattle   WA    P    Aug 25 80




Press Space Bar to continue []                            55K Avail.
```

Look the report over. Although some of the customer names are still truncated, you can see enough of them for the purposes of this telephone list. The report looks acceptable.

3. Press the spacebar to return to the Report Format screen.

Now that we know that the report is acceptable, let's print a hard copy.

Printing to the printer.   Again press OA-P to ask for a printout. The Print the Report menu will be displayed again. In this case you want your primary printer, so move the cursor to your printer name and press RETURN. Upon pressing RETURN the next screen will be displayed. As before, it informs you how to cancel the printing if you should want to. Also you are asked to enter a report date if you want to. You will normally wish to do this in order to keep track of how old a particular copy of the CIF Telephone List is and how recently it has been updated. If you do not wish to enter the date, simply press RETURN.

Press RETURN again to verify that you only want one copy of the report. As explained earlier, AppleWorks assumes that you want one copy and establishes that default for you. If you want a different number of copies, just enter the number (up to nine) and press RETURN.

The report should now be printing. If it is not, review the discussion of setting up the printer in Chapter 2 or Appendix A.

Saving the File

Since you have modified your data base file by creating a report format, the copy that was saved on disk earlier is no longer current. You need to update the saved version.

Save your report one final time by pressing OA-S. After a short wait your file and report formats will be saved for future use.

You have now completed the first exercise on the Apple-Works data base component. You can turn off your computer and continue later, or you can proceed either to Chapter 5 or to Chapter 7.

In Chapter 5, "Building A Spreadsheet," you will be introduced to the spreadsheet component of AppleWorks. If you are interested in continuing with the data base component, you can skip to Chapter 7, "Expanding Your Data Base Skills."

5

Building
A Spreadsheet

The spreadsheet component of AppleWorks, also called a *worksheet,* allows you to work with rows and columns of numbers, producing automatically anything you could produce on a columnar accounting pad or a manual spreadsheet. AppleWorks' spreadsheet gives you considerable power and flexibility in entering and editing information, setting up calculations with formulas and functions, and printing the results.

In Chapter 5 you will briefly review the spreadsheet concepts introduced in Chapter 1. Then you will learn to create a new spreadsheet file from scratch and to move the cursor around within the spreadsheet. You will also learn how to establish a format for the spreadsheet that suits your particular application. Next you will enter formulas, functions, and some data. Finally you will practice editing the file by both inserting new material and typing over existing material and "blanking out" units of information. At the end of the chapter you will save the file and print a spreadsheet report.

Getting Started

Spreadsheets are very powerful tools, but for this reason they require more planning and development. Before you enter the data itself, you need to design your spreadsheet by answering a series of questions. The first and most important question is, "What solution am I trying to develop?" From the answer to this question, you must determine what information you will need and how it should be arranged on the spreadsheet. You must also determine what formulas and functions the spreadsheet will require to perform its calculations.

Once you have established the basic structure of the spreadsheet, you'll be done with the hard work. Entering the data and printing the report are relatively easy procedures. What is more, you will have a model that you can use over and over again for a particular application, modifying it as necessary.

In this chapter, you build a spreadsheet for an accounts receivable invoice. In the process of building the spreadsheet model, you will be answering the questions you would normally have to answer and performing the steps you would normally perform to build other spreadsheets. Thus you should be able to use the process you practice in this chapter as the basis for building spreadsheet models that suit your particular needs.

The Elements of a Spreadsheet

Figure 5-1 presents the elements of a spreadsheet. It is composed of rows and columns. A *row* is a horizontal line of information, similar to a data base record. The rows are numbered on the left-hand side of the spreadsheet, and a spreadsheet can contain from 1 to 999 rows. A *column* is a vertical line of information and is identified by the letters along the top of the spreadsheet. Thus, in Figure 5-1, column A contains the NUM data, which is the customer number. Column C contains the CUSTOMER NAME data, column D is labeled DATE, and so on. Columns will be labeled A to Z, AA to AZ, BA to BZ, CA to CZ, and finally, DA to DW. This

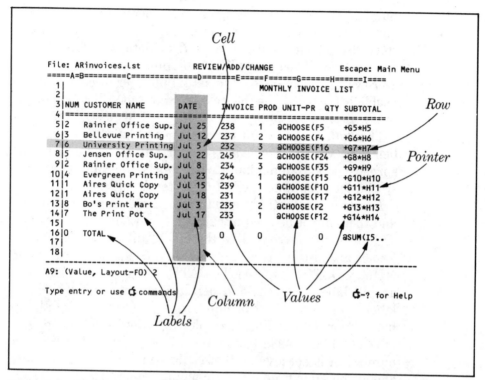

Figure 5-1.   Elements of a spreadsheet

amounts to 127 columns that can make up an AppleWorks spreadsheet.

Rows and columns intersect at cell locations. A *cell* is the same as a data base entry in that it is the basic unit of information in the spreadsheet. Cells are addressed by column and row: for example, cell B4 is the intersection of column B and row 4. Similarly, cell AB82 is the intersection of column AB and row 82. B4 and AB82 are called the *coordinates* of the cells.

Theoretically, with 127 columns and 999 rows, AppleWorks provides a total of 126,873 cells. But the actual number of cells in which you store information is a different story: the number of cells depends upon the amount of memory you have with your computer. With 128K of memory, you can store 2K (about 2000 characters) of data per row in your spreadsheet. If you used all 127 columns you could have about 28 rows. As you can see, the actual number of cells that are usable is far below the theoretical limit, but still adequate for many applications.

The data contained in the spreadsheet is of two types: labels and values. Since it is important in learning to use spreadsheets to understand what labels and values can consist of, let's examine each of these terms in turn.

Labels are essentially entries that have no numeric value and that cannot be used in calculations. Labels can be words or letters within cells, like the label "Jul 5" in Figure 5-1. Labels are also the titles for rows and columns; for example, NUM, CUSTOMER NAME, DATE, and so on, in Figure 5-1 are all labels. Finally, and perhaps somewhat surprisingly, labels can also consist of numbers that function like alphabetic information. For example, in a hypothetical column labeled "1988," 1988 would be a label; although 1988 is a number, it is not a value that could be used in a calculation, and at the same time it simply names something in a spreadsheet, just as the heading NINETEEN HUNDRED EIGHTY-EIGHT would. If you wish to use a number as a label, you must let AppleWorks know that the number is actually a label rather than a value by putting quotation marks in front of the number (for example, "1988).

Values are the opposite of labels: they are entries that can be used in calculations and that have a numeric value. That numeric value may be stated directly; that is, the value may simply be a number, like the numbers in columns A, E, and F in Figure 5-1.

Furthermore, values can consist of formulas and functions. *Formulas* are mathematical statements for calculating numbers. In Figure 5-1, the entries in column I, SUBTOTAL, are all formulas that will be calculated to produce numeric values. *Functions* are codes for commonly used calculations. @SUM(A2...D2), for example, is a function that tells AppleWorks to add the values of the numbers in cells A2 through D2. The result of this addition operation would be, once again, a numeric value. In Figure 5-1, the entries in column

G, UNIT-PR, are functions. In AppleWorks, functions are always preceded with the @ (at) sign.

Finally, in addition to being numbers, formulas, or functions, values can be *pointers*. Pointers are cell indicators that do exactly what their name implies: they point to a value in another cell, telling AppleWorks to reproduce that value in the cell containing the pointer. In Figure 5-1, H11 is a pointer, as are all the other cells named in the formulas listed in the SUBTOTAL column.

Like the data base, the spreadsheet has features that affect the format of the spreadsheet rather than its contents. You can set standard formats either for the spreadsheet as a whole or for a block of cells, which may consist of a single cell or a group of contiguous cells. This chapter will devote considerable space to the subject of standard formats.

Creating a New Spreadsheet File

If you have not started AppleWorks yet, do so now and bring up the Main Menu. If you have problems, reread the explanation of the procedure in Chapter 2. When you are at the Main Menu, select option 1, Add files to the Desktop, since we want to create a new spreadsheet file. If your assigned disk drive is drive 1, you must change it to drive 2. Then insert the AppleWorks1 disk that contains your word processing and data base files into drive 2. Now you're ready to create your first spreadsheet file.

To actually create the new spreadsheet file, select option 5, Spreadsheet, by typing **5** and pressing RETURN. You will be shown the Spreadsheet menu, which tells you that your new file can be created from scratch (which you want) or can be an accepted DIF file produced by a program other than AppleWorks. Your third option is to create a spreadsheet from a VisiCalc file.

Since you want From scratch, press RETURN. You will be asked to enter a name for your new file. Enter **ARinvoices.lst** for Accounts Receivable Invoices. You will see the pointing arrow that AppleWorks uses to tell you which option

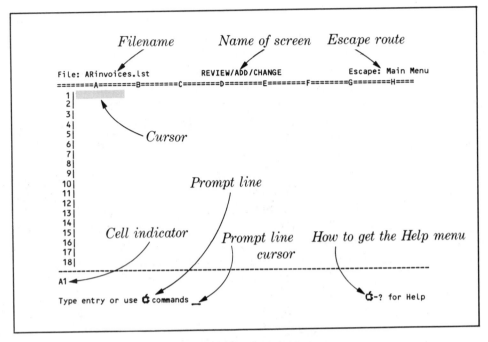

Figure 5-2. Elements of the Review/Add/Change screen

has been chosen. Press RETURN to complete the file-naming action. The Review/Add/Change screen will be displayed.

The Review/Add/Change Screen

The Review/Add/Change screen in the spreadsheet looks different from the corresponding screens in the data base and word processor, as you can see in Figure 5-2.

On the top of the screen is the name of the current file, the name of the screen, and the escape route. On the double line immediately beneath the screen name are letters that designate the columns. You can see columns A through H on the screen. On the left-hand side of the screen you can see the numeric row designators 1 to 18. At the bottom of the screen is the prompt line, which tells you what to do next, and the instruction for getting the Help menu.

The screen has two cursors—one on the prompt line and another highlighting cell A1. You'll soon see how having two cursors aids your data entry.

Also above the prompt line is the *cell indicator*, currently pointing to the cell you're on, A1. As you move the cursor this changes. The cell indicator not only tells you which cell you're on, it also describes the cell's content. In this case, the cell is blank, so all the cell indicator tells you is the name of the cell, A1.

The center of the screen is reserved for displaying data. But first, let's take a look at how to move the cursor, how the screen reflects your actions, and how you can correct mistakes.

Moving the Cursor From Cell to Cell

The cursor movements are similar to those you've experienced in the data base, but not identical.

Moving the UP, DOWN, RIGHT, and LEFT ARROW keys moves the cursor from cell to cell in the direction of the arrow. Let's try them out now. Press the DOWN, RIGHT, and LEFT ARROWS, keeping track of where you are on the screen by looking at the cell indicator. When you have moved down and to the right on the screen, press the UP ARROW key to return to the home position, cell A1. Now hold the RIGHT ARROW down and watch the cell indicator as the column identifiers sail past.

The arrow keys perform two functions. One is moving the cursor from one cell to another, as you've just seen. The second is to signal the program that entry of data is complete. In this regard, the arrow keys function like the RETURN key in the spreadsheet.

Continue to experiment with the arrow keys until you understand the scope and layout of the screen. You might experience a beep as AppleWorks informs you that you have reached the edge of the spreadsheet.

Another method of moving the cursor from cell to cell across the spreadsheet is with the TAB key. Try pressing the TAB key now to move the cursor forward—that is, to the right. To reverse the direction, press OA-TAB. You can use the TAB key as an alternative to the LEFT and RIGHT ARROW keys.

Moving From Screen to Screen

As with the data base and word processor, if you press simultaneously the OA key with the UP, DOWN, LEFT, or RIGHT ARROW the cursor will move quickly across the screen. It's particularly important to be able to move from screen to screen in the spreadsheet because spreadsheets usually occupy more than one screen.

To practice moving from screen to screen now, press OA-RIGHT ARROW once. The cursor jumps to the right edge of the screen, column H.

Now if you press OA-RIGHT ARROW three times, you will notice that the cursor moves across the spreadsheet one screen at a time. If you press OA-LEFT ARROW four times, you will return to the beginning of the spreadsheet. The first time you press OA-LEFT ARROW, the cursor jumps to the left-hand edge of the screen. Successive presses of the key move the cursor one screen at a time to the left, exactly like the OA-RIGHT ARROW key but in the opposite direction.

The OA-UP and DOWN ARROWs move the cursor in the same manner in a vertical direction. Try this now. Press the OA-DOWN ARROW once; the cursor jumps to the bottom of the screen. Press the OA-DOWN ARROW two more times; the cursor moves a full screen down each time. Now return to the top of the screen using the OA-UP ARROW. The first time you press the OA-UP ARROW the cursor moves to the top of the screen. Thereafter, it will leap to the next full screen until the cursor reaches the top of the spreadsheet.

As you have seen, the OA-ARROW key combinations enable you to move the cursor quickly from one part of the spreadsheet to another. Another command that is common to the three components and that is quite useful in the spreadsheet is the OA-1 to OA-9 key combinations, which allow you to thumb through the spreadsheet at relative intervals. Thus, pressing OA-1 positions the cursor at the beginning of the spreadsheet; OA-9 at the end; and OA-5 in the middle. Since our spreadsheet contains no data, however, there is nothing for AppleWorks to thumb through now. You will use these commands later.

Finding Specific Locations

Sometimes you want to move the cursor to a specific cell. To do this, you can use the Find command, OA-F. The Find command locates instances of whatever you wish to find one at a time, starting with the first instance relative to the cursor's position. Follow these steps now:

1. Press OA-F, for Find. This screen will be displayed:

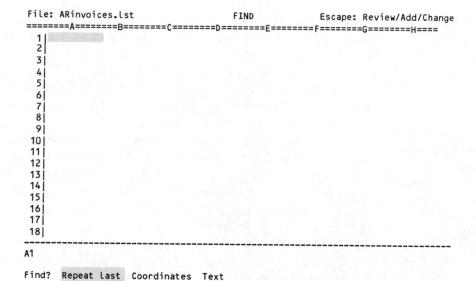

The prompt line shows that you have three options. If you have already entered a Find request, you can repeat it by simply selecting the default, Repeat last. If you are searching for a cell, you would select the Coordinates option and enter the column and row coordinates. If you are searching for the contents of a cell, you would select Text. You can specify up to 25 characters of text.

For practice using the Find command, try searching for a particular cell, G6.

2. Enter C for Coordinates.

3. Enter **G6** when prompted for the cell coordinates and then press RETURN.

Your cursor will go immediately to cell G6. If you were to request the Find command again, the G6 coordinates would be remembered, so that you could just select Repeat last. This feature makes it easy for you to return to a frequently used cell without reentering the coordinates.

Cells, cell indicator, and prompt line relationships. When you are entering or revising data in the spreadsheet, there are three areas to watch: the prompt lines (there are actually two of them), the cell indicator, and the cell cursor.

Normally you will see a single prompt line which describes exactly what you are doing (it will be blank if you are simply viewing the screen). But once you begin to enter data into a cell, the prompt line displays an informative message, and a second prompt line appears above it showing you exactly what is being entered into the cell. Above the second prompt line, the cell indicator always tells you the current contents of the cell: the type of data (label or value); whether it is a pointer, formula, or function; and the actual contents. The cell cursor shows you the cell contents (not always the actual contents, as you will see) unless instructed to display the pointer, formula, or function instead.

The following example illustrates the relationship between the prompt lines, the cell indicator, and the cell cursor. You'll write something into a cell and watch what happens in these areas as the data is first entered, then completed, and finally changed.

1. Move your cursor to cell B3.

2. Enter the word **dog**, but do not press RETURN or an arrow key.

Your screen should look like the following illustration.

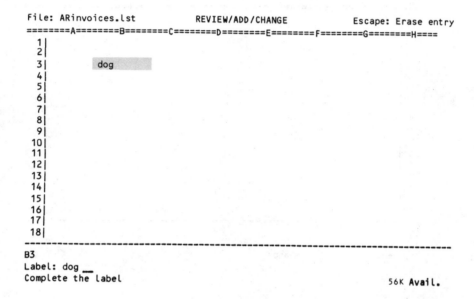

```
File: ARinvoices.lst          REVIEW/ADD/CHANGE          Escape: Erase entry
========A========B========C========D========E========F========G========H====
    1|
    2|
    3|       dog
    4|
    5|
    6|
    7|
    8|
    9|
   10|
   11|
   12|
   13|
   14|
   15|
   16|
   17|
   18|
-----------------------------------------------------------------------------
B3
Label: dog __
Complete the label                                        56K Avail.
```

The cell contains the word "dog," but you can see that the entry has not been completed because the cell indicator still shows the contents to be blank. Also the bottom prompt line displays a message informing you that a label has yet to be completed. Meanwhile, the upper prompt line displays the type of data (label since it's alphabetic) and the content.

3. Press the DOWN ARROW.

The word "dog" has disappeared from the prompt line but remains in the cell. The cell indicator now points to cell B4, which is blank.

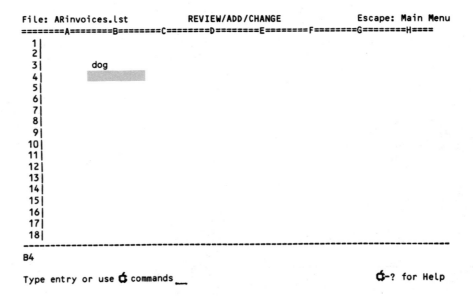

```
File: ARinvoices.lst            REVIEW/ADD/CHANGE              Escape: Main Menu
========A========B========C========D========E========F========G========H====
   1|
   2|
   3|        dog
   4|
   5|
   6|
   7|
   8|
   9|
  10|
  11|
  12|
  13|
  14|
  15|
  16|
  17|
  18|
-------------------------------------------------------------------------------
B4

Type entry or use ⌘ commands ___                            ⌘-? for Help
```

4. Press the UP ARROW.

Notice that the cell indicator, the line closest to the bottom border of the screen, now tells you both the type of data (label) and the contents of the cell (dog).

5. Enter the word **cat**. Do not press RETURN or an arrow key.

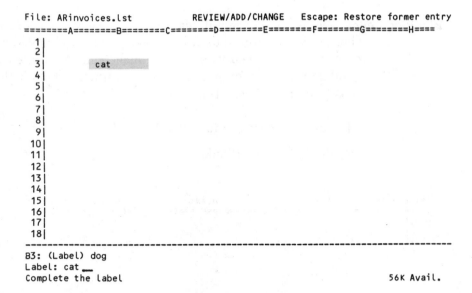

```
File: ARinvoices.lst            REVIEW/ADD/CHANGE   Escape: Restore former entry
========A========B========C========D========E========F========G========H====
  1|
  2|
  3|       cat
  4|
  5|
  6|
  7|
  8|
  9|
 10|
 11|
 12|
 13|
 14|
 15|
 16|
 17|
 18|
--------------------------------------------------------------------------------
B3: (Label) dog
Label: cat __
Complete the label                                              56K Avail.
```

The cell indicator tells you what the actual, original contents of cell B3 are, since the new entry has not been completed. That is, the original content is the word "dog." The word "cat" isn't in the cell indicator because you haven't pressed RETURN. The prompt line advises you that a new entry is waiting to be completed, and above that the type and contents of the new entry are displayed. The cell cursor shows the new entry.

6. Press RETURN to complete the entry.

The cell indicator now reflects the completed change of cell B3 to "cat."

Blanking cells.   Occasionally you will want to erase the contents of a cell when you have entered data incorrectly or have changed your mind about what you want to put in the cell. A simple command handles this for you: the Blank command. Follow these steps to blank out cell B3.

1. Move your cursor to cell B3.

2. Press OA-B for Blank.

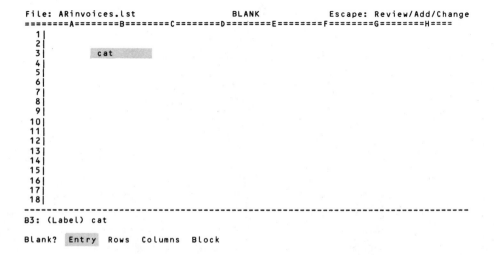

```
File: ARinvoices.lst                    BLANK               Escape: Review/Add/Change
========A========B========C========D========E========F========G========H====
   1|
   2|
   3|         cat
   4|
   5|
   6|
   7|
   8|
   9|
  10|
  11|
  12|
  13|
  14|
  15|
  16|
  17|
  18|
----------------------------------------------------------------------
B3: (Label) cat

Blank?  Entry   Rows  Columns  Block
```

The Blank screen prompt line tells you that you have a choice of blanking an entry (a cell, like B3), a whole column, a whole row, or any block of rows and columns that you specify. In this case you want to blank an entry.

3. Press RETURN to select the highlighted entry—that is, to blank out the current cell, cell B3.

Now that you know how to move the cell cursor and blank out a cell, and you understand how the two cursors relate to the cell indicator and the prompt lines, you have some familiarity with the techniques you'll need when you enter and manipulate data. The next step is to learn about setting up the physical design of the spreadsheet.

Preparing the Design of the Spreadsheet

The key to preparing the layout of the spreadsheet is standard values. Standard values can be assigned both to the spreadsheet as a whole and to individual cells. The worksheet standard values are in effect all the time and govern how your data will be formatted when it is entered. The cell standard values can either be entered as an afterthought—that is, when data already entered is seen to be incorrectly formatted—or they can be set up prior to data entry. You will want to set standard values for particular cells when the format of these cells differs from the values you set for the spreadsheet as a whole. You'll learn how to set the standard values of particular cells in a minute.

Setting Standard Values for the Whole Spreadsheet

To set and reset the worksheet standard values use the OA-V (for Values) command. Enter OA-V now to display the Standard Values menu.

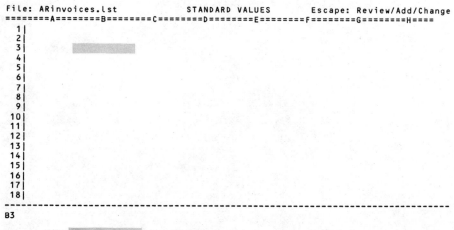

```
File: ARinvoices.lst          STANDARD VALUES        Escape: Review/Add/Change
========A========B========C========D========E========F========G========H====
    1|
    2|
    3|
    4|
    5|
    6|
    7|
    8|
    9|
   10|
   11|
   12|
   13|
   14|
   15|
   16|
   17|
   18|
-------------------------------------------------------------------------------
B3

Standards?  Value format  Label format  Column width  Protection  Recalculate
```

You will notice that there are five standards that you can set: Value format, Label format, Column width, Protection, and Recalculate. Value format allows you to define what the standard format will be for numeric data entered into each cell. You have five options that allow you to specify how the numbers in the cells will look. Press RETURN now to select Value format and see the five Value format options at the bottom of your screen.

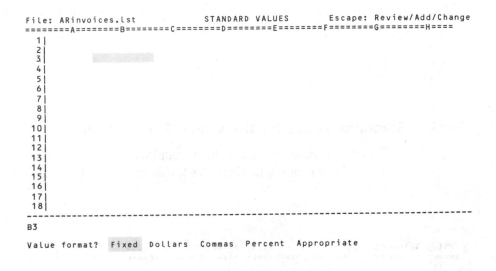

```
File: ARinvoices.lst          STANDARD VALUES       Escape: Review/Add/Change
========A========B========C========D========E========F========G========H====
    1|
    2|
    3|
    4|
    5|
    6|
    7|
    8|
    9|
   10|
   11|
   12|
   13|
   14|
   15|
   16|
   17|
   18|
-----------------------------------------------------------------------------
B3

Value format?  Fixed  Dollars  Commas  Percent  Appropriate
```

First, Fixed allows you to define a fixed number (0 to 7) of decimal places that will be displayed, like this: 25.1234567. Second, Dollars allows you to define a number that is formatted with a dollar sign, two fixed decimal places, and commas separating the thousands, like this: $1,536.82. Third, Commas separates the number by thousands, contains 0 to 7 fixed decimal places, and puts negative amounts in parentheses, like this: (1,234.8). Fourth, Percent displays the number as a percentage with 0 to 7 decimal places. The Percent format causes formatted numbers to be multiplied by 100 as they are entered, like this: .245 becomes 24.5%. Finally, the Appropriate format displays numbers as you enter them, or as closely as possible. Numbers are right-justified. Trailing zeros after a decimal place are dropped, a sure sign that the number is in Appropriate format.

Now press ESC and then OA-V again to return to your starting point in the Standard Values screen. Label format defines the formatting for label cells. Labels can be right-

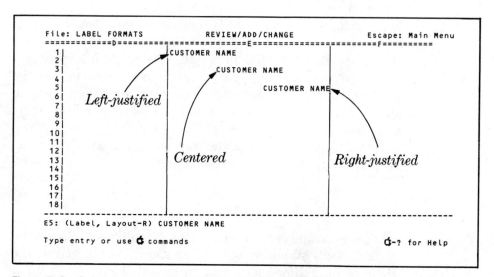

Figure 5-3. Labels centered, left-justified, and right-justified

justified, left-justified, or centered within a column, as shown in Figure 5-3.

The Column width feature allows you to change the standard column width for all the columns. Columns are initially set to be 9 characters wide. You can change this number for all columns using the OA-V command. To determine what width is appropriate, you need to look at all of the columns of data you will have in the worksheet and set your worksheet column width equal to the most common size. You can change the width for specific columns using the cell standard values, which you'll do in a moment.

The Protection feature allows you to protect labels and values from being inadvertently altered. Once a cell is protected, you cannot change its contents unless the protection is revoked. To set the protection for cells, you must use both the spreadsheet and the cell Protection features.

The Recalculate feature allows you to define whether you want the recalculations to be automatically done as you enter data or to be done only upon your command. Recalculations of the spreadsheet frequently cause data entry to be too slow. Therefore, disabling the automatic recalculation feature and having it performed at your express command makes the process faster. The Recalculate feature also allows you to determine the order of the calculation—by rows first, or by columns.

Now let's take a look at the worksheet standard values as they are currently set up.

Current spreadsheet standard values. The default settings for the spreadsheet's standard values are shown at the end of the Help menu. Follow these steps to look at them:

1. Press ESC to return to the Review/Add/Change screen.

2. Press OA-? for the Help menu.

3. Then press the DOWN ARROW until you reach the end of the menu (about 43 lines—don't give up).

This is what you'll see:

```
File: ARinvoices.lst                    HELP              Escape: Review/Add/Change
=========================================================================
                    @-Arrows        Move to another full screen

                    0-9 + - .       Type a value

                    " or letters    Type a label

                    @-1             Go to beginning of file
                      through              through
                    @-9             Go to end of file

                    Current settings of standard values
                    =====================================

                    Protection is       On
                    Label format is     Left justify
                    Value format is     Appropriate
                    Frequency is        Automatic
                    Order is            Columns
-------------------------------------------------------------------------

Use arrows to see remainder of Help __                        56K Avail.
```

You can see that Protection is On, indicating that you can set up protection for any cells (you'll learn later on to indicate which cells are to be protected with the cell standard value feature).

You can also see that the Label format is set by default to Left-justify. Value format is set to Appropriate by default, which means that the data is displayed just the way you enter it. Finally, recalculations are Automatic as the data is entered, and the calculations are performed first by Columns.

The @ signs in this depiction of the Help menu represent the OPEN-APPLE key.

4. Press ESC to leave the Help menu and return to the Review/Add/Change screen.

Resetting the standard values. Now let's look at how relevant the default standard values for the spreadsheet are to the particular spreadsheet you will be creating in this chapter. Figure 5-4 shows that spreadsheet. The most common column

```
File:    ARinvoices.lst                                                    Page  1
                                                                           7/15/87

                              MONTHLY INVOICE LIST

NUM CUSTOMER NAME        DATE      INVOICE PROD UNIT-PR QTY SUBTOTAL   TAX   FREIGHT   TOTAL
===================================================================================================
  2 Rainier Office Sup. Jul 25      238   1   25.00    5  125.00    9.88    2.50   137.38
  3 Bellevue Printing   Jul 12      237   2   32.00    4  128.00   10.11    2.35   140.46
  6 University Printing Jul 5       232   3   15.00   16  240.00   18.96    6.00   264.96
  5 Jensen Office Sup.  Jul 22      245   2   32.00   24  768.00   60.67    8.00   836.67
  2 Rainier Office Sup. Jul 8       234   3   15.00   35  525.00   41.48   24.00   590.48
  4 Evergreen Printing  Jul 23      246   1   25.00   15  375.00   29.62    5.00   409.62
  1 Aires Quick Copy    Jul 15      239   1   25.00   10  250.00   19.75    3.25   273.00
  1 Aires Quick Copy    Jul 18      231   1   25.00   17  425.00   33.58    6.24   464.81
  8 Bo's Print Mart     Jul 3       235   2   32.00    2   64.00    5.06    2.35    71.41
  7 The Print Pot       Jul 17      233   1   25.00   12  300.00   23.70    4.50   328.20

    TOTAL                                           3,200.00  252.80   64.19 3,516.99
```

Figure 5-4.   Spreadsheet to be created

width is 9 characters, so the Column width default value is acceptable. Most of the columns contain dollar information, however, making the default setting for the Value format—namely, the Appropriate format—not acceptable. The standard value for the numeric data in cells must be reset to Commas since the "Dollar" setting (normally the most reasonable choice for dollars and cents) would insert a dollar sign, which the spreadsheet doesn't have room for. Finally, notice that the Label format setting used most often in the worksheet is Centered. For this reason the default setting, Left-justified, will have to be changed as well. The Protection and Recalculate default settings are acceptable at the present time.

Follow these steps to reset the default values for the Value format and Label format features:

1. Press OA-V for Values.

2. Select the Value format option by pressing RETURN.

The screen will be displayed as shown in the following illustration.

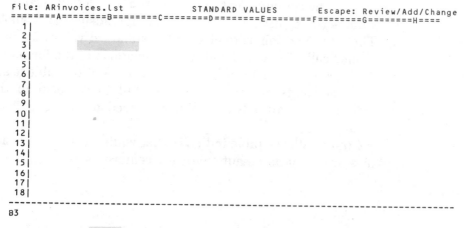

```
File: ARinvoices.lst          STANDARD VALUES          Escape: Review/Add/Change
========A========B========C========D========E========F========G========H====
    1|
    2|
    3|
    4|
    5|
    6|
    7|
    8|
    9|
   10|
   11|
   12|
   13|
   14|
   15|
   16|
   17|
   18|
-------------------------------------------------------------------------------
B3

Value format?  Fixed  Dollars  Commas  Percent  Appropriate
```

On it are the options available to you. You want the Commas option.

3. Enter C for Commas.

You will then be asked to enter the number of decimal places, a number from 0 to 7.

4. Enter 2 for two decimal places and press RETURN.

5. Press OA-V again to set the Label format.

6. Enter L for Label format.

7. Enter C for Centered.

Your worksheet standard values have now been altered. If you like, you can go back to the Help menu and look again at the Current Settings of Standard Values. You will find the Value format changed to Commas, with two decimal places, and the Label format changed to Centered.

Changing the Layout of Particular Cells

Before entering the title and column headings, you need to change the columns that will vary from the default standard value settings just established for the spreadsheet as a whole. The way to do this is to change the standard values for particular cells. Table 5-1 shows the variations in the format of different elements in the spreadsheet. Look at the table to see what elements of the spreadsheet fail to conform to the values you've already set. You will need to override those values.

First of all, the table indicates that while the column headings are going to be automatically centered according to the

COL	WIDTH	HEADING	LABEL FORMAT	CONTENT TYPE	VALUE FORMAT
A	3	NUM (customer number)	centered	value	fixed, 0 dec.
B	1	blank	—	—	—
C	20	CUSTOMER NAME	left-justified	label	—
D	9	DATE (invoice date)	left-justified	label	—
E	8	INVOICE (invoice number)	centered	value	fixed, 0 dec.
F	4	PROD (product type)	centered	value	fixed, 0 dec.
G	9	UNIT-PR (unit price)	centered	value	comma, 2 dec.
H	5	QTY (quantity)	centered	value	fixed, 0 dec.
I	9	SUBTOTAL (col.G * col.H)	centered	value	comma, 2 dec.
J	9	TAX (col.I * .079)	centered	value	comma, 2 dec.
K	9	FREIGHT	centered	value	comma, 2 dec.
L	9	TOTAL (cols. I + J + K)	centered	value	comma, 2 dec.

Table 5-1. Definition of the Column Formats and Contents

standard values set for the spreadsheet as a whole, the CUS-TOMER NAME and DATE headings should be left-justified. Also, some of the column widths do not conform to the spreadsheet default column width of nine characters. Finally, not all of the values entered will contain dollars and cents; four values that have fixed formats must be altered from the Commas default setting.

To sum up then, the spreadsheet will have 12 columns, which are formatted as listed in Table 5-1. For each column A through L, the table lists both the heading contents and formatting and the type of cell contents and the format of those cells. Three areas need to be changed: six column widths don't match the default of nine characters, two label formats are not to be centered, and six value formats are not dollars and cents.

To change the standard values—that is, the layout—for particular cells, you need to use a new command, OA-L, the Layout command. Press OA-L now to take a look at the options shown on the layout screen.

Looking at the prompt line, you can see that the Layout command offers you four different ways to establish standard values for particular cells or groups of cells in the spreadsheet. You can establish standard values for one cell or entry

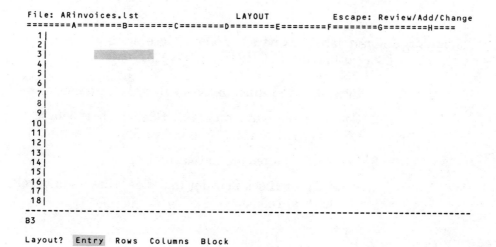

```
File: ARinvoices.lst                LAYOUT              Escape: Review/Add/Change
========A========B========C========D========E========F========G========H====
   1|
   2|
   3|
   4|
   5|
   6|
   7|
   8|
   9|
  10|
  11|
  12|
  13|
  14|
  15|
  16|
  17|
  18|
-------------------------------------------------------------------------------
B3

Layout?  Entry   Rows   Columns   Block
```

(this is the Entry option, highlighted on the prompt line). Or you can establish standard values for particular columns or rows (the Rows and Columns options on the prompt line). Finally, you can establish standard values for a particular Block of cells.

Although these four options are currently displayed on the layout screen's prompt line, there is a special rule about how they can be used that you should know about. Only two of the options, the Entry and the Block options, can be used *before* you have entered the data into your spreadsheet. The reason AppleWorks does not allow you to preset the layout of whole rows and columns is that it would waste the Desktop memory to do so: AppleWorks would continue to define standard values for all cells in a particular row or column, as it wouldn't know where the data ended and therefore where it could stop defining the formats. (Note that you can, however, use the Column option to change the width of columns that differ from the default before you have entered any data. But it's important to be clear about the fact that you can only change column width before data entry, not the format of what's inside the column.)

At this point, you can proceed to change the standard values for the format of some of the column labels, the column widths, and the value formats that differ from the default. Let's tackle the irregular label formats first.

Changing column label formats.   Follow these steps to change the Label format for the CUSTOMER NAME and DATE columns.

1. Press ESC to return to the Review/Add/Change screen.

2. Position your cursor on cell C3, which is where the CUSTOMER NAME column heading will begin.

3. Press OA-L to get the Layout options.

4. Enter **B** for Block in order to define what block of cells you wish to reformat.

5. Move your cursor down column C to cell C14, watching the cell indicator.

Notice how the block of cells you have specified is now highlighted.

6. Press RETURN to display the Block Cell Standard Value menu.

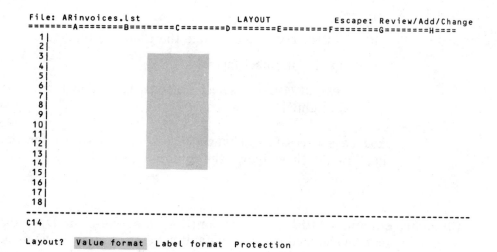

```
File: ARinvoices.lst                    LAYOUT              Escape: Review/Add/Change
========A=========B========C========D========E========F========G========H====
   1|
   2|
   3|
   4|
   5|
   6|
   7|
   8|
   9|
  10|
  11|
  12|
  13|
  14|
  15|
  16|
  17|
  18|
-----------------------------------------------------------------------------
C14

Layout?  Value format  Label format  Protection
```

AppleWorks now asks you whether you want to alter the Value format, the Label format, or the Protection feature of this particular block of cells.

7. Enter L for Label format.

Now you are offered a series of choices as to how exactly you want the label formatted. You want to change the column label from Centered to Left-justify.

8. Press RETURN to select the highlighted option, Left-justify.

Follow the same procedure for left-justifying the DATE column.

9. Move the cursor to cell D3, which heads the DATE column.

10. Press OA-L for the Layout menu.

11. Type **B** for Block.

12. Press the DOWN ARROW until the cell indicator reads D14.

13. Press RETURN to complete the Block definition.

14. Type **L** for Label format.

15. Press RETURN to select Left-justify, which is already highlighted.

You have sucessfully changed the standard values for the label fields. Now change the column widths.

Changing column widths. As mentioned earlier, the column widths can be changed from the default value prior to entering data. You have noticed that the column widths of six columns must be changed from the default of nine characters. First you will change column A, NUM, from nine to three characters, using these steps to do it:

1. Move your cursor to cell A3, the NUM column.

2. Press OA-L.

3. Enter C for Column.

This screen will be displayed:

```
File: ARinvoices.lst              LAYOUT           Escape: Review/Add/Change
========A========B========C========D========E========F========G========H====
  1|
  2|
  3|
  4|
  5|
  6|
  7|
  8|
  9|
 10|
 11|
 12|
 13|
 14|
 15|
 16|
 17|
 18|
---------------------------------------------------------------------
A3

Use cursor moves to highlight Columns, then press Return__        56K Avail.
```

Column A will be highlighted and you will be asked to move the cursor to highlight any other columns to be changed. You only want to modify Column A.

4. Press RETURN to indicate that the correct column is highlighted.

Again you will be given the options of changing the Value format, the Label format, Protection, or Column width.

5. Enter C for Column width.

You must tell AppleWorks how to change the column width by moving the cursor keys in the direction you want for the number of characters you want. In this case, you want to shorten the column (moving it to the left) by six characters.

6. Press OA-LEFT ARROW six times and press RETURN.

Column A will be reduced in width to three characters:

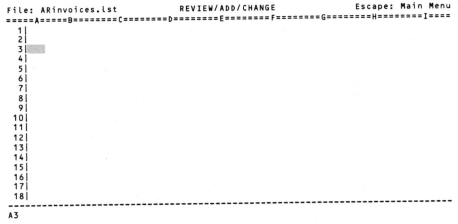

```
File: ARinvoices.lst         REVIEW/ADD/CHANGE          Escape: Main Menu
=====A=====B========C========D========E========F========G========H========I====
   1|
   2|
   3|
   4|
   5|
   6|
   7|
   8|
   9|
  10|
  11|
  12|
  13|
  14|
  15|
  16|
  17|
  18|
------------------------------------------------------------------------------
A3
Type entry or use @ commands                              @-? for Help
```

Now you must change the column widths of the other non-standard columns as well. Using the same procedure, change the cell standard values for the following columns:

- Column B—shorten by 8 characters to 1 character wide
- Column C—widen by 11 characters to 20 characters wide
- Column E—shorten by 1 to 8 characters
- Column F—shorten by 5 to 4 characters
- Column H—shorten by 4 to 5 characters

You are going to leave column B blank in order to separate columns A and C, as you'll see in a minute.

When you have finished, your screen will look like the following illustration.

```
File: ARinvoices.lst          REVIEW/ADD/CHANGE            Escape: Main Menu
=====A=B=========C===============D=======E=====F======G======H======I====
   1|
   2|
   3|
   4|
   5|
   6|
   7|
   8|
   9|
  10|
  11|
  12|
  13|
  14|
  15|
  16|
  17|
  18|
    -------------------------------------------------------------------------
H3

Type entry or use ⌂ commands __                        ⌂-? for Help
```

The change in column widths is clear if you look at the column indicators as the top of the screen. The last formatting step is to change the standard values for the nonstandard values that the cells will contain.

Changing value formats. In our spreadsheet, shown in Figure 5-4, there are four columns of values that do not conform to the standard of numbers with two decimal places. These are the customer number (column A), invoice number (column E), product type (column F), and quantity (column H). You will change these columns to reflect the fact that they are whole numbers with fixed values. Follow these steps:

1. Move your cursor to cell A5, which is where the first customer numbers will be entered.

2. Press OA-L for Layout.

3. Enter **B** to indicate that you want to define a block of cells.

4. Move the cursor down the column to row 17.

5. Press RETURN to cause the block to be highlighted.

6. Press RETURN to select Value format.

7. Press RETURN to select Fixed.

8. Press RETURN to indicate that you want zero decimal places.

Perform the same steps for columns E, F, and H. When you are finished, you will be ready to enter the title of the spreadsheet.

Entering the Title

Now enter the title of the spreadsheet. For the title to be centered on the page, it should be midway between the worksheet's 12 column headings, which will occupy cells A through L. Midway between A and L is column F. Start the title in that column in this way:

1. Move the cursor to cell F1.

2. Press the CAPS LOCK key.

3. Enter the title **MONTHLY INVOICE LIST** and press RETURN.

This is what your screen looks like:

```
File: ARinvoices.lst          REVIEW/ADD/CHANGE              Escape: Main Menu
=====A=B=========C==============D=======E=====F======G======H======I====
    1|                                    MONTHLY INVOICE LIST
    2|
    3|
    4|
    5|
    6|
    7|
    8|
    9|
   10|
   11|
   12|
   13|
   14|
   15|
   16|
   17|
   18|
----------------------------------------------------------------------------
F1: (Label) MONT

Type entry or use ⌘ commands __                        ⌘-? for Help
```

You can see that cell F1 contains only some of the title. It has spilled over into G1, H1, and I1 as well. The cell indicator shows only the contents of cell F1; to see the rest of the title, move your cursor over G1, H1, and I1 and watch the cell indicator change.

Entering the Column Headings

To enter the column headings, follow these steps:

1. Move your cursor to cell A3.

2. Enter **NUM** and press the RIGHT ARROW twice to confirm the entry and move two columns to the right.

You are skipping column B, which is simply a blank column separating the right-justified values in the NUM column from the left-justified names in the CUSTOMER NAME column. This is a convenient technique that you can use to handle many spacing problems.

3. In cell C3, enter **CUSTOMER NAME** and press the RIGHT ARROW to confirm the entry and move to the next column to the right.

4. Enter **DATE** and again press the RIGHT ARROW.

Notice how the two headings are left-justified. The rest of the titles will be centered as best they can be; it takes at least two extra spaces for the headings to be truly centered, and not all of the headings have that much extra space in their cells.

5. Enter **INVOICE** and press the RIGHT ARROW.

6. Enter **PROD** and press the RIGHT ARROW.

7. Enter **UNIT-PR** and press the RIGHT ARROW.

8. Enter **QTY** and press the RIGHT ARROW.

9. Enter **SUBTOTAL** and press the RIGHT ARROW.

10. Enter **TAX** and press the RIGHT ARROW.

11. Enter **FREIGHT** and press the RIGHT ARROW.

12. Enter **TOTAL** and press RETURN.

Your screen should look like those on the next page, with columns A through I showing on the first screen, and with columns D through L showing at the right on the next screen.

Entering a Heading Separator Line

One last task you must perform before entering data is to enter the line that separates the column headings from the actual data. This is a simple task that involves using the Copy

```
File: ARinvoices.lst          REVIEW/ADD/CHANGE              Escape: Main Menu
=====A=B=========C==============D=======E=====F======G=====H=====I====
   1|                                    MONTHLY INVOICE LIST
   2|
   3|NUM CUSTOMER NAME        DATE      INVOICE PROD UNIT-PR  QTY SUBTOTAL
   4|
   5|
   6|
   7|
   8|
   9|
  10|
  11|
  12|
  13|
  14|
  15|
  16|
  17|
  18|
-------------------------------------------------------------------------
A3: (Label) NUM

Type entry or use  commands __                              -? for Help
```

```
File: ARinvoices.lst          REVIEW/ADD/CHANGE              Escape: Main Menu
========D=======E=====F======G=====H======I========J========K=======L====
   1|                         MONTHLY INVOICE LIST
   2|
   3|DATE      INVOICE PROD UNIT-PR  QTY SUBTOTAL    TAX     FREIGHT  TOTAL
   4|
   5|
   6|
   7|
   8|
   9|
  10|
  11|
  12|
  13|
  14|
  15|
  16|
  17|
  18|
-------------------------------------------------------------------------
L3: (Label) TOTAL

Type entry or use  commands __                              -? for Help
```

command to copy the content of cells. Follow these steps:

1. Move your cursor to cell A4.

2. Type a quote mark (") and then three equal signs (=) to fill up the cell, and press RETURN.

Remember that the quote mark tells AppleWorks that you are entering a label, not a value. Now you are going to copy that one cell across the file from column B to column L.

3. Press OA-C for Copy.

You will be asked whether the copy is to be Within worksheet or To or From the Clipboard. It will be in the worksheet.

4. Press RETURN to select the Within worksheet option.

Now you will be asked to highlight the Source column.

5. Since cell A4 is already highlighted correctly, you only have to acknowledge it by pressing RETURN.

Now you must tell AppleWorks the destination of the copy. AppleWorks gives you a quick way to indicate where the copy is to be. If you are copying to a range of cells (as in this case), you would indicate the beginning of the copy by typing a period (.) at the first cell and RETURN at the last cell of the Destination range. (If it were a single cell copy, you would simply move the cursor to the destination cell and press RETURN.)

6. Move your cursor to cell B4, type a period to indicate the start of the range, move your cursor to cell L4 (you can use the OA-RIGHT ARROW), and press RETURN to indicate the end of the range.

You will see the double line duplicated across the spreadsheet.
Now you are ready to enter the formulas and functions required to handle the computing part of the spreadsheet.

Entering the Formulas and Functions

AppleWorks allows you to enter a variety of functions and formulas to be used in defining the contents of a cell. Chapter 8 will explore the formulas and functions available in more detail. For now let's just get acquainted with them.

If you look at Figure 5-4, you see that four of the columns of data are based upon calculations or functions. The first of these is G, or UNIT-PR. Its contents are based upon the value in PROD, which is a code for product type. Our fictitious company only has three products to sell, which have been coded 1, 2, and 3. Product type 1 costs $25.00; product type 2, $32.00; product type 3, $15.00. You will use a function called @CHOOSE, which allows AppleWorks to choose the unit price based upon the product type.

A second column that is based on calculations is I, the SUBTOTAL column. This column's value is based on quantity times unit price. You will use a formula for this.

The TAX column, column J, is based upon a sales tax rate times the SUBTOTAL. You will use a sales tax rate of 7.9% in this instance.

Finally, the TOTAL column, column L, is based on the sum of the SUBTOTAL, TAX, and FREIGHT. You'll use a function @SUM to handle this calculation.

Follow these steps to set up the cell definitions:

1. Move your cursor to cell G5, where the unit price value will first be entered.

You are going to tell AppleWorks that you want the value in G5 (unit price) to be based on the value in F5 (the product type). If the product type is type 1, the unit price is to be $25.00; if the product type is type 2, the unit price will be $32.00; if the product is type 3, the unit price will be $15.00.

Follow these steps:

2. Enter **@CHOOSE(F5,25.00,32.00,15.00)** and press
   RETURN.

You'll see the following screen.

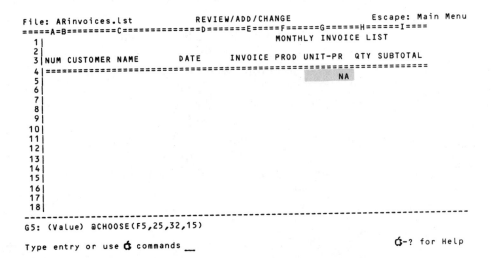

```
File: ARinvoices.lst              REVIEW/ADD/CHANGE              Escape: Main Menu
=====A=B=========C===============D=======E=====F======G======H======I====
   1|                                      MONTHLY INVOICE LIST
   2|
   3|NUM CUSTOMER NAME          DATE      INVOICE PROD UNIT-PR  QTY SUBTOTAL
   4|===============================================================
   5|                                                        NA
   6|
   7|
   8|
   9|
  10|
  11|
  12|
  13|
  14|
  15|
  16|
  17|
  18|
-------------------------------------------------------------------------
G5: (Value) @CHOOSE(F5,25,32,15)

Type entry or use Ǵ commands __                      Ǵ-? for Help
```

In cell G5 you'll see the notation NA instead of a value.
Unlike the labels you entered, function and formula are not
entered directly into the cell. The function in the cell indicator tells you that a value has been entered and what it is. In
the cell AppleWorks makes a notation, NA, which says that it
cannot calculate the value in this column because the values
on which it is based do not exist. That is, column F5 is blank
and so G5 cannot be calculated.

3. Move your cursor to cell I5, SUBTOTAL.

This time you will enter a formula. Because the cell names
start with letters, you must first enter a plus sign (+) or a
minus sign (−) to signal to AppleWorks that the cells contain

pointers (which are part of the formula) rather than labels. The formula will tell AppleWorks to multiply the contents of cell G5 (unit price) with the contents of cell H5 (quantity) and to place the result into cell I5.

4. Enter the formula **+G5*H5** and press RETURN.

5. Move your cursor to cell J5, TAX.

Now you must tell AppleWorks to multiply cell I5 (SUBTO-TAL) times a constant of 0.079, which represents the state sales tax amount.

6. Enter the formula **+I5*.079** and press RETURN.

Again notice the NA in the column indicating that Apple-Works cannot calculate the value since the source cell (in this case cell I5) is blank.

Finally, you want to place the sum of the SUBTOTAL, TAX, and FREIGHT values in the TOTAL column. You will use the @SUM function to do this.

7. Move your cursor to cell L5.

8. Enter **@SUM(** (be sure to enter the left parenthesis).

At this point you are going to enter pointers to cells I5, J5, and K5. You could enter the actual cell names, but Apple-Works provides a faster way for you to supply the cell names using your cursor.

9. Press the LEFT ARROW three times until you are in cell I5, SUBTOTAL.

You will see the cell indicator reflect the cells and their contents as you pass them. Cell I5 marks the beginning of the range of cells to be summed.

10. Type a period (.) at cell I5.

The period is a place marker for the start of a range of cells. It tells AppleWorks that the range of cells to be summed begins with cell I5. Because the period is just a place marker, it does not affect the contents of the cell in any way.

    11. Press the RIGHT ARROW twice until it is in cell K5, FREIGHT, and press RETURN.

This is the end of the range to be summed into cell L5. Now you must simply complete the entry.

    12. Type) to close the parentheses and press RETURN.

Your screen will look like this:

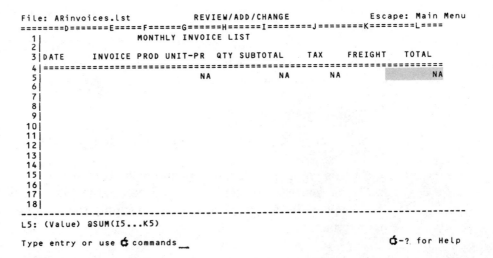

```
File: ARinvoices.lst          REVIEW/ADD/CHANGE              Escape: Main Menu
========D=======E=====F=====G=====H======I========J========K========L====
   1|                  MONTHLY INVOICE LIST
   2|
   3|DATE      INVOICE PROD UNIT-PR  QTY SUBTOTAL    TAX    FREIGHT    TOTAL
   4|=========================================================================
   5|                              NA          NA     NA              NA
   6|
   7|
   8|
   9|
  10|
  11|
  12|
  13|
  14|
  15|
  16|
  17|
  18|
------------------------------------------------------------------------------
L5: (Value) @SUM(I5...K5)

Type entry or use ⌂ commands __                         ⌂-? for Help
```

Once the formulas have been entered, they may be copied to the other appropriate cells, saving you the trouble of entering the same formulas and functions over and over again.

Copying the Cells

The formulas as they have been entered only apply to the data in cells G5, I5, J5, and L5. But you want them to apply to the data in all rows of those columns, not just in row 5. In order to make the formulas apply to all the cells in those columns, you need to use the Copy command, the command used a few moments ago to turn the three equal signs into a broken line separating the column headings from the data in the columns. When you copied the equal signs across the screen, you had to define both the source and the destination of the cells to be copied. When copying cell pointers, the definition process is a little more involved.

In the case of column I, you want to move the formula in I5 to cell I6 and so on. But you don't want the formula copied exactly; you want it corrected for the new row number, that is, the formula in I6 would be +G6*H6, not +G5*H5 as it is in cell I5. This is called *Relative copying*. There will be times when you do want the exact same pointer maintained, however. This is called *No change* copying. You must tell Apple-Works whether to change the pointer relative to a new position or to copy the pointer with no change.

Follow these steps to copy the functions and formulas you have entered.

1. Press the OA-LEFT ARROW key twice to place your cursor on cell A5 (the leftmost cell of the range you are copying).

2. Press OA-C for Copy.

3. Press RETURN to copy Within worksheet.

You will be asked to define the Source range of the copy operation by moving the cursor or pressing RETURN.

4. Move the cursor across row 5 to column L.

The cursor should rest in cell L5, according to the cell indicator. At this point row 5 should be highlighted, defining the source to be copied.

5. Press RETURN to tell AppleWorks that the source is now defined.

Now you must define the destination of the copy. The destination will be columns A through L in rows 6 through 17.

6. Press the DOWN ARROW to move the cursor to row 6 and type a period (.) to start the definition of the range.

The highlighted row will move from row 5 to row 6.

7. Move the cursor with the DOWN ARROW to cell A17.

The screen will be almost completely highlighted.

8. Press RETURN to tell AppleWorks that the destination is now defined.

Next you will be asked to decide whether each pointer should be copied as is or changed to be relative to its new location. The screen should now look like this:

```
File: ARinvoices.lst                    COPY              Escape: Review/Add/Change
=====A=B=========C=============D=======E=====F======G======H======I====
  1|                                        MONTHLY INVOICE LIST
  2|
  3|NUM CUSTOMER NAME    .   DATE      INVOICE PROD UNIT-PR  QTY SUBTOTAL
  4|=====================================================================
  5|                                                   NA              NA
  6|
  7|
  8|
  9|
 10|
 11|
 12|
 13|
 14|
 15|
 16|
 17|
 18|
-------------------------------------------------------------------------
G5: (Value) @CHOOSE(F5,25,32,15)
@CHOOSE(F5,25,32,15)
Reference to F5?  No change  Relative
```

The first pointer, F5 (product type) in the @CHOOSE function, is highlighted. You must tell AppleWorks whether to make it relative or not. You want this pointer and all the others in this exercise to be corrected for location—in other words, you want copying to be relative.

9. Enter **R** for Relative.

AppleWorks presents to you next the formulas for calculating the subtotal column. Pointer G5 (unit price) and then pointer H5 (quantity) will be highlighted.

10. Enter **R** for Relative for both of the pointers.

Highlighted next will be the formula from cell J5, the tax calculation.

11. Enter **R** for Relative for the pointer in the tax calculation.

The final total function will be presented, first pointer I5 (subtotal), and then K5 (freight).

12. Enter **R** for Relative for each of the two pointers presented.

```
File: ARinvoices.lst            REVIEW/ADD/CHANGE              Escape: Main Menu
=====A=B==========C==============D=======E=====F======G======H======I====
  1|                                    MONTHLY INVOICE LIST
  2|
  3|NUM CUSTOMER NAME        DATE      INVOICE PROD UNIT-PR  QTY SUBTOTAL
  4| =======================================================================
  5|                                                   NA            NA
  6|                                                   NA            NA
  7|                                                   NA            NA
  8|                                                   NA            NA
  9|                                                   NA            NA
 10|                                                   NA            NA
 11|                                                   NA            NA
 12|                                                   NA            NA
 13|                                                   NA            NA
 14|                                                   NA            NA
 15|                                                   NA            NA
 16|                                                   NA            NA
 17|                                                   NA            NA
 18|
------------------------------------------------------------------------
A5: (Value, Layout-F0)

Type entry or use ⌘ commands _                        ⌘-? for Help
```

You will immediately see AppleWorks try to calculate the formulas as they are copied. A row of NA's will be displayed for each of the columns containing functions or formulas as shown in the illustration at the bottom of the previous page.

Zooming In

At times like this you want to verify that the results of the procedures you asked AppleWorks to program are what you expected. You may use the OA-Z command to zoom into the spreadsheet and examine the formulas you have just entered. In contrast to the Zoom command in the word processor or data base, the spreadsheet Zoom command lets you see the formulas, functions, and pointers for each column instead of the actual data contents. The Zoom command lets you switch back and forth between the data and the other values connected with a column.

1. Move your cursor to cell L5 so you can see the formulas and functions entered.

2. Press OA-Z to see that the formulas and functions have in fact been copied to the correct cells.

```
File: ARinvoices.lst          REVIEW/ADD/CHANGE          Escape: Main Menu
========D=======E=====F=====G======H=======I========J========K=======L====
  1|                  MONTHLY INVOICE LIST
  2|
  3|DATE     INVOICE PROD UNIT-PR  QTY SUBTOTAL    TAX      FREIGHT   TOTAL
  4|===========================================================================
  5|            0       0  aCHOOSE(FO   +G5*H5    +I5*.079           aSUM(I5..
  6|            0       0  aCHOOSE(FO   +G6*H6    +I6*.079           aSUM(I6..
  7|            0       0  aCHOOSE(FO   +G7*H7    +I7*.079           aSUM(I7..
  8|            0       0  aCHOOSE(FO   +G8*H8    +I8*.079           aSUM(I8..
  9|            0       0  aCHOOSE(FO   +G9*H9    +I9*.079           aSUM(I9..
 10|            0       0  aCHOOSE(FO   +G10*H10  +I10*.079          aSUM(I10.
 11|            0       0  aCHOOSE(FO   +G11*H11  +I11*.079          aSUM(I11.
 12|            0       0  aCHOOSE(FO   +G12*H12  +I12*.079          aSUM(I12.
 13|            0       0  aCHOOSE(FO   +G13*H13  +I13*.079          aSUM(I13.
 14|            0       0  aCHOOSE(FO   +G14*H14  +I14*.079          aSUM(I14.
 15|            0       0  aCHOOSE(FO   +G15*H15  +I15*.079          aSUM(I15.
 16|            0       0  aCHOOSE(FO   +G16*H16  +I16*.079          aSUM(I16.
 17|            0       0  aCHOOSE(FO   +G17*H17  +I17*.079          aSUM(I17.
 18|
---------------------------------------------------------------------------
L5: (Value) aSUM(I5...K5)

Type entry or use & commands __                         &-? for Help
```

3. Press OA-Z to return to the normal viewing display.

You can use the Zoom command whenever you want to check the formulas, pointers, and functions in the columns.

Entering Data

Figure 5-5 contains the invoice records for the month of July. You should enter them as is, including the errors, which you'll correct later. If you make other mistakes, either ignore them or correct them using the DELETE key or the Blank command. Later you'll learn other methods for correcting them.

Follow these steps to enter the first invoice record. After that, you will enter the rest of the records in the same way.

1. Release the CAPS LOCK key.

2. Position your cursor on cell A5, enter **2**, and press the RIGHT ARROW twice.

3. Enter the customer name, **Rainier Office Sup.**, and press the RIGHT ARROW to move to the next column.

4. Enter **Jul 15** and press the RIGHT ARROW to move to the next column.

5. Enter invoice number **238** and press the RIGHT ARROW to move to the next column.

6. Enter product type **1** and press the RIGHT ARROW two times to move to QTY (quantity) (the unit price will automatically be filled in).

7. Enter **5**, and press the RIGHT ARROW three times.

Notice how the subtotal and tax figures have been filled in for you. Even the total is calculated, although it is inaccurate at this point since the freight charges are still missing.

8. Enter **2.50** in the FREIGHT column and press RETURN.

```
File:   INVOICE DATA                                            Page  1
                                                                7/15/87

                              AR INVOICES FOR JULY

NUM  CUSTOMER NAME          DATE      INVOICE  PROD   QTY   FREIGHT
=========================================================================
  2  Rainier Office Sup.    Jul 15      238     1      5     2.50
  3  Bellevue Printing      Jul 12      237     2      4     2.35

  6  University Printing    Jul 5       232     3     16     6.00
  5  Jensen Office Sup.     Jul 22      245     2     24     8.00

  2  Rainer Office Sup.     Jul 8       234     3     35    24.00
  4  Evergreen Printing     Jul 23      246     1     15     5.00

  1  Aires Quick Copy       Jul 15      239     1     10     3.25
  1  Aires Quick Copy       Jul 18      231     1     17     6.24

  8  Bo's Print Mart        Jul 3       235     2      2     2.35
  7  The Print Pot          Jul 17      233     1     12     4.50
```

Figure 5-5. Invoice data to be entered into the spreadsheet

The total amount will be automatically updated. Your screen now looks like this:

```
File: ARinvoices.lst         REVIEW/ADD/CHANGE           Escape: Main Menu
========D=======E=====F======G======H======I========J=======K=======L====
 1|                    MONTHLY INVOICE LIST
 2|
 3|DATE     INVOICE PROD UNIT-PR  QTY SUBTOTAL    TAX      FREIGHT    TOTAL
 4|========================================================================
 5|Jul 15     238    1   25.00     5   125.00    9.88      2.50     137.38
 6|                                NA          NA       NA            NA
 7|                                NA          NA       NA            NA
 8|                                NA          NA       NA            NA
 9|                                NA          NA       NA            NA
10|                                NA          NA       NA            NA
11|                                NA          NA       NA            NA
12|                                NA          NA       NA            NA
13|                                NA          NA       NA            NA
14|                                NA          NA       NA            NA
15|                                NA          NA       NA            NA
16|                                NA          NA       NA            NA
17|                                NA          NA       NA            NA
18|
--------------------------------------------------------------------------
K5: (Value) 2.5

Type entry or use ⌂ commands __                            ⌂-? for Help
```

Continue by entering the rest of the records, as shown in Figure 5-5, in the same way. As you enter the numeric amounts in columns A, E, F, H, and K, notice that you are forced to pause while the spreadsheet is recalculated. A message appears at the bottom of the screen explaining that AppleWorks is "Calculating columns A − L." To avoid this delay the automatic recalculation may be turned off on larger spreadsheets. When you finish, your screens should look like the ones in the following illustrations.

```
File: ARinvoices.lst              REVIEW/ADD/CHANGE               Escape: Main Menu
=====A=B=========C===============D=======E=====F======G======H======I====
  1|                                        MONTHLY INVOICE LIST
  2|
  3|NUM CUSTOMER NAME        DATE       INVOICE PROD UNIT-PR  QTY SUBTOTAL
  4|======================================================================
  5|  2 Rainier Office Sup.  Jul 15        238   1   25.00     5   125.00
  6|  3 Bellevue Printing    Jul 12        237   2   32.00     4   128.00
  7|  6 University Printing  Jul 5         232   3   15.00    16   240.00
  8|  5 Jensen Office Sup.   Jul 22        245   2   32.00    24   768.00
  9|  2 Rainer Office Sup.   Jul 8         234   3   15.00    35   525.00
 10|  4 Evergreen Printing   Jul 23        246   1   25.00    15   375.00
 11|  1 Aires Quick Copy     Jul 15        239   1   25.00    10   250.00
 12|  1 Aires Quick Copy     Jul 18        231   1   25.00    17   425.00
 13|  8 Bo's Print Mart      Jul 3         235   2   32.00     2    64.00
 14|  7 The Print Pot        Jul 17        233   1   25.00    12   300.00
 15|                                                          NA        NA
 16|    TOTAL                                                 NA        NA
 17|                                                          NA        NA
 18|
--------------------------------------------------------------------------
A14: (Value, Layout-F0) 7

Type entry or use ⌘ commands __                         ⌘-? for Help
```

```
File: ARinvoices.lst              REVIEW/ADD/CHANGE               Escape: Main Menu
========D=======E=====F======G======H======I========J========K========L====
  1|                 MONTHLY INVOICE LIST
  2|
  3|DATE       INVOICE PROD UNIT-PR  QTY SUBTOTAL     TAX   FREIGHT    TOTAL
  4|======================================================================
  5|Jul 15        238   1   25.00     5   125.00     9.88     2.50   137.38
  6|Jul 12        237   2   32.00     4   128.00    10.11     2.35   140.46
  7|Jul 5         232   3   15.00    16   240.00    18.96     6.00   264.96
  8|Jul 22        245   2   32.00    24   768.00    60.67     8.00   836.67
  9|Jul 8         234   3   15.00    35   525.00    41.48    24.00   590.48
 10|Jul 23        246   1   25.00    15   375.00    29.62     5.00   409.62
 11|Jul 15        239   1   25.00    10   250.00    19.75     3.25   273.00
 12|Jul 18        231   1   25.00    17   425.00    33.58     6.24   464.81
 13|Jul 3         235   2   32.00     2    64.00     5.06     2.35    71.41
 14|Jul 17        233   1   25.00    12   300.00    23.70     4.50   328.20
 15|                             NA           NA       NA               NA
 16|                             NA           NA       NA               NA
 17|                             NA           NA       NA               NA
 18|
--------------------------------------------------------------------------
L14: (Value) @SUM(I14...K14)

Type entry or use ⌘ commands __                         ⌘-? for Help
```

Entering Column Totals

The spreadsheet you've created is able to give you total invoice amounts on the four calculated values: SUBTOTAL, TAX, FREIGHT, and TOTAL. To develop these, you first need to enter a title in the CUSTOMER NAME column and then create a formula in the SUBTOTAL column to be copied to the other three columns. Follow these steps to enter these final calculations:

1. Press the CAPS LOCK key to enter the row heading.

2. Place your cursor in cell C16.

3. Enter **TOTAL** and press the RIGHT ARROW six times until you are at cell I16.

4. Enter @**SUM(** (be sure to enter the opening parenthesis).

5. Move your cursor to the top of the row, to cell I5.

6. Enter a period (.) to start the range of cells to be summed.

7. Move the cursor down to cell I14 so that the range covers all values entered in the SUBTOTAL column.

8. Press RETURN.

9. Enter **)** (closing parenthesis) and press RETURN.

You should immediately see the calculation of the total dollars on your screen. The amount is $3,200.00.

Since you originally copied the formulas for the TAX and TOTAL columns down to row 17, you don't need to change them; they are still valid for the grand TOTAL row. You do need to sum the FREIGHT column, which you can do by copying the SUBTOTAL formula to that column. To copy the formula to the FREIGHT column, follow these steps:

10. Press OA-C for Copy.

11. Press RETURN to accept the Within worksheet option.

12. Press RETURN to acknowledge that cell I16 is the correct source.

13. Move the RIGHT ARROW twice to cell K16 and press RETURN.

14. Enter **R** for Relative twice, once for each of the pointers in the range.

AppleWorks will recalculate the totals in each newly totaled column. After moving your cursor to cell L16, your screen should look like this:

```
File: ARinvoices.lst              REVIEW/ADD/CHANGE              Escape: Main Menu
========D=======E=====F======G======H======I========J========K=======L====
    1|               MONTHLY INVOICE LIST
    2|
    3|DATE      INVOICE PROD UNIT-PR  QTY SUBTOTAL      TAX   FREIGHT   TOTAL
    4|======================================================================
    5|Jul 15       238    1   25.00    5   125.00     9.88     2.50   137.38
    6|Jul 12       237    2   32.00    4   128.00    10.11     2.35   140.46
    7|Jul 5        232    3   15.00   16   240.00    18.96     6.00   264.96
    8|Jul 22       245    2   32.00   24   768.00    60.67     8.00   836.67
    9|Jul 8        234    3   15.00   35   525.00    41.48    24.00   590.48
   10|Jul 23       246    1   25.00   15   375.00    29.62     5.00   409.62
   11|Jul 15       239    1   25.00   10   250.00    19.75     3.25   273.00
   12|Jul 18       231    1   25.00   17   425.00    33.58     6.24   464.81
   13|Jul 3        235    2   32.00    2    64.00     5.06     2.35    71.41
   14|Jul 17       233    1   25.00   12   300.00    23.70     4.50   328.20
   15|                         NA          NA        NA                 NA
   16|                         NA      3,200.00   252.80    64.19  3,516.99
   17|                         NA          NA        NA                 NA
   18|
---------------------------------------------------------------------------
L16: (Value) aSUM(I16...K16)

Type entry or use á commands __                       á-? for Help
```

Tidying Up

You will notice that there are several columns containing irrelevant NA notations across the worksheet. To remove the NA code from rows 15 and 17 and from cell G16, follow these steps:

1. Place your cursor on any cell in row 15.
2. Press OA-B for Blank.
3. Enter **R** to indicate that you want to blank a row.
4. Press RETURN to acknowledge that the highlighted row 15 should be blanked.

The row will be blanked of all NA's.

5. Move your cursor to cell G16.
6. Press OA-B for Blank.
7. Press RETURN to acknowledge that the entry should be blanked.

The cell is immediately blanked. Now NA's remain only in row 17.

8. Move your cursor to any cell in row 17.
9. Press OA-B for Blank.
10. Enter **R** for Row.
11. Press RETURN to verify that the correct row is highlighted.

The screen will be cleared of the rest of the NA's.

Editing the File

Editing a spreadsheet file is somewhat different from editing a data base or word processing file. The heart of the editing process in all three components is the OA-E command, which enables you to move back and forth between the insert and overstrike modes. But in the spreadsheet, you must use the OA-U command first before using the OA-E command if you wish to edit the characters within a cell. The OA-U command puts you, in effect, in a different mode, which allows you to use the LEFT and RIGHT ARROW keys to move inside a cell rather than through it to the next entry. (Normally, as you know, using the ARROW keys in the spreadsheet signals to AppleWorks that you wish to confirm the entry and move in the direction of the arrow toward the next entry.)

Just as a quick review of overstrike and insert modes, remember from the earlier chapters that you can tell when you're in insert mode because your cursor is a blinking underline. In the overstrike mode, your cursor is a flashing block. When you are inserting, you insert new characters between existing characters, pushing the existing ones to the right as you insert. In overstrike mode, however, you type over the existing data.

Let's practice editing spreadsheet cells now. Suppose that you decide to change the date of the first order listed on our spreadsheet (from Rainier Office Supplies) from July 15 to July 25. Follow these steps to correct the date entry:

1. Position your cursor on cell D5.

2. Press OA-U to signal AppleWorks that you wish to edit the contents of the cell.

In the first line of the prompt line area, the contents of the cell are displayed. This is where your editing will be visible:

```
File: ARinvoices.lst              EDITING MODE          Escape: Review/Add/Change
=====A=B=========C===============D=======E=====F======G======H======I====
 1|                                              MONTHLY  INVOICE  LIST
 2|
 3|NUM CUSTOMER NAME          DATE      INVOICE PROD UNIT-PR  QTY SUBTOTAL
 4|==================================================================
 5|    2 Rainier Office Sup.  Jul 15       238   1   25.00     5  125.00
 6|    3 Bellevue Printing    Jul 12       237   2   32.00     4  128.00
 7|    6 University Printing  Jul 5        232   3   15.00    16  240.00
 8|    5 Jensen Office Sup.   Jul 22       245   2   32.00    24  768.00
 9|    2 Rainer Office Sup.   Jul 8        234   3   15.00    35  525.00
10|    4 Evergreen Printing   Jul 23       246   1   25.00    15  375.00
11|    1 Aires Quick Copy     Jul 15       239   1   25.00    10  250.00
12|    1 Aires Quick Copy     Jul 18       231   1   25.00    17  425.00
13|    8 Bo's Print Mart      Jul 3        235   2   32.00     2   64.00
14|    7 The Print Pot        Jul 17       233   1   25.00    12  300.00
15|
16|    TOTAL                                                    3,200.00
17|
18|
----------------------------------------------------------------------------
D5: (Label, Layout-L) Jul 15
Jul 15
Type entry or use Ć commands                                    54K Avail.
```

3. Move your cursor over the "1" in "15."

4. Press OA-E to get into overstrike mode.

5. Enter 2 and press RETURN.

You can see the date corrected in the cell as soon as RETURN is pressed.

Another error you have noticed is that row 9 contains a spelling error. The CUSTOMER NAME in this row should be "Rainier," not "Rainer." To insert the missing "i,"

6. Move your cursor to cell C9, and release the CAPS LOCK key.

7. Press OA-U for Use Edit.

8. Press OA-E to restore the insert mode.

The cursor will change from a flashing block to a blinking underline.

9. Move your cursor over the "e" in Rainer.

10. Enter **i** and then press RETURN.

The spelling will be corrected to "Rainier."

If you see any other mistakes, correct them in this same way. After all your mistakes have been corrected, you should save your file before printing a report of it. Your spreadsheet files must be saved just as any other file. To save your files and continue with your work, simply press OA-S for Save.

After a few seconds, your file will be safely saved onto disk and you can continue with your work.

Preparing to Print

Printing the spreadsheet file requires that you change several of the printer options. Printer options are instructions from AppleWorks to the printer about how to format your files. Chapter 8 will explore the printer options in more depth, but for now, you need to alter some familiar printing options and then print the file.

Altering the Printer Options

The printer options that need altering are the platen width and the margins. The platen width measures the distance that the printer head will travel across the printer. It should be 8 1/2 inches. The top margin should permit some space at the top of the page, just as the left and right margins should allow space on the edges of the page. The bottom margin is not too important since the report has only a few lines of data.

You'll also want to verify that the other printer options will serve your needs. Let's examine them now.

1. Press OA-O for Options.

Printer Options menu will be displayed, like this:

```
File: ARinvoices.lst          PRINTER OPTIONS        Escape: Review/Add/Change
===============================================================================


-------Left and right margins--------        ------Top and bottom margins-------
PW: Platen Width          8.0 inches     PL: Paper Length          11.0 inches
LM: Left Margin           0.0 inches     TM: Top Margin             0.0 inches
RM: Right Margin          0.0 inches     BM: Bottom Margin          0.0 inches
CI: Chars per Inch        10             LI: Lines per Inch         6

    Line width            8.0 inches         Printing Length       11.0 inches
    Char per Line (est)   80                 Lines per page        66

         -------------------Formatting options-------------------
    SC:  Send Special Codes to printer                       No
    PH:  Print report Header at top of each page             Yes
         Single, Double or Triple Spacing (SS/DS/TS)         SS



------------------------------------------------------------------------------
Type a two letter option code __                              54K Avail.
```

You can see that the platen width (PW) is set to 8.0 inches. It must be changed. The left, right, and top margins are set to 0.0 inches, which will also need changing.

2. Enter **PW** for Platen Width and press RETURN.

You will be asked for the width in inches.

3. Enter **8.5** and press RETURN.

You will see the width change reflected on the screen in two places. The number next to Platen Width will now show

8.5 inches and the estimated Char per Line reading will be increased from 80 to 85 characters. Char per Inch (CI) should be at least 95 characters to accommodate the total characters on the spreadsheet (calculated by adding up the number of characters in each column). Try changing the Char per Inch from 10 to 12.

4. Enter **CI** for Char per Inch and press RETURN.

5. Enter **12** to change the characters per inch and press RETURN.

You'll see that the Char per Line (est) has changed from 85 to 102. Let's see what the margin settings will do to this figure.

6. Enter **LM** for Left Margin and press RETURN.

7. Enter **.2** inches and press RETURN.

8. Enter **RM** for Right Margin and press RETURN.

9. Enter **.2** for inches and press RETURN.

The Char per Line (est) is reduced to 97 characters, still enough for a 95-character spreadsheet.

10. Enter **TM** for Top Margin and press RETURN.

11. Enter **2** to indicate that you want a two-inch top margin and press RETURN.

Your screen should show that the left and right margins have reduced your Char per Line (est) to 97 characters, and the top margin has reduced the Lines per page to 54 lines. These are the only changes in printer options necessary at this time.

12. Press ESC to return to the Review/Add/Change screen.

Printing the File

Follow these steps to quickly print your file:

1. Press OA-P for Print.

You will be shown the following menu, which gives you the
option to print all of the worksheet, certain rows, certain
columns, or a block of cells you define.

```
File: ARinvoices.lst              PRINT           Escape: Review/Add/Change
=====A=B=========C==============D=======E=====F======G=====H======I====
   1|                                 MONTHLY INVOICE LIST
   2|
   3|NUM CUSTOMER NAME        DATE      INVOICE PROD UNIT-PR  QTY SUBTOTAL
   4|====================================================================
   5|   2 Rainier Office Sup.  Jul 25       238    1   25.00    5   125.00
   6|   3 Bellevue Printing    Jul 12       237    2   32.00    4   128.00
   7|   6 University Printing  Jul 5        232    3   15.00   16   240.00
   8|   5 Jensen Office Sup.   Jul 22       245    2   32.00   24   768.00
   9|   2 Rainier Office Sup.  Jul 8        234    3   15.00   35   525.00
  10|   4 Evergreen Printing   Jul 23       246    1   25.00   15   375.00
  11|   1 Aires Quick Copy     Jul 15       239    1   25.00   10   250.00
  12|   1 Aires Quick Copy     Jul 18       231    1   25.00   17   425.00
  13|   8 Bo's Print Mart      Jul 3        235    2   32.00    2    64.00
  14|   7 The Print Pot        Jul 17       233    1   25.00   12   300.00
  15|
  16|   TOTAL                                                  3,200.00
  17|
  18|
---------------------------------------------------------------------------
C9: (Label, Layout-L) Rainier Office Sup.

Print?  ALL  Rows  Columns  Block
```

2. Press RETURN to select All of the worksheet.

You will be shown another screen which informs you how
wide your report will be and gives you several options about
where to print. Your selection now should be to your named
printer. But in the future you may also choose to print to the

Clipboard in order to transfer spreadsheet data to a word processing file. Or you can print to an ASCII or DIF file on disk. In this case, you may use the spreadsheet data in a software package other than AppleWorks.

3. Press RETURN to select your named printer.

4. Type the date of the report, **7/15/87**, and press RETURN.

5. Press RETURN to confirm that you want to print one copy.

The printer should now be printing. If it is not, verify that your printer is plugged in and turned on, and has the paper and ribbon correctly mounted. If all of these are OK, refer to the procedures outlined in Chapter 2 or in Appendix A.

Figure 5-6 shows you what your report should look like.

Removing Your File From the Desktop

Now that you are finished with the ARinvoices.lst file, you should remove it from the Desktop so that you can continue to work with other files. If you are leaving AppleWorks, this is not necessary since you saved your finished file to disk before printing it. However, if you want to continue working with another AppleWorks file, you need to clear the Desktop of unnecessary files. Follow these steps to clear the Desktop:

1. Press ESC to return to the Main Menu.

2. Select option 4, Remove files from the Desktop.

3. Select the file ARinvoice.lst by pressing RETURN.

```
File:   ARinvoices.lst                                        Page  1
                                                              7/15/87

                           MONTHLY INVOICE LIST

NUM CUSTOMER NAME        DATE    INVOICE PROD UNIT-PR QTY SUBTOTAL  TAX   FREIGHT  TOTAL
======================================================================================
  2 Rainier Office Sup.  Jul 25    238   1   25.00    5  125.00    9.88   2.50   137.38
  3 Bellevue Printing    Jul 12    237   2   32.00    4  128.00   10.11   2.35   140.46
  6 University Printing  Jul 5     232   3   15.00   16  240.00   18.96   6.00   264.96
  5 Jensen Office Sup.   Jul 22    245   2   32.00   24  768.00   60.67   8.00   836.67
  2 Rainier Office Sup.  Jul 8     234   3   15.00   35  525.00   41.48  24.00   590.48
  4 Evergreen Printing   Jul 23    246   1   25.00   15  375.00   29.62   5.00   409.62
  1 Aires Quick Copy     Jul 15    239   1   25.00   10  250.00   19.75   3.25   273.00
  1 Aires Quick Copy     Jul 18    231   1   25.00   17  425.00   33.58   6.24   464.81
  8 Bo's Print Mart      Jul 3     235   2   32.00    2   64.00    5.06   2.35    71.41
  7 The Print Pot        Jul 17    233   1   25.00   12  300.00   23.70   4.50   328.20

    TOTAL                                              3,200.00  252.80  64.19 3,516.99
```

Figure 5-6.   Final printed Monthly Invoice List report

4. Press RETURN twice more when prompted to save your file to disk.

Your new file is now safely on disk and your Desktop space is cleared for other AppleWorks tasks.

This concludes the introduction to the spreadsheet component. If you decide to proceed immediately to another chapter, select either Chapter 6, which delves into more advanced uses of word processing, or Chapter 8, which discusses more advanced uses of the spreadsheet component.

6

Expanding
Your Word
Processing Skills

In Chapter 3 you learned the basics of word processing with AppleWorks. Now you are ready to move on to more advanced word processing concepts.

In Chapter 6 you will produce a partial business plan for adding a new store to ABC Company. Of course, the business plan presented here is not as thorough or complete as you would actually produce if that were your sole intent. But in producing the plan, you will learn how to move and copy text within the document, how to perform replacement functions both to streamline the typing process and to correct errors that are duplicated throughout the document, and how to place markers in your text for future searches with the Find command.

In this chapter, you will also learn more about printing options, using the most important ones in the process. You will create headers and footers, change margins, and center titles. And you will learn to calculate page breaks and to change the layout of your documents as you see the need.

The business plan you create in this chapter will be used again in Chapter 9 to demonstrate AppleWorks' integration power. In Chapter 9 you will merge an inventory list from the data base component and a budget from the spreadsheet component into the business plan. Your job in this chapter is to prepare the text of the business plan, leaving blanks where pieces from the other components will be integrated later.

Printer Options

The ability to set and change printing options for formatting your documents is a very important feature because it allows you to control how your documents will look. In Chapter 3 you used a few of the printing options to format the Order Acknowledgment letter. In this chapter you will use many more printing options to create a formal business plan.

A survey of the printing options and other formatting commands provided by AppleWorks will help you appreciate the wide range of possibilities it gives you.

Your Formatting Choices

Most formatting options, but not all, are chosen from the Printer Options menu, which you have probably already used on several occasions. Let's take another look at this menu now, so that you can refer to it as we go over some of the options you may not have used yet.

```
File: Busplan88.unf          PRINTER OPTIONS      Escape: Review/Add/Change
=====|====|====|====|====|====|====|====|====|====|====|====|====|====|====|===
```

```
      PW=8.0  LM=1.0   RM=1.0  CI=10  UJ  PL=11.0  TM=0.0  BM=2.0  LI=6  SS
Option:_                   UJ: Unjustified    GB: Group Begin      BE: Boldface End
                           CN: Centered       GE: Group End        +B: Superscript Beg
PW: Platen Width           PL: Paper Length   HE: Page Header      +E: Superscript End
LM: Left Margin            TM: Top Margin     FO: Page Footer      -B: Subscript Begin
RM: Right Margin           BM: Bottom Margin  SK: Skip Lines       -E: Subscript End
CI: Chars per Inch         LI: Lines per Inch PN: Page Number      UB: Underline Begin
P1: Proportional-1         SS: Single Space   PE: Pause Each page  UE: Underline End
P2: Proportional-2         DS: Double Space   PH: Pause Here       PP: Print Page No.
IN: Indent                 TS: Triple Space   SM: Set a Marker     EK: Enter Keyboard
JU: Justified              NP: New Page       BB: Boldface Begin   MM: Mail Merge
```

The printer options that are in effect by default are displayed in a row above the list of options; that is, AppleWorks has already set values for the options listed on this line, but you can change them if you wish. If the default settings are acceptable to you, you are saved the trouble of defining them.

The printing options can be divided by function into six groups: horizontal spacing, vertical spacing, page layout, pagination, special printing effects, and miscellaneous features. This chapter will discuss only selected, frequently used printing options since many are quite obvious in their use and function.

In addition to the printing options, AppleWorks includes some formatting commands that can be entered directly from the keyboard without accessing the Printer Options menu. These are commands that control frequently used features like boldface or underlining. The commands are invoked either with OA or CONTROL key combinations, or through the Printer Options menu. It is faster and more convenient, of course, to enter commands directly from the Review/Add/Change screen. In the following discussion, you will find mention of the CONTROL and OA key commands whenever appropriate.

Horizontal spacing. Horizontal spacing controls the spacing of the characters on a line of text. Some of the options that affect horizontal spacing include Platen Width (PW), Left Margin (LM), Right Margin (RM), Tabs (OA-T), Characters per Inch (CI), and Proportional Spacing (P1 or P2).

Figure 6-1 illustrates some of the effects you can achieve by adjusting the horizontal spacing. As shown there, the *platen width* is the maximum distance across the page that the printer can move and print. This distance is reduced, of course, by any left and right margins you may set. For example, the default text width is 6 inches: the platen width of 8.0 inches minus a left margin of 1.0 inch and a right margin of 1.0 inch.

In AppleWorks, tabs are used in a way that is very similar to how they're used on typewriters. You can set and clear tabs easily using the OA-T (for Tab) command directly from the Review/Add/Change screen rather than going into the Printer Options menu. Tabs are preset at intervals of five spaces. To use tabs in your document, simply press the TAB key to advance the cursor five spaces or OA-TAB to reverse the direction.

The number of characters per inch is determined in Apple-Works by the CI option (normally referred to as CPI, but CI in AppleWorks). Characters per inch is another name for *printer pitch;* both refer to the number of characters your printer will print in one inch.

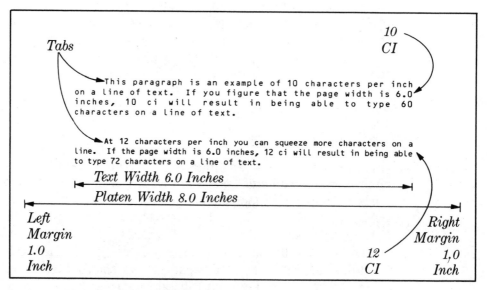

Figure 6-1. Examples of horizontal spacing

The characters per inch setting you specify can make quite a difference in horizontal spacing. If you use the default of 10 characters per inch, you will be able to print 60 characters on a six-inch text line. If you change the pitch from 10 characters per inch to 12, you will be able to print 72 characters in the same line. You change the CI to get more or fewer characters on a line. You might need, for example, to squeeze more letters into smaller spaces when you fill in printed forms. Or you might want to make your text easier to read by decreasing the number of letters on a line.

Another way to control the density of a line of text is through *proportional spacing*, which controls the spacing between characters by varying the space allotted to each character. Thus, for example, because an "I" requires less space than an "M," space can be saved by allotting the "I" less room. Normal spacing, in contrast, would allot each character the same printed space regardless of size. In order for you to take advantage of proportional spacing, your printer must support it. If your printer supports proportional spacing you will be able to print more formal-looking documents, since this is the technique used in books and newspapers.

AppleWorks lets you specify two different proportional print modes (P1 and P2). Since printers vary in their handling of proportional spacing, you'll have to experiment with yours to discover how it treats each of the proportional print modes. You should not try to use proportional spacing with tabular text, however, since the variations in the space allotted to each letter tend to ruin the columnar spacing.

Vertical spacing.   Vertical spacing controls the spacing of the lines of text on a page from its top to its bottom. Some of Apple-

Works' printer options that affect vertical spacing are Paper Length (PL), Top Margin (TM), Bottom Margin (BM), Single, Double, or Triple Spacing (SS, DS, TS), Lines per Inch (LI), and Skipping Lines (SK). Figure 6-2 shows some examples of vertical spacing.

To determine the length of your text, subtract the top and bottom margins from the paper length. The default setting is 9 inches, which assumes a paper length of 11 inches, minus a top margin default of 0.0 inches and a bottom margin default of 2.0 inches. If you use a setting of six lines per inch, you will be able to print 54 lines per page with nine inches of text. Figure 6-2 compares two kinds of vertical spacing. As you can see, printing with eight lines per inch packs the line closer than with six lines and allows you to print more lines in the same space. Nine inches of text, for example, would contain 72 lines at eight lines per inch.

Page layout.   Page layout controls the appearance of the text on a page. Some of AppleWorks' most useful page layout options include Indenting (IN), Justification or Unjustification (JU, UJ), and Centering text (CN). Figure 6-3 shows some examples of these options.

Indenting is used to set up paragraphs that have an "over-hanging" first line, as you would find in bulleted or numbered lists (remember that to AppleWorks a paragraph is any section of text that ends with a RETURN). An example of this is shown in Figure 6-3. The effects of the indent are that the first line extends from the established left margin to the right, and the second line and subsequent lines are indented in from the left margin by the number of characters you specify. The indent ends with a RETURN.

Justified and *unjustifed text* refers to the appearance of the right margin of the text. If the lines of text end evenly at the right margin, the text is justified. If the right margin is ragged, the text is unjustified. You'll usually find justified text only in books or newspapers. It gives your documents a more formal look.

Centering centers a line of text, such as a title, between the left and right margins. Your line can be either centered, jus-

Top
Margin
1.0
Inch

```
1001 South First
Santa Fe, NM 87340
December 14, 1988
```

Single
Spacing

```
Ms. Kim Long, Vice President
Accounting Systems Consultants
14000 NW Rolling Hills
Houston, TX  85660

Dear Ms. Long:
```

Printed
At
6 Lines
Per Inch

```
As we discussed on the telephone last Friday, I am enclosing
the specifications for a new computer system that we are
interested in purchasing for our expanding business.

We want to find a good accounting system that has all the
basic functions such as General Ledger, Accounts Receivable,
Accounts Payable, Payroll, Inventory, and Fixed Assets to
start with.  We have listed our priorities below.  In
addition to the specific operating features, we want these
characteristics:

1.  A User friendly system that takes minimal training for
new personnel that will be hired after the initial training
has been completed.

2.  An integrated system between the accounting modules.
This is so we do not have to enter the same accounting
transactions more than once in the various modules.

3.  A speedy system, or at least responsive.  We do not want
to wait undue time for transactions to complete.

4.  A computer system that is easy to change without
additional cost to us.  We realize that some future
requirements might require special programming assistance,
but we don't want to pay extra for such necessities as
simple new reports.

5.  An inexpensive computer system.  We know we'll have to
pay something for the computer equipment and software, but
we want to limit our investment to under $12,000 if
possible.

6.  Customer service representatives that are truly
interested in assisting customers get the most out of their
computer.  We heard too many times about the problems with
inadequate computer assistance.
```

Printed
At
8 Lines
Per Inch

Skipped
Lines

Figure 6-2.   Examples of vertical spacing

tified, or unjustified. It cannot be more than one of these at a time.

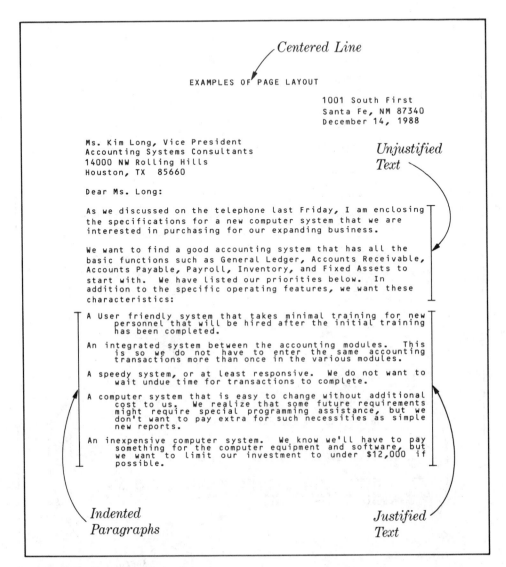

Figure 6-3.   Examples of page layout

Pagination.   Pagination determines such formatting issues as where to start a new page, where and how to print page numbers, and how to avoid splitting text between two pages that should be on the same page. The printer options for page formatting are New Page (NP), Page Number (PN), Print Page Number (PP), Calculate Page Breaks (OA-K), and Group Begin (GB) and Group End (GE).

The New Page option allows you to override AppleWorks' automatic calculation of page breaks as you enter text. For example, you may want to break a page early to keep a title with the paragraph that follows it. If you don't invoke the New Page option, AppleWorks calculates the page breaks based on the page length and margin settings you have established.

AppleWorks actually does more than calculate where a page break should be; it also tries to eliminate "orphans" and "widows." An *orphan* is a single line of a paragraph at the bottom of the page, and a *widow* is a single line of a paragraph at the top of a page. While AppleWorks tries not to break paragraphs at a point where less than two lines would appear at the end or beginning of a page, it may not position a single-line paragraph or a title properly.

To weed out any persisting widow and orphan problems, you may determine where the pages are going to break by using the OA-K command (for Calculate Page Break). Apple-Works will calculate the page breaks before the document is printed, allowing you to scan the document to see if the pages are the way you want them to be. You may need to move a stranded line from one page to the next or insert a forced page break. AppleWorks will not override any forced page breaks you may make.

Another way to oversee page breaks is to group the text to be printed on the same page using the Group Begin (GB) and Group End (GE) options. For example, you may want to group a single-line paragraph or title with the text imme-diately following it. To do this, you mark the beginning and ending of the group to be kept together on one page by invok-ing the GB option at the beginning of the group and GE at the end. AppleWorks will break the page either before or after the group, but not in the middle.

AppleWorks also calculates and prints page numbers for you when you use the Print Page Number (PP) option. To override its calculations for any page number, you may insert your own with the Page Number (PN) option. AppleWorks will number the following pages continuing from the number you entered.

Special printing effects.   AppleWorks offers a variety of special printing effects for altering the appearance of characters. These include several printing options and two CONTROL key command sequences. To create boldfaced printing or underlining, for example, invoke the Printer Options menu and access the BB and BE (for Boldface Begin and Boldface End) options or the UB and UE (for Underline Begin and Underline End) options. Or use CONTROL key commands directly for the Review/Add/Change screen to mark the beginning and end of the text you wish to boldface or underline. This second method has the advantage of being faster. For boldface, the CONTROL sequence is CONTROL-B; for underlining, it is CONTROL-L. Both boldface and underlining will last until end markers are encountered, regardless of how many lines or pages.

Subscripting and superscripting, on the other hand, will automatically stop at the end of the line. Of course, to use any of the special printing effects, you must have a printer that supports the feature. The printer options for creating subscripts and superscripts are $-B$ and $-E$ for subscripts and $+B$ and $+E$ for superscripts. Both are accessed through the Printer Options menu.

Sticky spaces are used to force two or more words to be printed together on one line. You can create a sticky space by pressing OA simultaneously with the spacebar. You might want to use a sticky space for names. For example, to ensure that the name Samuel E. Whitaker appears on only one line, you would use sticky spaces between the first, middle, and last names.

How do you know when a special printing effect has been used in a document? AppleWorks marks all special printing effects with carets ($^$). To see what particular special effects a caret signifies, place your cursor over the mark and watch the message line on your screen: the particular feature in question will be named.

Miscellaneous features.   Other printing options that will give you flexibility in preparing your documents are the Set a Marker (SM), Pause Each Page (PE), Pause Here (PH), Enter Keyboard (EK), and Mail Merge (MM) options.

The Set a Marker feature is a way of marking places in your text that you will want to get to quickly. You might want to rewrite a particular section of your text. Or you may be in the middle of a complicated move where you want to shift several locations around; finding each of them may be time-consuming without markers.

The next three options allow you to take some action while your document is actually printing. For example, the Pause Each Page option halts the printing at the end of each page. This pause allows you time to feed single sheets of paper, perhaps letterhead stationery or preprinted forms, into the printer. The Pause Here option halts the printing at a specific location in the document, not just at the end of a page. You might, for example, want to change print wheels at that spot. Finally, the Enter Keyboard option is particularly useful for filling out forms from the keyboard. Our Order Acknowledgment letter is an example of how the Enter Keyboard option might be used. When the letter is printed, the printer automatically stops at each occurrence of the Enter Keyboard caret so that you can type in the name and address, the delivery date, and the order detail. The printer resumes printing when you press the RETURN key after entering each piece of information.

The last option, Mail Merge, allows you to print customized form letters. It merges a form letter created in word processing with a list (of names and addresses, for example) created in the data base. You will use the Mail Merge option in Chapter 9.

Let's now begin entering the business plan. In the process

you'll use many of the printing options that were just discussed.

Entering the Business Plan

Figure 6-4 displays the business plan as you will be entering it. You can see that two sections of the business plan depend upon documents from other components: the list of inventory items must come from the data base and the financial plan must come from the spreadsheet. Thus it will not be possible to complete the writing of the business plan in this chapter. But in Chapter 9 the three documents will be integrated into one.

If you have not booted the computer, do so now. Position yourself at the Main Menu of AppleWorks. Insert the unused AppleWorks2 disk into disk drive 2. Change the disk drive assignment to be disk drive 2. If you have questions about booting or changing the disk assignment, review the discussion of these topics in Chapter 2.

To create a file for the business plan, follow these familiar steps:

1. On the Main Menu press RETURN to select Add files to the Desktop.

2. On the Add Files menu, select option 3, Make a new file for the Word Processor.

3. Direct AppleWorks to create a fresh file by pressing RETURN (thus selecting the highlighted option From scratch).

4. When prompted for the filename, enter **Busplan88.unf** and press RETURN.

The "unf" stands for "unfinished." When the business plan is completed through the inclusion of the data base and spreadsheet portions in Chapter 9, you'll change the filename to reflect its finished status.

At this point the blank Review/Add/Change screen will be displayed for you to begin entering the business plan. The first task will be to set up the margins for the document.

Changing Margins

Because the default settings of 0.0 for the top margin and 2.0 for the bottom margin are not appropriate for a business plan that will have both a header and a footer, you must change both the top and bottom margins. A one-inch margin for each is ample.

Since you set margins in Chapter 3, you probably need just briefly to review the procedure here. Follow these steps to change the default settings for the document's margins:

1. Press OA-O to access the Printer Options menu.

The familiar Printer Options menu will be displayed with the line above the menu highlighting the values that have been previously set or that are predefined by AppleWorks. As you change the options, the results will be shown both on the highlighted line and on the top of the screen. Watch the code for Top Margin (TM) change as you complete the next two steps.

2. Type **TM** for Top Margin and press RETURN.

3. Enter **1.0** to direct AppleWorks to set the top margin at one inch and press RETURN.

Notice that the TM in the highlighted default line has been changed from 0.0 inches to 1.0 inches and that the formatting message "----Top Margin" has appeared on the top of the screen. Remember that you can enter the formatting code in lowercase (**tm**), even though it appears in uppercase on the

ABC COMPANY

Plan to Add Store, 1988

This section of the business plan addresses the opening
of an additional store in 1988.

OBJECTIVE

abc plans to open one new retail store in 1988 which is
to be profitable within eight months from opening.

THE PLAN

The plan is composed of three sections: a description
of the new store, the startup plans, and the financial plan.

DESCRIPTION

abc's new store will be named om. It will appeal to
small businesses in and near the city of Bellevue,
Washington. om will sell office supplies and accessories.
Paper and film products will be stressed in the product
lines sold.

STARTUP PLAN

The startup plan for om involves two areas: the
physical startup and the marketing plans.

Physical Startup

Many of the startup personnel will initially be
transferred from the Renton store. These employees will be
returned to the Renton store after two weeks time, except
for the store manager who is to be permanently promoted from
the Renton store.

The rest of the employees will be hired especially for
the new store. The details concerning the number of persons
hired and the skills needed are described under the
Financial Plan.

One month prior to opening the store, space will be
leased. At that time the new equipment, inventory, and
displays will be moved into the store. Also the new
personnel training will begin. The training will teach the
new employees about abc and about the product lines that om
carries.

The list of startup inventory items which will be used
to initially stock the store is as follows:

(from data base)

CONFIDENTIAL   PAGE 15

Figure 6-4. Business plan to be created

```
                          ABC COMPANY


Marketing Plan
        Advertising will begin one month prior to opening.
There will be weekly 1/2 page advertisements in the leading
Bellevue newspapers.   In addition, a direct mail campaign
will  be  used  to  distribute  announcements  to  Bellevue
businesses.  One week before the opening, a daily radio ad
will announce the opening of om.   The ads will be timed to
reach the Bellevue business during the noon news hour.   The
financial costs are described under the Financial Plan.

FINANCE PLAN
        The following budget covers the new store for one year
beginning one month prior to the opening:

(from spreadsheet)
```

```
CONFIDENTIAL                                          PAGE 16
```

Figure 6-4.   Business plan to be created (*continued*)

Printer Options menu. Codes will usually appear in upper-case throughout this book.

4. Type **BM** for Bottom Margin and press RETURN.

5. Type **1.0** to change the bottom margin from 2.0 inches to 1.0 inch and press RETURN.

Again you can see the change reflected in the default line and on the top of the screen.

6. Press ESC to return to the Review/Add/Change screen.

Zooming In on Format Controls

As you enter text, you will occasionally want to be reminded of the formatting specifications you've entered — that is, the ones that differ from the default values. The Zoom command, as you will recall from Chapter 3, allows you to zoom in and out on the formatting you've done so far. If you press OA-Z right now, for example, you should see some messages in the top left corner of the screen telling you that the top and bottom margins have been specially set at 1.0 inches. The Zoom command is a toggle: if you press OA-Z again, the messages regarding margins will disappear.

Use the Zoom command as a way of keeping track of the formatting you've done. You can always go back and undo formatting commands that you've entered by mistake or that are not to your liking.

Entering the Header, Footer, and Title

The business plan contains both a header and a footer, and the latter will contain the page number as well. AppleWorks allows you to establish a one-line header or footer, or both, which will be generated on all following pages until you specify otherwise. In addition, there are several formatting functions that you will perform in entering these items, such as centering and underlining.

Adding a header and title.   Headers are printed on the first text line immediately following the top margin and are followed by two blank lines and then the text. Consequently, when you think about how large a top margin you want, you need to consider your header line plus the two blank lines used as separators between the header and the text. While the top margin is unaffected by the header, the header does cause three lines to be subtracted from the body of text. Thus, if you have decided on vertical spacing of six lines per inch, the header would take up one-half inch.

Your header must be entered at the top of the first page on which it is to appear. Setting up your header requires that you first call up the Printer Options menu and request the Page Header option (HE). Then, before you leave the menu to enter the header on the Review/Add/Change screen, you need to specify the centering option. Let's see how this is done:

1. Press OA-O to get the Printer Options menu.

2. Type **HE** to request a header line and press RETURN.

You will see the formatting message "----Page Header" on your screen. At this point, you will continue to give Apple-Works directions about the header although you will not type it in until you leave the Printer Options menu.

3. Type **CN** to indicate that the header is to be centered and press RETURN.

4. Now press ESC to return to the full Review/Add/Change screen so that the header line can be typed in.

5. Press OA-Z so that you can see what formatting options you've specified.

Your screen should look like this:

```
File: Busplan88.unf          REVIEW/ADD/CHANGE          Escape: Main Menu
=====|====|====|====|====|====|====|====|====|====|====|====|====|====|====|===
--------Top Margin:  1.0 inches
--------Bottom Margin:  1.0 inches
--------Page Header
--------Centered
```

Type entry or use Ć commands   Line 5 Column 1   Ć-? for Help
```

At this point you can type in the header, in this case the name of the company for which the business plan is being written. It must be done right now before you enter any other text, because AppleWorks will accept the next line as the header, whatever it is.

    6. Press the CAPS LOCK key and enter **ABC COMPANY** and then press RETURN to end the header.

While in the centering mode, type in the title of the document, underlining it in the process.

    7. Press the CAPS LOCK key to disable it since the title will contain both upper- and lowercase letters.

    8. Press CONTROL-L to begin the underlining.

A caret (^) will be placed right before the words to be underlined. This formatting mark will not be printed; it only
```

appears on the screen to inform you that the line is being underlined.

9. Enter **Plan to Add Store, 1988.**

10. Press CONTROL-L to end the underlining and press RETURN to confirm your entry.

Your screen should look like the one in the following illustration.

```
File: Busplan88.unf            REVIEW/ADD/CHANGE            Escape: Main Menu
=====|====|====|====|====|====|====|====|====|====|====|====|====|====|===
--------Top Margin:  1.0 inches
--------Bottom Margin:  1.0 inches
--------Page Header
--------Centered
                       ABC COMPANY※
                 ^Plan to Add Store, 1988^※
※
░
```

```
-----------------------------------------------------------------------
Type entry or use ⌂ commands          Line 7  Column  1        ⌂-? for Help
```

Now that you've finished with the titles and header, you can eliminate the centering feature. To reset the centering feature to justified,

11. Press OA-O.

12. Enter **JU** to change from centering to justified and press RETURN.

You're now ready to tackle the footer and page numbering options.

Setting up footers and page numbering. In order to ensure that the business plan is kept private, put the word CONFIDEN-TIAL at the bottom of the page for emphasis. You can enter a footer anywhere on the first page it is to appear on. It will be printed, however, on the last text line immediately before the bottom margin and will be preceded by two blank lines. Just as with the header, when you establish a footer, three lines will be subtracted from the body of text, while the bottom margin will remain unchanged.

For this exercise, you are also going to put the page number in the footer. Since this plan for opening a store is just one part of a larger business plan, the page numbering will not start with 1 but with 15. Follow these steps to correct the page number and set up the footing.

1. Enter **PN** for Page Number and press RETURN.

2. In response to the message "Number:" enter **15** and press RETURN.

You have now changed the page number so that the page numbering will begin with Page 15 and be numbered sequentially from there.

3. Enter **FO** for Page Footer and press RETURN.

4. Now press ESC to return to the full Review/Add/Change screen so that you can type in the footing text.

Since AppleWorks will accept whatever is typed next as the footer, the footer must be entered immediately after the footer line message.

5. Again press the CAPS LOCK for uppercase letters.

6. Enter the word **CONFIDENTIAL**.

7. By pressing the spacebar, move the cursor over to

column number 53, type the word **PAGE**, and press the spacebar once more.

Your screen should look like this:

```
File: Busplan88.unf            REVIEW/ADD/CHANGE              Escape: Main Menu
=====|====|====|====|====|====|====|====|====|====|====|====|====|====|===
--------Top Margin:  1.0 inches
--------Bottom Margin:  1.0 inches
--------Page Header
--------Centered
                        ABC COMPANY▓
                 ^Plan to Add Store, 1988^▓
--------Justified
--------Page Number: 15
--------Page Footer
CONFIDENTIAL                                    PAGE▓




-------------------------------------------------------------------------
Type entry or use ⌘ commands        Line 10  Column 58      ⌘-? for Help
```

At this point you must direct AppleWorks to calculate the page number and place it immediately following the word "PAGE." This requires that you go back into the Printer Options menu to request the Page Number option.

8. Press OA-O, enter **PP** for Print Page Number, and press RETURN.

9. Press ESC to return to the Review/Add/Change screen.

A caret will be inserted after the word "PAGE" to indicate that the page number will be printed there. The next screen shows what your document looks like with the margins reset and the header and footer lines established.

```
File: Busplan88.unf              REVIEW/ADD/CHANGE                Escape: Main Menu
=====|====|====|====|====|====|====|====|====|====|====|====|====|====|====|===
--------Top Margin:  1.0 inches
--------Bottom Margin:  1.0 inches
--------Page Header
--------Centered
                           ABC COMPANY▒
                  ^Plan to Add Store, 1988^▒
--------Justified
--------Page Number: 15
--------Page Footer
CONFIDENTIAL                                          PAGE ^▒




----------------------------------------------------------------------------
Type entry or use ⌕ commands          Line 10  Column 59      ⌕-? for Help
```

10. Press RETURN to end the Page Footer operation.

11. Release the CAPS LOCK key.

This is a good time to test the Zoom command. Press OA-Z a few times to see the formatting instructions appear and disappear. Leave the Zoom feature activated for the time being.

You have successfully changed your top and bottom margins and entered a header, a title, and a footer and set up automatic page numbering for the business plan.

Entering the Text of the Business Plan

Figure 6-4 shows the business plan you should now proceed to enter. Type the text exactly as you see it in Figure 6-4— that is, with references to "abc," which stands for "ABC Company," and with the abbreviation "om," which stands for the store's new name, Office Mart. These shortened names make entering the text faster. After you finish entering the text, you'll have a chance to use the Replace command to replace the abbreviations with the full names.

Some of the printer options you will need include the Centered option (CN); the Justified option (JU) to turn off centering and return to normal justified text, and the Underline

Begin (UB) and Underline End (UE) options to begin and end underlining. All of these options must, of course, be accessed through the Printer Options menu. An alternative method of underlining is to press CONTROL-L to begin and end underlining.

Remember to use RETURN only to end paragraphs or enter blank lines. Use the TAB key to indent the first word of each paragraph.

If you make any mistakes, correct them using the editing techniques explored in Chapter 3.

When you reach the end of the business plan, you should save it. To do this press OA-S for Save. AppleWorks will quickly save the document so that you can safely continue with your editing.

Using the Replace Command

You were able to save time in typing the text by entering shortened names for ABC Company and Office Mart. Now get AppleWorks to do the work of entering the longer names.

The Replace command can replace all occurrences of a word or phrase or only the occurrences you specify. In addition, you can choose whether to replace text that is "case sensitive." For example, if you want to specifically replace only uppercase occurrences of "ABC," then "abc" and "Abc" will not be replaced. If your replacement is not case sensitive, all will be replaced.

AppleWorks keeps track of the last Replace operation you performed. The next time you use the Replace command, AppleWorks will select your last replacement as its default. You can either use the same replacement again, or specify new terms.

Here are the steps involved in replacing one group of characters with another:

1. Press OA-1 to position your cursor at the beginning of the document.

Since the Replace command only works forward, from the

cursor position to the end of the document, you want to ensure that you start at the correct location. In this case, because you want to find all occurrences of "abc" so that they can be replaced with the actual company name, you want to start at the beginning of the document.

2. Press OA-R for Replace.

You are asked to choose between Case sensitive text and all Text, that is, whether AppleWorks should preselect for replacement only those words that are in a particular case. Since you have consistently entered the company name in lowercase, as "abc," except for the header line, you should only replace lowercase occurrences of "abc" with the longer

```
File: Busplan88.unf                REPLACE              Escape: Review/Add/Change
=====|====|====|====|====|====|====|====|====|====|====|====|====|====|====|===
--------Top Margin:  1.0 inches
--------Bottom Margin:  1.0 inches
--------Page Header
--------Centered
                            ABC COMPANY▓
                    ^Plan to Add Store, 1988^▓
--------Justified
--------Page Number: 15
--------Page Footer
CONFIDENTIAL                                          PAGE ^▓
▓
      This section of the business plan addresses the opening
of an additional store in 1988.▓
▓
--------Centered
                        OBJECTIVE▓
--------Justified
     abc plans to open one new retail store in 1988 which is
to be profitable within eight months from opening.▓
▓
-------------------------------------------------------------------------
Replace?  Text  Case sensitive text
```

company name. Otherwise, the header line will be included in the replacement and will be changed to read "ABC COMPANY COMPANY."

3. To make the replace operation case sensitive, type **C** to select Case sensitive text.

You will be asked to enter the text to be searched for.

4. In response to the question Replace what?, enter **abc** and press RETURN.

Next you will be asked to enter the replacement text that will overwrite the abbreviation you typed in the business plan.

5. In response to the question Replace with what?, enter **ABC Company** and press RETURN.

Finally, you will be asked whether AppleWorks should replace All occurrences of "abc" or replace them One at a time, to enable you to verify the replacement before it occurs.

6. In response to the question Replace?, enter **a** for All.

This step automatically replaces all occurrences of "abc" with "ABC Company." There really is no need to verify each replacement in this case since "abc" is a very distinctive abbreviation and no other combination of these letters is likely to have occurred.

7. Press OA-1 to return to the beginning of the document.

Now look through your document using the OA-DOWN and UP ARROWs. Notice how all occurrences have been changed. Wasn't this a fast way to type in the long company name? Text replacement is one of the greatest productivity tools in word processing.

Now change all occurrences of "om" to "Office Mart." Follow these steps:

8. Press OA-1 to return to the beginning of the document, if you are not already there.

9. Press OA-R for Replace.

10. Enter C to select Case sensitive text.

Selecting the Case sensitive text option restricts the replacement to exactly the same case, lowercase in this instance. You'll need to blank out "abc" and enter **om** over it. You can do this using the overstrike mode.

11. Enter overstrike mode by pressing OA-E.

12. Type **om** as the text to be replaced, use the spacebar to delete the "c" in "abc," and press RETURN.

Notice that the "om" is now followed by a space. You'll need to maintain that space to avoid running words together during the replacement. Be careful, however, not to enter extra spaces when you enter the search text because AppleWorks considers spaces to be characters, and it may not find the words you think you are asking it to find.

13. Type **Office Mart** followed by a space as the replacement text, typing over "ABC Company," and press RETURN

14. Press RETURN to accept the default One at a time option.

This ensures that you have the opportunity to verify the replacements. Your screen should now look like the following illustration.

```
File: Busplan88.unf              REPLACE            Escape: Review/Add/Change
=====|====|====|====|====|====|====|====|====|====|====|====|====|====|===
--------Page Footer
CONFIDENTIAL                                        PAGE ^
     This section of the business plan addresses the opening
of an additional store in 1988.
--------Centered
                    OBJECTIVE
--------Justified
     ABC Company plans to open one new retail store in 1988
which is to be profitable within eight months from opening.
--------Centered
                     THE PLAN
--------Justified
     The plan is composed of three sections: a description
of the new store, the startup plans, and the financial plan.
DESCRIPTION
     ABC Company's new store will be named om.  It will
--------------------------------------------------------------------------
Replace this one?  No  Yes
```

You can immediately see why you chose the option to approve each replacement one at a time. Your first opportunity to replace "om" is in the word "from." The way to avoid this problem is to be sure to put a space before the whole words you're searching for. Thus, if you entered a space before entering om, you would have prevented the Replace command from finding letters that are embedded in other words.

15. Press RETURN to select No, thereby directing Apple-Works not to replace the "om" in "from."

Change the search to eliminate the embedded letters within words.

16. In response to the question Find next occurrence?, press RETURN to accept the default option, No.

17. Press OA-R for Replace.

18. Type C for Case sensitive text.

19. Type a space, **om**, and then press RETURN to enter the text to be searched for.

20. Also enter a space before **Office Mart** and then press RETURN immediately after the "t" to verify that **Office Mart** is still the replacement text you want.

21. Press RETURN to select One at a time.

You are now presented with a valid replacement candidate since you are searching for the letters alone, not for the letters embedded within other words.

22. Type **Y** for Yes to direct AppleWorks to replace the displayed candidate.

You will see the replaced word immediately.

23. Enter **Y** for Yes to direct AppleWorks to continue the search.

Continue this sequence of actions until all replacements have been completed. For each replacement possibility you will direct AppleWorks to replace the text or not, and then to proceed to the next occurrence. You should find four more occurrences of "om" to replace.

When all occurrences of "om" have been found, Apple-Works will beep and stop, displaying a message that no more occurrences can be found and instructing you to press the spacebar to continue.

24. Press the spacebar to continue.

Note that AppleWorks puts a limit on the size of both the text it searches for and the replacement text. Neither can be more than 30 characters long.

Moving and Copying Text

Suppose that in reading over the plan, you decide that there are some confusing sentence arrangements in the "Physical Startup" section. The third paragraph seems like a more suitable way to begin the section than the first paragraph. Let's switch them around.

Follow these steps to move the two paragraphs:

1. Move the cursor to the third paragraph under "Physical Startup," which begins "One month prior...."

Be sure to position the cursor at the left margin, rather than on the first word of the paragraph, "One."

2. Press OA-M to activate the Move command.

AppleWorks will ask you where you want to move the text. If you were moving text to or from another file, you would use the Clipboard. But here you are just switching paragraphs within the document.

3. In response to the question Move text?, press RETURN to accept the default option, Within document.

4. Move your cursor down six times to mark the paragraph to be moved.

The text will be highlighted as shown in the following illustration.

```
File: Busplan88.unf              MOVE TEXT            Escape: Review/Add/Change
=====|====|====|====|====|====|====|====|====|====|====|====|====|====|===
※
^Physical Startup^※
       Many of the startup personnel will initially be
transferred from the Renton store.  These employees will be
returned to the Renton store after two weeks time, except
for the store manager who is to be permanently promoted from
the Renton store.※
※
       The rest of the employees will be hired especially for
the new store.  The details concerning the number of persons
hired and the skills needed are described under the
Financial Plan.※
※
       One month prior to opening the store, space will be
leased.  At that time the new equipment, inventory, and
displays will be moved into the store.  Also the new
personnel training will begin.  The training will teach the
new employees about ABC Company and about the product lines
that Office Mart carries.※
※
-------------------------------------------------------------------------
Use cursor moves to highlight block, then press Return※              54K Avail.
```

5. Press RETURN to tell AppleWorks that you have defined the text to be moved to the new location.

Now you must specify where the highlighted text is to be moved. This is the left margin of the first line of the first paragraph, which begins "Many of the startup personnel...."

6. Move your cursor to the left margin of the first line of the first paragraph and press RETURN.

The third paragraph should now begin the section, like this:

```
File: Busplan88.unf          REVIEW/ADD/CHANGE          Escape: Main Menu
=====|====|====|====|====|====|====|====|====|====|====|====|====|====|===
※
^Physical Startup^※
[]    One month prior to opening the store, space will be
leased. At that time the new equipment, inventory, and
displays will be moved into the store. Also the new
personnel training will begin. The training will teach the
new employees about ABC Company and about the product lines
that Office Mart carries.※
※
      Many of the startup personnel will initially be
transferred from the Renton store. These employees will be
returned to the Renton store after two weeks time, except
for the store manager who is to be permanently promoted from
the Renton store.※
※
      The rest of the employees will be hired especially for
the new store. The details concerning the number of persons
hired and the skills needed are described under the
Financial Plan.※
※
--------------------------------------------------------------------------
Type entry or use Ć commands          Line 38  Column  1       Ć-? for Help
```

You can use this technique to move text of any size, from one word to several pages. You need only to highlight the text to be moved and then tell AppleWorks where to place it.

The Copy command is very similar to the Move command. The major difference is that the Copy command, OA-C, does not change the position of the original as it moves a copy of it to another position. This command is particularly useful for moving standard text to other files. You can define paragraphs that you want to use in many documents: for example, boilerplate proposals where much of the content is the same from proposal to proposal. You are able to select and copy those paragraphs that apply to each new proposal you write.

You will learn more about the Copy command in Chapter 9, which covers integration.

Setting Markers

Occasionally you want to mark certain positions in your text so that you can quickly and easily find them again. Apple-Works lets you insert numeric markers, up to 254 of them in one file. After the markers are set, you can quickly get to them using the Find command.

There are two areas in the business plan where markers are appropriate. You will be inserting text into this document from the data base and spreadsheet components in Chapter 9. It will be faster to do this if you set markers in your text.

1. Press OA-1 to position your cursor at the beginning of the text.

2. Press OA-F for Find to locate the first spot to be marked.

3. Press RETURN to verify that you want to search for Text.

Again, watch the spaces carefully. In this case there are no spaces at the end of the word "base."

4. Be sure you are in overstrike mode; enter the words **data base** and press RETURN.

Once you press RETURN, the words will be found and high-lighted. At this point you want to end the search process and insert the markers within your text.

5. Press RETURN to indicate that you do not want to con-tinue searching.

6. Press OA-O and enter **SM** for Set a Marker and press RETURN.

7. Type the number **1** and then press RETURN to indicate that this is the first marker.

8. Press ESC to return to the Review/Add/Change screen.

You should see the marker formatting message "Set a Marker: 1," just above the words "data base." If you don't, be sure you can see the formatting characters by pressing OA-Z (for Zoom).

```
File: Busplan88.unf              FIND         Escape: Review/Add/Change
=====|====|====|====|====|====|====|====|====|====|====|====|====|====|===
▓
      The rest of the employees will be hired especially for
the new store.  The details concerning the number of persons
hired and the skills needed are described under the
Financial Plan.▓
▓
      .The list of startup inventory items which will be used
to initially stock the store is as follows:▓
--------Set a Marker: 1
▓
(from data base)▓
▓
^Marketing Plan^▓
      Advertising will begin one month prior to opening.
There will be weekly 1/2 page advertisements in the leading
Bellevue newspapers.  In addition, a direct mail campaign
will be used to distribute announcements to Bellevue
businesses.  One week before the opening, a daily radio ad
will announce the opening of om.  The ads will be timed to
reach the Bellevue business during the noon news hour.  The
-----------------------------------------------------------------------
Find next occurrence?  No  Yes
```

Follow the same procedure to find the second site for the marker and to set that second marker.

9. Press OA-F for Find to locate the second spot to be marked.

10. Press RETURN to verify your search for Text.

11. In overstrike mode, enter the word **spreadsheet** and press RETURN.

12. When the location has been highlighted, press RETURN to stop the search.

13. Press OA-O to get the Printer Options menu.

14. Enter the code for Set a Marker, **SM**, and press RETURN.

15. Enter the number **2** and press RETURN to indicate the second marker.

16. Press ESC to return to the Review/Add/Change screen.

The two markers are now set, defining where the additions will be inserted in Chapter 9.

Finding Markers

Now that the markers are set within the business plan, let's see how to jump to the places where the markers are located. Follow these steps to find your first marker:

1. Press OA-1 to return to the beginning of the document.

2. Press OA-F to activate the Find command.

3. Type **M** for Marker.

4. In response to question Marker number?, enter the number **1** and press RETURN.

The data base marker will be highlighted.

5. Press RETURN to end the search for markers.

You have seen how easily you can set markers and then find them in your text. Using this technique you can mark any portion of your text so that you can come back to it later to edit, move, or correct it. Markers can be very useful tools.

Calculating Page Breaks

Before printing the business plan, let's take a look at how the document is currently paginated. As you enter text, Apple-

Works calculates pages according to the printing options you have set; it takes into account the top and bottom margins, for example. As AppleWorks prints, however, it recalculates the paging, so that the current paging may not be what you see on the screen.

Let's have AppleWorks paginate the business plan so that any needed adjustments can be made before the plan is printed.

Here's the way to do it:

1. Press OA-1 to position the cursor at the beginning of the document.

The pagination calculation will be done starting from the current position of the cursor, so you want to be sure that you're at the start of the file.

2. Press OA-K for Calculate.

A message is displayed asking you to verify which printer will be used to print the business plan after the page breaks have been calculated.

3. Move the cursor to the name of the printer you will be using and press RETURN.

You will see the disk light and hear the disk movements as the pagination is being performed. This will take about two seconds. When the pagination process is complete, you can verify that your page breaks are correct.

4. Press the OA-DOWN ARROW a total of four times, looking for the page breaks as you go.

Your page break appears as a dotted line with the words End of Page 15 in the middle of the line, as shown in the following illustration.

```
File: Busplan88.unf          REVIEW/ADD/CHANGE              Escape: Main Menu
=====|====|====|====|====|====|====|====|====|====|====|====|====|====|===
(from data base)▒
▒
- - - - - - - - - - - - End of Page 15- - - - - - - - - - - - - - - - - -
^Marketing Plan^▒
      Advertising will begin one month prior to opening.
There will be weekly 1/2 page advertisements in the leading
Bellevue newspapers.  In addition, a direct mail campaign
will be used to distribute announcements to Bellevue
businesses.  One week before the opening, a daily radio ad
will announce the opening of Office Mart.  The ads will be
timed to reach the Bellevue business during the noon news
hour.  The financial costs are described under the Financial
Plan.▒
▒
FINANCE PLAN▒
      The following budget covers the new store for one year
beginning one month prior to the opening:▒
▒
--------Set a Marker: 2
◖(from spreadsheet)▒
------------------------------------------------------------------------
Type entry or use ⌘ commands        Line 80  Column  1      ⌘-? for Help
```

The two page breaks seem to be acceptable; there are no stranded titles or one-line paragraphs.

Before continuing, save the business plan. To do this, simply press OA-S and wait for the file to be saved. Now go ahead with printing the document.

ABC COMPANY

Plan to Add Store, 1988

This section of the business plan addresses the opening
of an additional store in 1988.

OBJECTIVE
ABC Company plans to open one new retail store in 1988
which is to be profitable within eight months from opening.

THE PLAN
The plan is composed of three sections: a description
of the new store, the startup plans, and the financial plan.

DESCRIPTION
ABC Company's new store will be named Office Mart. It
will appeal to small businesses in and near the city of
Bellevue, Washington. Office Mart will sell office supplies
and accessories. Paper and film products will be stressed
in the product lines sold.

STARTUP PLAN
The startup plan for Office Mart involves two areas:
the physical startup and the marketing plans.

Physical Startup
One month prior to opening the store, space will be
leased.   At that time the new equipment, inventory, and
displays will be moved into the store.   Also the new
personnel training will begin. The training will teach the
new employees about ABC Company and about the product lines
that Office Mart carries.

Many of the startup personnel will initially be
transferred from the Renton store. These employees will be
returned to the Renton store after two weeks time, except
for the store manager who is to be permanently promoted from
the Renton store.

The rest of the employees will be hired especially for
the new store. The details concerning the number of persons
hired and the skills needed are described under the
Financial Plan.

The list of startup inventory items which will be used
to initially stock the store is as follows:

(from data base)

CONFIDENTIAL   PAGE 15

Figure 6-5. Final printed report

ABC COMPANY

Marketing Plan
        Advertising will begin one month prior to opening.
There will be weekly 1/2 page advertisements in the leading
Bellevue newspapers.   In addition, a direct mail campaign
will be used to distribute announcements to Bellevue
businesses.   One week before the opening, a daily radio ad
will announce the opening of Office Mart.   The ads will be
timed to reach the Bellevue business during the noon news
hour.   The financial costs are described under the Financial
Plan.

FINANCE PLAN
        The following budget covers the new store for one year
beginning one month prior to the opening:

(from spreadsheet)

CONFIDENTIAL   PAGE 16

Figure 6-5.   Final printed report (*continued*)

Printing the Business Plan

Follow these steps to print the business plan. You have already set the Printer Options. All that's needed now is to invoke the Print command, like this:

1. Press OA-P for Print.

2. Press RETURN to instruct AppleWorks to print from the Beginning of the business plan.

3. Move the cursor over the name of the printer you're using and press RETURN.

4. Press RETURN to tell AppleWorks that you do in fact wish to print one copy of the business plan.

5. When the printer finishes, save the file by pressing OA-S.

When the business plan has been printed, compare it to Figure 6-5. Correct any inaccuracies, resave, and reprint it. The document will be used again in Chapter 9, so you will want to be sure to save the file again if you change it.

Having completed Chapter 6, you should now return to the Main Menu. For your next exercise, go on to either the first data base chapter, Chapter 4, or to Chapter 7.

7

Expanding Your Data Base Skills

In Chapter 7 you will expand your data base skills by learning more advanced functions. The emphasis will be on formatting reports and on changing the structure of your data base. You will create a new report for the CIF file you created in Chapter 4 and then build a new inventory file. Later on, in Chapter 9, you will integrate the inventory file with the business plan you created in Chapter 6.

If you have not already done so, turn on your computer and bring up AppleWorks. Then, if necessary, change the disk assignment to disk drive 2 and insert the AppleWorks1 disk containing the CIF file created in Chapter 4.

Creating Mailing Labels

You learned in Chapter 4 that there are two types of reports that AppleWorks allows you to create. One is the tables-style report that you used in Chapter 4 to build a telephone list. This type is a line-by-line list of all the records, each line showing data for one record only. The other type is a labels-style report; it prints several lines per record. You can see more information about each record in the labels-style report.

Name and address labels are, naturally enough, created from the labels-style data base report. Most businesses use mailing labels at some time, for advertising, special promotions, billing, or simply for holiday cards. In the following exercise, you will use the existing CIF file to build a list of customer labels.

Let's get started by bringing the CIF file onto the Desktop so you can format the labels. From the Main Menu, press RETURN to ask AppleWorks to Add files to the Desktop. So from the Add Files menu, press RETURN to select the first option, The current disk. Then place the cursor on the CIF filename, CIF.LST, and press RETURN again. The CIF file will be displayed for you on the Review/Add/Change screen.

Formatting a Report

To create the labels, you must design—or format—the report. To do this, AppleWorks must know which categories to include and exclude, how wide the categories should be, how they are arranged on the page, which records to include in the reports, and in what sequence the records are to be printed.

Follow these steps to format your name and address labels:

1. Press OA-P for Print.

AppleWorks will display the Report menu:

```
File: CIF.LST                    REPORT MENU          Escape: Review/Add/Change
Report: None
```

```
=============================================================================
```

```
                      1.  Get a report format
                      2.  Create a new "tables" format
                      3.  Create a new "labels" format
                      4.  Duplicate an existing format
                      5.  Erase a format
```

```
---------------------------------------------------------------------------
Type number, or use arrows, then press Return _              55K Avail.
```

You have five options to choose from. The first option, Get a report format, lists all of the report formats that currently exist for this file. There is only one right now, the CIF Telephone List created in Chapter 4. (You can press RETURN to see it and press ESC to return to the Report menu.) The second option, Create a new "tables" format, allows you to create a report that looks like a list, similar to the CIF Telephone List. The third option, Create a new "labels" format, is what you want for the name and address labels. The fourth option, Duplicate an existing format, allows you to copy and then modify an existing report format to give a slightly different look to your data base. For example, you may want to look at the CIF Telephone List in sequence by product type rather than alphabetically by name.

The fifth option, Erase a format, allows you to delete report formats that no longer apply to the data base. A sixth option, which does not currently appear on the screen, is

Keep working with current format. You can see this sixth option after you have been working with one of the report formats. It allows you to return quickly to the format you were working on previously and can be used only when you have already established formats for your data base.

2. Select the third option by typing **3** and pressing RETURN.

You will be asked to enter a name for the report. The name can have up to 19 characters, either letters, numbers, or special characters, or a combination.

3. Type in the name **Address Labels** and press RETURN.

This is what your screen should look like:

```
File: CIF.LST                 REPORT FORMAT            Escape: Report Menu
Report: Address Labels
Selection: All records


================================================================================
CUST
CUSTOMER NAME
STREET 1
STREET 2
CITY
STATE
ZIP CODE
TELEPHONE
CONTACT NAME
CREDIT LIMIT
PRODUCT TYPE
1ST ORDER DATE
----------------------Each record will print 12 lines--------------------


---------------------------------------------------------------------------
Use options shown on Help Screen                              ⌂-? for Help
```

Notice that the top of the screen lists the name of the file, the report, and the record selection. The selection All records indicates that all records in the data base will be included in the report. If the report were printed as is, each category would take up one line, causing each record to occupy 12 lines. Formatting this report will involve deleting the unwanted lines and then rearranging the categories on the page as you want them to appear on the labels.

Getting help.   The Help menu lists the commands available for formatting your report: what keys to press to move the cursor, to move categories, to insert and delete categories, and many other commands. To look at your options, press OA-? to get the Help menu and briefly look over the commands listed on the screen.

```
File: CIF.LST                      HELP              Escape: Report Format
Report: Address Labels
Selection: All records


===========================================================================
                -->   <--    Move cursor location
                a-arrows     Move category location
                   > a <     Next or previous record
                a-1...a-9    Go to beginning...end of file
                a-A         Arrange (sort) on this category
                a-D         Delete this spacing line or category
                a-I         Insert a spacing line or
                            a previously deleted category
                a-J         Left justify this category
                a-N         Change report name and/or title
                a-O         Printer options
                a-P         Print the report
                a-R         Change record selection rules
                a-V         Print category name AND entry
                a-Z         Zoom between category names, entries
-----------------------------------------------------------------------------
Press Space Bar to continue _                                    54K Avail.
```

Notice that all the OA keys are represented by @ signs in our depiction of this screen. The first three commands listed are the cursor movement commands. Since you'll be using these commands throughout the advanced work on the data base, take a moment now to recall how they work.

To format this report, you will be using not only the three cursor movement commands, but also the Delete, Insert, and

Left-Justify commands, the printer options, and the Print the Report command.

When you are finished examining the data base Help screen, press the spacebar to return to the Report format screen. To move the cursor from category to category, simply use the UP and DOWN ARROWS or the RETURN keys. To move to the right or left, use the RIGHT and LEFT ARROWS. Try these keys now. If you happen to push the cursor past the last category, additional blank lines will be inserted. If you do this, don't be alarmed. You'll delete the extra lines in a minute.

Deleting categories and blank lines.   One of your first tasks is to delete the unneeded categories. For mailing labels you will need to retain only name and address categories. Deleting categories in the Report Format screen never changes your actual data, just its appearance in a specific report. Thus, even though the category will no longer be on the screen or in the report, it is still in the data base.

Follow these steps to delete the unwanted categories:

1. Position your cursor on the "C" in CUST (for Customer Number) and press OA-D for Delete.

The category name has disappeared, but you'll notice that there is a blank line where the category was. You'll want to delete all unnecessary blank lines since you want your labels to have six lines per record, not the current 12, so that they will fit on the standard-size labels produced for computer printing. If you are printing six lines per inch, you can fit six lines on a one-by-three-inch label. Six lines should be adequate for most mailing programs (you may want eight lines per label for some foreign country mailings).

To rid yourself of the extra blank line, follow this step:

2. Place your cursor on the blank line and press OA-D.

Continue to delete the other unwanted categories—TELE-

PHONE, CONTACT NAME, CREDIT LIMIT, PRODUCT TYPE, and finally 1ST ORDER DATE—by moving the cursor to the first letter of each category and pressing OA-D twice, first to delete the category, and then again to delete the remaining blank line.

Now all of your unwanted categories and blank lines should be eliminated, and your screen should look like this:

```
File: CIF.LST                        REPORT FORMAT                     Escape: Report Menu
Report: Address Labels
Selection: All records



=======================================================================================
CUSTOMER NAME
STREET 1
STREET 2
CITY
STATE
ZIP CODE
-------------------------Each record will print  6 lines-------------------------




---------------------------------------------------------------------------------
Use options shown on Help Screen                                    ᘌ-? for Help
```

Should you want to reinsert a category, simply press OA-I for Insert. All deleted categories will be presented to you in a list and you can select the ones you want to reinsert. If you choose to look at this list right now, use the ESC key to return to the Report format screen without changing it.

Moving categories.   You now want to move the categories so that they are placed on the page as they will be on the mailing labels. To accomplish this, you must use the OA-RIGHT, -LEFT, -DOWN, and -UP ARROWS. Place your cursor on a category and push one of the keys; the category will move one position for each press of the key. You must be sure that your cursor is on the first character of the category, otherwise the category won't move.

Follow these steps to move the categories around:

1. Place your cursor on the "S" in STATE and press OA-RIGHT ARROW six times.

2. Now press OA-UP ARROW one time.

The STATE category should be next to the CITY category.

3. Place your cursor on the "Z" in ZIP CODE and press OA-RIGHT ARROW 13 times.

4. Next press OA-UP ARROW two times.

The ZIP CODE should be on the same line as CITY and STATE.

Left-justifying categories.   If you were to print the report right now, you would notice that the categories don't print properly. The CITY, STATE, and ZIP CODE categories are not properly spaced; the CITY is overwritten by the STATE. If you were to print the report to the screen, you would see how the city name, Bellevue, is cut off by the state, WA:

```
Aires Quick Copy
1345 South 8th
BellevWA      98004


Rainier Office Supply
Suite 501
5327 148th Street
BellevWA      98004


Bellevue Printing Co.
456 East Bellevue Way
BellevWA      98005
```

To provide proper spacing (that accepts longer names while omitting extra spacing in shorter names), you must left-justify the STATE and ZIP CODE categories. Left-justification ensures that spacing between categories is determined according to the actual length of the information in the entry.

Follow these steps to left-justify the two categories in question.

1. Place your cursor on the first character of STATE.

2. Press OA-J for Justify.

A less than sign ($<$) will be inserted to the left of the STATE category to indicate that the category is justified. The $<$ won't be printed.

3. Place your cursor on the first character of ZIP CODE and press OA-J.

The $<$ will appear on the ZIP CODE category, indicating that it is also left-justified. If you were to print the report to the screen right now, this is what it would look like:

```
Aires Quick Copy
1345 South 8th
Bellevue WA 98004


Rainier Office Supply
Suite 501
5327 148th Street
Bellevue WA 98004


Bellevue Printing Co.
456 East Bellevue Way
Bellevue WA 98005




Press Space Bar to continue _                      54K Avail.
```

The city is no longer truncated by the state. Now let's sort the records.

Arranging the records. You may also want to sort or arrange your records by ZIP code in order to get special discount rates from the post office. Remember from Chapter 4 that in order to sort by two categories, you must perform two sort operations, sorting the minor or least significant category first.

Follow these steps to arrange the labels alphabetically by name within ZIP code sequence.

1. Place the cursor on the CUSTOMER NAME category.

2. Press OA-A for Arrange.

3. From the Arrange (Sort) records menu, select option 1, From A to Z, by pressing RETURN.

4. Move the cursor to the less than sign (<) preceding ZIP CODE.

5. Press OA-A again.

6. This time on the Arrange (Sort) records screen select option 3, From 0 to 9, by typing **3** and pressing RETURN.

The records will be sorted first alphabetically by customer name and then numerically by ZIP code.

Modifying printer options. As you may recall from Chapter 4 and other chapters, printer options communicate certain facts to the printer about your document; for example, the size of your text, the margins, the characters per inch and the lines per inch. Whenever you wish to change the appearance of the final product in AppleWorks, you must change the printer options. So in producing the mailing labels, you'll need to change certain default printer option settings that are not appropriate for labels. To modify the printer options:

1. Press OA-O for Options to get the Printer Options menu.

The labels-style Printer Options screen will be displayed:

```
File: CIF.LST                    PRINTER OPTIONS           Escape: Report Format
Report: Address Labels
================================================================================

-------Left and right margins--------          ------Top and bottom margins------
PW: Platen Width            8.0 inches    PL: Paper Length          11.0 inches
LM: Left Margin             0.0 inches    TM: Top Margin             0.0 inches
RM: Right Margin            0.0 inches    BM: Bottom Margin          0.0 inches
CI: Chars per Inch          10            LI: Lines per Inch         6

    Line width              8.0 inches        Printing Length       11.0 inches
    Char per line (est)     80                Lines per page        66

        --------------------Formatting options-------------------
        SC:  Send Special Codes to printer                        No
        PD:  Print a Dash when an entry is blank                  No
        PH:  Print report Header at top of each page              Yes
        OL:  Omit Line when all entries on line are blank         Yes
        KS:  Keep number of lines the Same within each record     Yes



--------------------------------------------------------------------------------
Type a two letter option code _                            54K Avail.
```

As you can see, it differs somewhat from the other Printer Options screens. It contains two printer options that apply specifically to mailing labels: the OL and the KS options. Because these options are set to apply to labels, there is no need to change them. The OL option stands for Omit Line and allows you to omit a line when all entries on the line are blank. The OL option is set at a default of Yes, indicating that if a category contains no data, a blank line is not to be maintained to mark its place. Thus, for example, for every address without a Street 2, no blank line will be printed.

The KS option stands for Keep number of lines the Same within each record. This option guarantees that the same number of lines will be printed for each record whenever the OL option is set to Yes. It adds the omitted blank line to the bottom of the label to maintain the six lines per label. If OL is No, the KS option is revoked.

Remember that AppleWorks recalculates the line width and characters per line based upon values assigned to the printer options. It will, for example, take an 8-inch platen width (that is, the distance that the printer head travels from left to right) and decrease that width by the left and right margins to arrive at the line width. The line width is then multiplied by the characters per inch to arrive at the characters per line. Currently, the figures look like this: the platen width of 8.0 inches minus left and right margins of 0.0 equals a line width of 8.0 inches. The line width of 8.0 inches times 6 characters per inch equals 48 characters per line. The results of these calculations are on the Printer Options screen.

In order to generate standard label forms, you need to change the platen width from the default of 8.0 inches to 3.5 inches. You also need to change the left margin from the default of 0.0 inches to 0.3 inches, to leave a small margin so that printing doesn't start on the edge of the label. The paper length must be changed from the default of 11 inches to the standard one-inch label. And finally, the Print Header option must be changed from the default of Yes to No, since the labels don't need headers.

To continue changing these options,

2. Enter **PW** for Platen Width and press RETURN.

3. When prompted, enter **3.5** inches for the standard label form width and press RETURN.

4. Enter **LM** for Left Margin and press RETURN.

5. When prompted, enter **.3** and press RETURN.

6. Enter **PL** for Paper Length and press RETURN.

7. When prompted, enter **1** inch (for the standard length of labels) and press RETURN.

8. Enter **PH** for Print Header and then press RETURN to change the default from Yes to No.

All of these changes will be reflected on the screen as you change them:

```
File: CIF.LST                    PRINTER OPTIONS         Escape: Report Format
Report: Address Labels
================================================================================

-------Left and right margins--------      ------Top and bottom margins-------
PW: Platen Width              3.5 inches    PL: Paper Length            1.0 inches
LM: Left Margin               0.3 inches    TM: Top Margin              0.0 inches
RM: Right Margin              0.0 inches    BM: Bottom Margin           0.0 inches
CI: Chars per Inch            10            LI: Lines per Inch          6

     Line width               3.2 inches         Printing Length        1.0 inches
     Char per line (est)      32                 Lines per page         6
        --------------------Formatting options--------------------
     SC:  Send Special Codes to printer                         No
     PD:  Print a Dash when an entry is blank                   No
     PH:  Print report Header at top of each page               No
     OL:  Omit Line when all entries on line are blank          Yes
     KS:  Keep number of lines the Same within each record      Yes


-------------------------------------------------------------------------------
Type a two letter option code _                            54K Avail.
```

9. Press ESC to return to the Report format menu.

Printing the Labels

Now that you have deleted unnecessary categories, designed the data base report so that it will fit the mailing labels, and changed the printer options, it is time to print the labels. You are familiar with printing, but here is a quick review of the steps.

1. Press OA-P for Print.

2. From the Print the Report menu, move the cursor to your printer and press RETURN.

3. Press RETURN to verify that you want one copy of the labels.

Your labels should now be printing. Figure 7-1 shows how the labels look when printed. When the labels have been printed, press ESC twice to return to the Review/Add/ Change screen from the Report format screen. Save the new Address Labels report format so that it can be used again.

Saving the Report Format

When you save your file, any newly created report formats will be saved as well. AppleWorks considers the report formats a part of the data base, just like the actual data. That means you must save the whole file in order to save any report formats you intend to use again.

1. Press OA-S for Save.

2. Press ESC to return to the Main Menu.

The next file you will learn to create will require some more advanced data base functions. First remove your Apple-Works1 disk and replace it with the AppleWorks2 disk.

Building an Inventory Data Base

The new data base file you will create will become part of the business plan begun in Chapter 6. Figure 7-2 contains a list of inventory items needed for your business plan. The list shows the items that will be required when you open the new store. Notice that many of the entries are very similar except for a few characters; some entries, such as those in the VENDOR and COST categories, are identical. These similarities will simplify data entry, as you will see.

The first step is to build a file for the data base. Next, the categories of data to be contained in it must be defined and named. Finally, you will enter the data, changing the layout of the input screen as you go.

The procedure for creating a new file is not new to you. From the Main Menu select the first option, Add files to the Desktop. Then select the fourth option, Make a new file for

```
Aires Quick Copy
1345 South 8th
Bellevue WA 98004


Best and Marsh's
Department C
10476 NE 8th Street
Bellevue WA 98004


Bo's Print Mart
7264 Northrup Way South
Bellevue WA 98004


Evergreen Printing Supply
4769 NE 20th Street
Bellevue WA 98004


Jensen Office Supply
800 East 8th Street
Bellevue WA 98004


Rainier Office Supply
Suite 501
5327 148th Street
Bellevue WA 98004


Bellevue Printing Co.
456 East Bellevue Way
Bellevue WA 98005


University Print Shop
10056 Roosevelt Ave.
Seattle WA 98123


The Print Pot
801 NW Adamson
Seattle WA 98134


Foster's Printing Presses
83658 Pacific Hwy. South
Renton WA 98526
```

Figure 7-1.   Printed labels

```
File:     Inventory List                                          Page   1
Report: Figure 7-2
ITEM NAME  DESCRIPTION                     VENDOR    COST    MIN.QTY.
----------  ---------------------------  -------  -------  --------
 f100       Dupe film 12x18                 85      9.00      25
 f25        Photostat screen 1/2            85     10.25      25
 f30        Photostat screen 10x12          85     10.50      20
 f35        Line Film 1/2                   85      8.00      25
 f40        Line Film 10x12                 85      8.50      30
 f50        Line Film 12x18                 85      9.25      15
 f55        Halftone film                   85     12.00      12
 f70        Film photostat 1/2              85      8.00      10
 f80        Film photostat 10x12            85      8.50      12
 p01wh      8.5x11 16# white bond          102      5.20      10
 p03wh      8.5x11 20# white bond          102      6.48      10
 p03bl      8.5x11 20# blue  bond          102      6.48       5
 p03bu      8.5x11 20# buff  bond          102      6.48       5
 p03go      8.5x11 20# gold  bond          102      6.48       5
 p03iv      8.5x11 20# ivory bond          102      6.48      15
 p07wh      8.5x11 60# white bond          102     11.82      12
 p07bl      8.5x11 60# blue  bond          102     11.82      10
 p07go      8.5x11 60# gold  bond          102     11.82      10
 p07iv      8.5x11 60# ivory bond          102     11.82       7
```

Figure 7-2. List of inventory items to be entered

the Data base, from the Add Files menu. At that point, select the first option, From scratch, and when prompted enter **Inventory.lst** as the data base name. You will be shown the Change Name/Category screen.

Naming Categories

When entering the category names, notice that the names are *not* in the same order as shown in Figure 7-2. This difference in order will allow you to practice correcting the input layout later.

Follow these steps. If you make a typing mistake, use the DELETE key to delete characters and then retype them. Use the UP and DOWN ARROWS to change categories when you are not using RETURN.

1. Press the CAPS LOCK key.

2. Press OA-E to get into the overstrike edit mode.

3. Enter **ITEM NAME**, one space, and press RETURN.

4. Enter **DESCRIPTION** and press RETURN.

5. Enter **COST** and press RETURN.

6. Enter **VENDOR** and press RETURN.

7. Enter **MIN.QTY.** and press RETURN.

Your screen should look like this:

```
File: Inventory.lst          CHANGE NAME/CATEGORY     Escape: Review/Add/Change




Category names
==============================================================================
ITEM NAME
DESCRIPTION                            | Options:
COST                                   |
VENDOR                                 | Type category name
MIN.QTY.                               | Up arrow   Go to previous category
□                                      |
                                       |
                                       |
                                       |
                                       |
                                       |
                                       |
------------------------------------------------------------------------------
Type entry or use Ć commands                                    53K Avail.
```

8. Press ESC to notify AppleWorks that you are finished naming your categories.

9. Release the CAPS LOCK key.

You will be notified that you have no existing data for the file. You will be automatically placed in the Insert New Records screen.

10. Press the spacebar.

Entering Data

Now enter the first two records, f100 and f25, as shown here, using the blank form as it is displayed on the Insert New

Records screen. Notice that the VENDOR and COST entries are in reverse order from that shown on the screen.

ITEM NAME	DESCRIPTION	VENDOR	COST	MIN. QTY.
f100	Dupe film 12 x 18	85	9.00	25
f25	Photostat screen 1/2	85	10.25	25

As you enter the records, remember the following:

- If you make a typing error, use the DELETE key to erase and retype.

- End each entry with a RETURN.

- Use the UP and DOWN ARROWs and the RETURN key to move between categories. When you are prevented from using the cursor keys, use the TAB and OA-TAB keys to move from category to category in the multiple-record layout.

- Use the RIGHT and LEFT ARROWs to move within an entry.

- To erase an entire entry, press ESC, and then reenter it.

- To erase a partial entry, move your cursor to the point where you wish to begin replacing, press CONTROL-Y, and reenter the balance of the entry.

- Use OA-E to alternate between the insert and overstrike modes to enter and correct information.

Before you continue by entering the rest of the records, let's see if there isn't an easier way.

Changing the insert layout.   When you have entered the two records, press OA-Z for Zoom to see the records in multiple-record layout. The screen should look like this:

```
File: Inventory.lst            REVIEW/ADD/CHANGE           Escape: Main Menu

Selection: All records


ITEM NAME        DESCRIPTION    COST          VENDOR         MIN.QTY.
=====================================================================================
f100             Dupe film 12x18 9.00          85             25
f25              Photostat scree 10.25         85             25
```
```
------------------------------------------------------------------------
Type entry or use ⌂ commands                               ⌂-? for Help
```

You'll notice two things. First the records, as you planned
them, are in an inconvenient order to enter; the COST and
VENDOR categories are in reverse order from Figure 7-2.
It would be easier to enter the data if the VENDOR and the
COST categories were reversed. Second, the DESCRIPTION
category is cut off by the COST category, making it difficult
to read. But there is enough room on the screen to show the
whole DESCRIPTION category if the COST, VENDOR, and
MIN. QTY. categories are shortened.

Let's switch the placement of the VENDOR and COST
categories and change the width of the categories.

1. While in the multiple-record layout, press OA-L for
Layout.

You'll be shown the familiar Change Record Layout screen.

```
File: Inventory.lst          CHANGE RECORD LAYOUT     Escape: Review/Add/Change



=================================================================================
                  --> or <--   Move cursor
                     >  a  <    Switch category positions
                  -->  a  <--   Change column width
                  a-D           Delete this category
                  a-I           Insert a previously deleted category

       ---------------------------------------------------------------------

ITEM NAME       DESCRIPTION     COST           VENDOR          MIN.QTY.
-----------    ---------------  --------------  ---------------  ---------------
f100           Dupe film 12x18 9.00            85              25
f25            Photostat scree 10.25           85              25

                                                           ------ More --->
-----------------------------------------------------------------
Use options shown above to change record layout             53K Avail.
```

2. Move your cursor to the VENDOR category by pressing the RIGHT ARROW three times.

3. To switch the VENDOR and COST categories, press the OA-< (LESS THAN key without the SHIFT key) once.

The COST and VENDOR categories will be switched. Now widen the DESCRIPTION category.

4. Press the LEFT ARROW once to move the cursor to the DESCRIPTION category.

5. Press OA-RIGHT ARROW 12 times to make the category wide enough for future descriptions.

Now some of the categories have been pushed off the screen. You must shorten other categories to make room on the screen for all of them.

6. Place your cursor on the ITEM NAME category by pressing the LEFT ARROW once.

7. Press OA-LEFT ARROW five times to shorten the category name.

8. Move the cursor to the VENDOR category by pressing the RIGHT ARROW two times.

9. Press OA-LEFT ARROW five times to shorten it.

10. Move the cursor to COST by pressing the RIGHT ARROW once.

11. Press OA-LEFT ARROW eight times.

At this point you should be able to see all categories on the screen, as shown in the following illustration.

```
File: Inventory.lst          CHANGE RECORD LAYOUT      Escape: Review/Add/Change




================================================================================
                 --> or <--   Move cursor
                  >   a   <    Switch category positions
                 --> a <--     Change column width
                  a-D          Delete this category
                  a-I          Insert a previously deleted category
--------------------------------------------------------------------------------

ITEM NAME  DESCRIPTION                  VENDOR    COST     MIN.QTY.      M
---------  --------------------------   -------   ▣-----   ------------  A
f100       Dupe film 12x18               85       9.00     25            R
f25        Photostat screen 1/2          85       10.25    25            G
                                                                         I
                                                                         N
--------------------------------------------------------------------------------
Use options shown above to change record layout              53K Avail.
```

The word MARGIN displayed vertically on the right-hand edge of the screen indicates where the right edge of the screen is—and the end of your records.

12. Press ESC once to exit the Change Record Layout screen.

Changing cursor direction.   Upon leaving the Change Record Layout screen, you will be asked to indicate in which direction, down or right, the cursor is to go when you press RETURN. For now, select the Right option. Later you will use the standard Down direction and see how and when it's appropriate to use it. To set the cursor to move right, type **2** and press RETURN. The Review/Add/Change screen will be displayed with the first two records you've entered.

Copying one record.   As mentioned earlier, many of the records in the Inventory List are similar. The Copy command will allow you to use this similarity to your advantage. The Copy command can be used in three ways: (1) to copy one category only; (2) to copy the whole record; or (3) to copy groups of records.

You will notice that the third record, f30, is very similar to the second, f25. Let's copy f25 and then modify it as needed.

1. Move the cursor to f25 and then press OA-C for Copy.

The f25 record will be highlighted.

```
File: Inventory.lst            COPY RECORDS          Escape: Review/Add/Change

Selection: All records


ITEM NAME  DESCRIPTION                 VENDOR    COST    MIN.QTY.
================================================================================
f100       Dupe film 12x18             85        9.00    25
f25        Photostat screen 1/2        85        10.25   25




                      
                      
                      

-------------------------------------------------------------------------------
Copy?  Current record  To clipboard  From clipboard
```

On the message line, the Current record option will also be highlighted as the default. You want to copy the current record.

2. Press RETURN to copy the current record.

3. Enter **1** and press RETURN when prompted for the number of copies.

A duplicate of f25 will be displayed:

```
File: Inventory.lst              REVIEW/ADD/CHANGE              Escape: Main Menu

Selection: All records


ITEM NAME  DESCRIPTION                    VENDOR     COST     MIN.QTY.
=======================================================================================
f100       Dupe film 12x18                85         9.00     25
f25        Photostat screen 1/2           85         10.25    25
f25        Photostat screen 1/2           85         10.25    25




------------------------------------------------------------------------------
Type entry or use ⌂ commands                                     ⌂-? for Help
```

Editing a record.   Now edit the duplicate record so that it becomes the third inventory record, as shown in Figure 7-2. Follow these steps:

1. Place your cursor on the "2" in the second f25 category name.

2. Type **30** over the "25" and press RETURN. (Be sure you are in the overstrike mode.)

3. Move your cursor to the "/" and type **0x12** and press RETURN.

4. Press RETURN to skip the VENDOR category as there is no change.

5. Move the cursor to ".25," type in **.50**, and press RETURN.

6. Replace the "5" in "25" with a **0** and press RETURN.

Although the third record has been modified from the copy, there are still quite a few records to be inserted. This is when the Ditto command proves handy.

Inserting records using the Ditto command. You can duplicate information from the previous category into a current one using the Ditto command. Copying data from a model record into a number of blank records saves you from enterig the information piece by piece. Later you can go back and enter the information in each record that varies from the model.

1. Position your cursor on the last record in the data base by pressing OA-9.

2. Press OA-Z to get into the single-record layout.

3. Press the DOWN ARROW key until you are past the last category.

AppleWorks will ask you if you want to insert additional records since you are trying to go beyond the end of the data base:

```
File: Inventory.lst          INSERT NEW RECORDS       Escape: Review/Add/Change

Selection: All records


Record 3 of 3
================================================================================




                 You are now past the last record
                 of your file and can now start
                 typing new records at the end.




-------------------------------------------------------------------------------
Do you really want to do this?  No  Yes
```

4. Enter **Y** for Yes.

A blank Insert New Records screen will be displayed. Now enter the fourth record, whose contents will be dittoed into other blank records.

5. Enter the fourth record, f35, as shown here:

f35 Line Film 1/2 Cost:8.00 Vendor:85 Min.Qty.:25

After the last RETURN, a blank screen for the fifth record will be displayed. This will become a blank record to be added to the end of the file. After you create duplicates of the blank record, you will then copy data from the fourth record just entered into the blank records.

6. Press RETURN five times, skipping through each of the categories and leaving each blank, to create a fifth blank record.

7. When the new blank screen for the sixth record is displayed, press OA-Z to return to the multiple-record layout.

You will see the blank record at the end of the list of records:

```
File: Inventory.lst              REVIEW/ADD/CHANGE               Escape: Main Menu

Selection: All records


ITEM NAME  DESCRIPTION                 VENDOR    COST    MIN.QTY.
=================================================================================
f100       Dupe film 12x18             85        9.00    25
f25        Photostat screen 1/2        85        10.25   25
f30        Photostat screen 10x12      85        10.50   20
f35        Line film 1/2               85        8.00    25
-          -                           -         -       -




----------------------------------------------------------------------------
Type entry or use ⚼ commands                               ⚼-? for Help
```

Now we will create seven blank records.

8. Place your cursor on the blank record and press OA-C for Copy.

9. Press RETURN to indicate that the copy is for the Current record.

10. Then enter **7** to get seven blank records and press RETURN.

Your screen should now look like this:

```
File: Inventory.lst          REVIEW/ADD/CHANGE              Escape: Main Menu

Selection: All records


ITEM NAME DESCRIPTION                      VENDOR     COST     MIN.QTY.
================================================================================
f100      Dupe film 12x18                    85       9.00      25
f25       Photostat screen 1/2               85      10.25      25
f30       Photostat screen 10x12             85      10.50      20
f35       Line film 1/2                      85       8.00      25
⊟         -                                   -        -         -
-         -                                   -        -         -
-         -                                   -        -         -
-         -                                   -        -         -
-         -                                   -        -         -
-         -                                   -        -         -
-         -                                   -        -         -


------------------------------------------------------------------------------
Type entry or use ⌂ commands                               ⌂-? for Help
```

Now you are ready to enter the data. Although you have the option of just entering the data, it is easier to copy the information from the preceding record by using the Ditto command. Then you can go back to correct entries that are different from the copied record in Figure 7-2.

Try this technique to enter record f40.

11. Place your cursor on the first blank record.

12. Type **f40** and press RETURN.

13. Press OA-" (double quotes without the SHIFT key) to activate the Ditto command.

The contents of the DESCRIPTION category from f35 will be copied into the entry. (Corrections will be made later.)

14. Press OA-" to copy the contents of the VENDOR category.

15. Enter the cost of **8.50** and press RETURN.

16. Enter the quantity of **30** and press RETURN.

The cursor will be advanced to the next blank record. Using Figure 7-2, continue to enter only the next six records, f50 through p03wh. Type in any information that is different from the preceding record. Press OA-" to copy the contents of the DESCRIPTION categories when they are mostly alike and of the other categories when they are the same. You should be able to enter the records very rapidly. Do not bother to make corrections yet.

Your screen will look something like the one in the following illustration. It may be somewhat different, depending on the categories you chose to ditto.

```
File: Inventory.lst           REVIEW/ADD/CHANGE              Escape: Main Menu

Selection: All records


ITEM NAME  DESCRIPTION              VENDOR     COST     MIN QTY
===============================================================================
f100       Dupe film 12x18          85        9.00      25
f25        Photostat screen 1/2     85        10.25     25
f30        Photostat screen 10x12   85        10.50     20
f35        Line film 1/2            85        8.00      25
f40        Line film 1/2            85        8.50      30
f50        Line film 1/2            85        9.25      15
f55        Halftone film            85        12.00     12
f70        Film photostat 1/2       85        8.00      10
f80        Film photostat 1/2.      85        8.50      12
p01wh      8.5x11 16# white bond    102       5.20      10
p03wh      8.5x11 16# white bond    102       6.48      10
□          -                        -         -         -



-------------------------------------------------------------------------------
Type entry or use ⌂ commands                                  ⌂-? for Help
```

When you have finished, go back and edit records f40 through p03wh. Using the overstrike mode, correct the entries that contain errors. The finished screen should look like this:

```
File: Inventory.lst              REVIEW/ADD/CHANGE              Escape: Main Menu

Selection: All records


ITEM NAME  DESCRIPTION                    VENDOR    COST    MIN.QTY.
===================================================================================
f100       Dupe film 12x18                85        9.00     25
f25        Photostat screen 1/2           85       10.25     25
f30        Photostat screen 10x12         85       10.50     20
f35        Line film 1/2                  85        8.00     25
f40        Line film 10x12                85        8.50     30
f50        Line film 12x18                85        9.25     15
f55        Halftone film                  85       12.00     12
f70        Film photostat 1/2             85        8.00     10
f80        Film photostat 10x12           85        8.50     12
p01wh      8.5x11 16# white bond         102        5.20     10
p03wh      8.5x11 20# white bond         102        6.48     10
⊟          -                              -         -        -



-----------------------------------------------------------------------------------
Type entry or use ⌂ commands                                      ⌂-? for Help
```

Copying a record several times.   Notice that record p03wh is very similar to the next four records—so similar, in fact, that record p03wh through record p03iv could be seen as a series. For convenience, quickly copy that one record four times and then edit the duplicates as needed. Do this now:

1. Place your cursor on p03wh and press OA-C for Copy.

2. Press RETURN to indicate that the copy is for the current record.

3. Enter 4 to get four extra records—the four duplicates of record p03wh—and press RETURN.

Your screen is changed to this:

```
File: Inventory.lst            REVIEW/ADD/CHANGE           Escape: Main Menu
Selection: All records


ITEM NAME  DESCRIPTION                   VENDOR    COST    MIN.QTY.
==================================================================================
f100       Dupe film 12x18               85        9.00    25
f25        Photostat screen 1/2          85        10.25   25
f30        Photostat screen 10x12        85        10.50   20
f35        Line film 1/2                 85        8.00    25
f40        Line film 10x12               85        8.50    30
f50        Line film 12x18               85        9.25    15
f55        Halftone film                 85        12.00   12
f70        Film photostat 1/2            85        8.00    10
f80        Film photostat 10x12          85        8.50    12
p01wh      8.5x11 16# white bond         102       5.20    10
p03wh      8.5x11 20# white bond         102       6.48    10
p03wh      8.5x11 20# white bond         102       6.48    10
p03wh      8.5x11 20# white bond         102       6.48    10
p03wh      8.5x11 20# white bond         102       6.48    10
p03wh      8.5x11 20# white bond         102       6.48    10
----------------------------------------------------------------------------------
Type entry or use ⌘ commands                              ⌘-? for Help
```

Now edit the duplicates.

4. Place your cursor on the first copy of p03wh and move your cursor to the "w" under ITEM NAME.

5. Replace "wh" with **bl** and press RETURN.

6. Move your cursor to the word "white" and replace it with **blue**, overwriting the extra letter with the space-bar (you can delete the extra space with the DELETE key, but it's not necessary).

7. Skip the next two categories by pressing RETURN twice.

8. Enter the new minimum quantity of **5** and press RETURN.

The cursor will have advanced to the next record. Continue to edit and correct the rest of the records according to Figure 7-2 until the series has been corrected.

Copying groups of records.   Refer to the completed Inventory List in Figure 7-2 again and notice that records p07wh through p07iv form a series, just as records p03wh through p03iv did. What is more, the two series of records share similar data. Again, you will save time if you copy records p03wh through p03iv and modify these records for the second series. To do this, use the Copy command to copy a group of records. You will use the Clipboard—another area of memory that AppleWorks uses to temporarily hold data being moved or copied. To move groups of records by first "cutting" the records to the Clipboard and then "pasting" them back into the text. Follow Steps 1 through 3.

1. Move your cursor to record p03wh and press OA-C for Copy.

2. Select the Clipboard option by positioning the cursor on To Clipboard and pressing RETURN.

3. Move the cursor by pressing the DOWN ARROW four times to highlight the whole series of records starting with p03wh and ending with p03iv.

The screen should look like this:

```
File: Inventory.lst              COPY RECORDS          Escape: Review/Add/Change

Selection: All records


ITEM NAME  DESCRIPTION                   VENDOR     COST      MIN.QTY.
========================================================================================
 f30       Photostat screen 10x12        85        10.50      20
 f35 ·     Line film 1/2                 85         8.00      25
 f40       Line film 10x12               85         8.50      30
 f50       Line film 12x18               85         9.25      15
 f55       Halftone film                 85        12.00      12
 f70       Film photostat 1/2            85         8.00      10
 f80       Film photostat 10x12          85         8.50      12
 p01wh     8.5x11 16# white bond         102        5.20      10
 p03wh     8.5x11 20# white bond         102        6.48      10
 p03bl     8.5x11 20# blue  bond         102        6.48       5
 p03bu     8.5x11 20# buff  bond         102        6.48       5
 p03go     8.5x11 20# gold  bond         102        6.48       5
 p03iv     8.5x11 20# ivory bond         102        6.48      15
 -         -                             -          -

---------------------------------------------------------------------------------------
Use cursor moves to highlight records, then press Return☐        53K Avail.
```

4. Press RETURN to indicate that you have marked the group of records to be moved to the Clipboard.

5. Using OA-9, move the cursor to the end of the file on the last blank record displayed.

6. Press OA-C and select the From the Clipboard option by moving the cursor over it and pressing RETURN.

7. Press OA-9 to look at the end of the file.

Your screen should look like the one in the following illustration.

```
File: Inventory.lst              REVIEW/ADD/CHANGE              Escape: Main Menu

Selection: All records


ITEM NAME  DESCRIPTION                    VENDOR    COST     MIN.QTY.
=================================================================================
f55        Halftone film                  85        12.00    12
f70        Film photostat 1/2             85        8.00     10
f80        Film photostat 10x12           85        8.50     12
p01wh      8.5x11 16# white bond          102       5.20     10
p03wh      8.5x11 20# white bond          102       6.48     10
p03bl      8.5x11 20# blue  bond          102       6.48     5
p03bu      8.5x11 20# buff  bond          102       6.48     5
p03go      8.5x11 20# gold  bond          102       6.48     5
p03iv      8.5x11 20# ivory bond          102       6.48     15
p03wh      8.5x11 20# white bond          102       6.48     10
p03bl      8.5x11 20# blue  bond          102       6.48     5
p03bu      8.5x11 20# buff  bond          102       6.48     5
p03go      8.5x11 20# gold  bond          102       6.48     5
p03iv      8.5x11 20# ivory bond          102       6.48     15
▣          -                              -         -
---------------------------------------------------------------------------------
Type entry or use Ć commands                                   Ć-? for Help
```

The series formed by records p03wh through p03iv has been duplicated in full. Now you can go back through the duplicated series to change any entries that deviate from the norm.

Editing the categories. At this point you may find that the direction of the cursor is not as efficient as it could be. Since you are now dealing with groups of records which need to be edited, it would be more convenient if the cursor moved down through the records in each category when RETURN was pressed, instead of across the screen from category to category within one record. That is, if the cursor advanced down instead of to the right, you could edit one category very quickly and then go on to the next and edit it.

To change the direction of the cursor key, proceed as you did previously: press OA-L for Layout, and then press ESC to skip the first menu screen and go directly to the menu explaining cursor direction. Press RETURN to select the Down (Standard) option.

Now you will edit the new records by going completely through one category to correct it before continuing on to the next category. These steps will help you quickly correct the new records:

1. Place your cursor over the second p03wh record.

2. Move the cursor to the "3" with the right arrow, replace it with 7, and press RETURN.

3. Change the next record p03bl to **p07bl** in the same way.

4. Since there is no p07bu record, delete it by pressing OA-D for Delete and then press RETURN.

5. Correct the next two records by replacing the "3" with 7 and pressing RETURN.

6. Using the UP ARROW and the TAB keys, return to the first p07wh record and place the cursor on the DE-SCRIPTION category.

7. Move the cursor to the "2" with the RIGHT ARROW, replace it with 6, and then press RETURN.

Perform the same steps for each of the remaining p07 records.

8. Move the cursor past the VENDOR category since that

category is correct.

9. Place the cursor on the COST category of the p07wh record.

10. Change the cost to **11.82** and press RETURN.

11. Now press OA-" to ditto the previous entry.

12. Press OA-" two more times to complete all four records.

13. Move the cursor to the MIN. QTY. category of the p07wh record.

14. Replace the "10" with **12** and press RETURN.

15. Replace the "5" with **10** and press RETURN.

16. Press OA-" to ditto the "10."

17. Replace the "15" with **7** and press RETURN.

You may delete the extra blank record added because you specified one too many records to copy. It's easy to end up with blank records, and even easier to get rid of them. Make sure your cursor is on the blank record, and then:

18. Press OA-D and then RETURN to delete the extra blank record.

You have now entered all the records for the Inventory List data base in a fast and efficient manner using the Copy and Ditto commands. The records now need to be saved.

Saving the Records

This would be a good time to save the records you have just entered. Press OA-S for Save. After a short wait the records will be saved onto disk for you. Now you needn't fear losing, through human error or a power or hardware failure, the work you put into entering the data.

Finding Records

If you want to search your data base for specific information, you can use the Find command to do just that. For example, suppose you have just learned that your 20-pound bond paper has suffered an increase in price to $6.80. Use the following steps in order to quickly find and update those records in your Inventory List.

1. Press OA-1 to place the cursor at the beginning of the file.

2. Press OA-F for Find.

3. When prompted for comparison information, enter **20#** and press RETURN.

The data base will be searched from beginning to end for any records containing "20#" in any location. All the records containing "20#" will be listed:

```
File: Inventory.lst              FIND RECORDS            Escape: Review/Add/Change

Find all records that contain 20#
Press a-F to change Find.

ITEM NAME  DESCRIPTION                     VENDOR    COST    MIN.QTY.
=====================================================================================
p03wh      8.5x11 20# white bond           102       6.48     10
p03bl      8.5x11 20# blue  bond           102       6.48      5
p03bu      8.5x11 20# buff  bond           102       6.48      5
p03go      8.5x11 20# gold  bond           102       6.48      5
p03iv      8.5x11 20# ivory bond           102       6.48     15




-----------------------------------------------------------------------------------
Type entry or use ₲ commands                                     ₲-? for Help
```

4. Position your cursor on the COST category by pressing OA-TAB once.

5. Replace "48" with **80** and press RETURN.

6. Press OA-" to ditto the entry.

The updated cost figure will be copied from the previous entry, and the cursor will be advanced to the next entry. Continue using OA-" with the remaining three entries. When all costs have been updated, press ESC to return to the Review/Add/Change screen.

Record Selections

Another feature, similar to the Find command, is the Record Selection feature. The Find command searches the entire record for the text you specify, regardless of which category holds the information. The Record Selection feature lets you name the specific category to compare against the selected information. In other words, this feature lets you establish comparisons so that you can print, or look at, only certain records. For example, you could select all records that show costs over $10 or all records that show a particular vendor.

When you first create a data base file, the selection criteria listed in the upper left-hand corner of the screen is All Records. You can change both the screen display and report formats to select certain records using the Record Selection feature. For example, to change the screen display so that it shows only the records from vendor 85 that cost over $10.00, you would

1. Press OA-R for Record selection rules.

A list of category names, as shown here, will be displayed:

```
File: Inventory.lst              SELECT RECORDS        Escape: Review/Add/Change

Selection:


================================================================================
   1.  ITEM NAME
   2.  DESCRIPTION
   3.  COST
   4.  VENDOR
   5.  MIN.QTY.
```

```
----------------------------------------------------------------------------
Type number, or use arrows, then press Return                 52K Avail.
```

2. Position your cursor on the VENDOR category name by pressing the DOWN ARROW three times and pressing RETURN.

A list of operations will be displayed:

```
File: Inventory.lst              SELECT RECORDS        Escape: Review/Add/Change

Selection: VENDOR


================================================================================
   1.  equals
   2.  is greater than
   3.  is less than
   4.  is not equal to
   5.  is blank
   6.  is not blank
   7.  contains
   8.  begins with
   9.  ends with
  10.  does not contain
  11.  does not begin with
  12.  does not end with
```

```
----------------------------------------------------------------------------
Type number, or use arrows, then press Return                 52K Avail.
```

3. You want all vendors equal to 85, so press RETURN to select the first option.

4. In response to the prompt Type comparison information, enter **85** and press RETURN.

You will now be asked to specify the relationship of this first comparison to the next condition to be entered.

```
File: Inventory.lst          SELECT RECORDS          Escape: Review/Add/Change

Selection: VENDOR equals 85


================================================================================
1.  and
2.  or
3.  through




- - - - - - - - - - - - - - - - - - - - - - - - - - - - - - - - - - - - - - - -
Type number, or use arrows, then press Return                     52K Avail.
```

There are three ways in which the second part of your comparison can be related to the first. The And option indicates that you want the next condition to be true in addition to the one you just specified. The Or option indicates that either the first comparison or the one to be entered next can be true for the record selection to be valid. The Through option indicates that a range of values, beginning with the value entered initially and ending with the next value entered, will make the selection valid. When a record meets the conditions you've established, the record is selected and displayed on the screen. In this instance, you want the And option because you want vendor 85 *and* a cost exceeding $10.00.

5. Press RETURN to select the And option.

6. Position the cursor on the COST category and press RETURN.

7. Type **2** for the Is greater than option and press RETURN.

8. Enter **10.00** and press RETURN.

The selection notation at the top of your screen now shows the criteria you've entered: "VENDOR equals 85" and "COST is greater than $10.00." You have now entered all the criteria for the comparison—all inventory items from vendor 85 costing more than $10.00.

9. Press ESC to exit from the Select Records screen.

The results of the Select Records operation are shown here:

```
File: Inventory.lst              REVIEW/ADD/CHANGE              Escape: Main Menu

Selection: VENDOR equals 85
   and      COST is greater than 10.00

ITEM NAME  DESCRIPTION                    VENDOR   COST    MIN.QTY.
===============================================================================
  f25      Photostat screen 1/2            85      10.25    25
  f30      Photostat screen 10x12          85      10.50    20
  f55      Halftone film                   85      12.00    12




------------------------------------------------------------------------------
Type entry or use ⌂ commands                              ⌂-? for Help
```

The selection criteria reflected in the upper left-hand corner of your screen will continue to be in effect until you cancel the selection. You can use any of the normal commands with these selected entries.

10. Return now to Selection: All records by pressing OA-R for Record selection rules again.

11. Move the cursor over the Yes option and press RETURN.

You will be returned to the Review/Add/Change screen.

Renaming the File

The name of the file, Inventory.lst, will prove too general if you have many inventory lists. Rename this file BegInv.lst (shortened to fit the maximum 15 characters allowed in a filename) since it is the list of items you need to begin your new store. Follow these quick steps to rename the file:

1. Press OA-N for Name. You will be shown the Change Name/Category screen.

2. In overstrike mode, enter **BegInv.lst**, three spaces, three deletes, and press RETURN.

3. Press ESC to exit the Change Name/Category screen.

The new name of the file will be displayed in the upper left-hand corner of the screen.

Generating Final Reports

You have used the CIF data base to format and print a labels-style report: namely, the name and address mailing labels. Now you are going to format and print a tables-style report which will be used as a checklist of the inventory items. In addition, it will calculate the total dollars tied up in the start-up inventory. Finally, you will create two versions of the report: one that selects specific records as well as one showing all inventory items.

Formatting a Tables-Style Report

Several new formatting options are presented here. Follow these steps to format the report:

1. Press OA-P for Print.

The Report menu will be displayed. The second option, Create a new "tables" format, is highlighted.

2. Press RETURN to select this option.

3. In response to the request for the title of the report, enter **Startup Inventory** and press RETURN.

The Report format screen will be displayed (remember that the @ signs represent OA keys).

```
File: BegInv.lst               REPORT FORMAT              Escape: Report Menu
Report: Startup Inventory
Selection: All records


========================================================================
--> or <--  Move cursor                    a-J  Right justify this category
  >  a  <   Switch category positions      a-K  Define a calculated category
--> a  <--  Change column width            a-N  Change report name and/or title
a-A  Arrange (sort) on this category       a-O  Printer options
a-D  Delete this category                  a-P  Print the report
a-G  Add/remove group totals               a-R  Change record selection rules
a-I  Insert a prev. deleted category       a-T  Add/remove category totals
------------------------------------------------------------------------

ITEM NAME    DESCRIPTION  COST       VENDOR       MIN.QTY.      L
A----------  -B---------- -C-------- -D---------- -E----------  e
f100         Dupe film 12 9.00       85           25            n
f25          Photostat sc 10.25      85           25            6
f30          Photostat sc 10.50      85           20            5

------------------------------------------------------------------------
Use options shown above to change report format              52K Avail.
```

The Report format screen shows the options available to

you for formatting reports. There are four options listed here that are new.

Categories can be totaled and subtotaled using OA-T for Total and OA-G for Group Total commands. The OA-T command allows you to designate a category to be totaled. The OA-G command allows you to indicate which category will trigger the subtotaling of the totaled column; that is, when a category changes in value, a subtotal will be taken.

The OA-J command for Justify allows you to right-justify categories in your report. This is especially useful for columns of numbers, as you will see.

You can define a category that contains calculations performed on other categories by using the OA-K command for Calculate. When you use this command, you must specify the formula that applies to the calculated category.

Now let's see how some of the new commands work. Since you have already been exposed to several of the options, you won't need to go through all of them.

Switching columns.   As you can see, the VENDOR and COST columns have been saved in the order in which you originally entered them. You changed their order once to make the input screen more convenient to use. Now you want to be able to see the COST AND MIN. QTY. columns together so that the TOTAL COST cateogry, which will be entered next, will be clearly understood.

Follow these steps to switch the two columns:

1. Position your cursor over the COST category by pressing the RIGHT ARROW key twice.

2. Press OA-> (the GREATER THAN key without the SHIFT key) once.

The COST and VENDOR categories will be switched.

Right-justifying columns.   The VENDOR, COST, and MIN. QTY. columns are not aligned as they should be, with an even right edge.

The numbers are left-justified rather than right-justified. This means that the even edge is on the left-hand side, rather than on the right, which is what you need for figures.

To right-justify these two columns, follow these steps:

1. Since the cursor is on the COST column, press OA-J for Justify.

AppleWorks will ask you for the number of decimal places to include in the justified column. It assumes that you want zero decimal places, which you would if you were entering alphabetic information or integers. Since you want two decimal places for dollar amounts, however, you should

2. Enter 2 and press RETURN.

Now you are asked for the number of blank spaces to skip after each entry in the category so that the spacing between this category and the next will be correct.

3. Press RETURN to accept the default of three spaces.

AppleWorks will fill the category with the number "9" to show you how the category is formatted. Don't be alarmed: your data is intact. Only real numbers will be printed.

4. Move the cursor to the VENDOR category.

5. Press OA-J for Justify.

6. Press RETURN to accept the default of zero decimal places.

7. Press RETURN to accept the default of three trailing blank spaces.

8. Move the cursor to the MIN. QTY. category.

9. Press OA-J to right-justify the MIN. QTY. category.

10. Press RETURN to accept AppleWorks' default of zero decimal places.

11. Press RETURN to accept AppleWorks' default of three
    blank spaces to follow the category entries.

Your screen looks like this, with 9s in the right-justified
categories.

```
File: BegInv.lst                  REPORT FORMAT              Escape: Report Menu
Report: Startup Inventory
Selection: All records


===============================================================================
--> or <--  Move cursor                      @-J  Right justify this category
 >   @   <  Switch category positions        @-K  Define a calculated category
--> @  <--  Change column width               @-N  Change report name and/or title
@-A  Arrange (sort) on this category          @-O  Printer options
@-D  Delete this category                     @-P  Print the report
@-G  Add/remove group totals                  @-R  Change record selection rules
@-I  Insert a prev. deleted category          @-T  Add/remove category totals
-------------------------------------------------------------------------------

ITEM NAME   DESCRIPTION  VENDOR      COST          MIN.QTY.      L
-A--------- -B--------- -C--------   -D--------    ⊟E--------    e
f100        Dupe film 12 9999999999  9999999.99    9999999999    n
f25         Photostat sc 9999999999  9999999.99    9999999999    6
f30         Photostat sc 9999999999  9999999.99    9999999999    5


-------------------------------------------------------------------------------
Use options shown above to change report format                    52K Avail.
```

Calculating categories. One essential category that the Startup Inventory
list lacks is a category showing total costs of your inventory
at the outset of your new business. You can obtain a category
called TOTAL COST by multiplying the totals in MIN. QTY.
times the totals in COST. This calculation will yield the cost
of your starting inventory.

AppleWorks' OA-K command allows you to create a new
category for this purpose. Follow these steps:

1. Position your cursor to the right of column E, on the
   letter "e" contained in the vertical margin delimiter set
   up by AppleWorks.

2. Press OA-K to indicate that you wish to calculate the new
   category.

You will see a new column F labeled Calculated. It is filled with 9s, indicating that the contents are to be numeric. On the prompt line you are asked to name the column. You can overwrite the assumed name, Calculated, and enter your own name of up to 20 characters.

3. In overstrike mode, enter **TOTAL COST** and press RETURN.

Your screen should look like this:

```
File: BegInv.lst              DEFINE CALCULATED            Escape: Report Format
Report: Startup Inventory
Selection: All records


===============================================================================
--> or <--   Move cursor               a-J  Right justify this category
  >  a  <    Switch category positions a-K  Define a calculated category
--> a  <--   Change column width        a-N  Change report name and/or title
a-A  Arrange (sort) on this category    a-O  Printer options
a-D  Delete this category               a-P  Print the report
a-G  Add/remove group totals            a-R  Change record selection rules
a-I  Insert a prev. deleted category    a-T  Add/remove category totals
-------------------------------------------------------------------------------

ITEM NAME    DESCRIPTION VENDOR      COST          MIN.QTY.     TOTAL COST   L
-A---------- -B--------- -C--------  -D--------  . -E--------   -F---------- e
f100         Dupe film 12 9999999999 9999999.99    9999999999   9999999999  n
f25          Photostat sc 9999999999 9999999.99    9999999999   9999999999  7
f30          Photostat sc 9999999999 9999999.99    9999999999   9999999999  8
-------------------------------------------------------------------------------
Type calculation rules (Example: A+B+C/5.75):□
```

When asked to enter the calculation rules or formulas, you may add (+), subtract (−), multiply (*), or divide (/). The columns named for the letters of the alphabet are used as the identifiers. For example, the formula A / B + C would divide column A by column B and add the result to column C. The calculations always work from left to right. You may use constants instead of column names.

4. To multiply COST by MIN. QTY., enter **D*E** and press RETURN.

5. When prompted, enter the number of decimal places to be included in the calculated category: **2**.

You will then be asked for the number of blank spaces to skip following each entry in the category. Since this is the last category of the report and the data base, this number isn't critical.

6. Just press RETURN to accept AppleWorks' default of three spaces.

You have now set up a new calculated category that will be displayed for you when the report is printed, either on the screen or on paper.

Calculating totals.   Suppose, however, that at this point you want to total this calculated category in order to know how much capital you have invested in the startup inventory. Follow these steps to total the column:

1. Position the cursor on the TOTAL COST category.

2. Press OA-T for Total.

You will be asked for the number of decimal places to include. The previously entered value of two decimal places is assumed for you.

3. Accept the default of two decimal places by pressing RETURN.

AppleWorks will then ask you for the number of blank spaces to skip after printing the total.

4. Press RETURN to accept the assumed three blank spaces.

At the bottom of the category you will see a double line,

which indicates that a total will be taken on this category. (To remove the total, place your cursor on the category with the total and press OA-T, but don't do this now.)

Setting group totals.   Group totals allow you to define subtotals based on the value of another category. For example, suppose you needed to keep track of the total cost by vendor. When a value in the VENDOR category changed, you could request that AppleWorks perform a subtotal.

Follow these steps to get a group subtotal:

1. Place the cursor on the VENDOR category since it controls whether the subtotal is to be calculated.

2. Press OA-G for Group Total.

You will be asked if you want to print only the totals or the detail of the records as well. In this case, you only have a few records, so printing the details is acceptable and desirable.

3. Choose No since you want to see the detailed records by pressing RETURN.

You will be asked if you want the report to skip to a new page after each subtotal.

4. Choose No by pressing RETURN since you don't have enough volume in this data base to justify separate pages for each vendor.

Now let's see what we can do about lengthening the DESCRIPTION category.

Changing column widths.   In looking at the screen, you can see that the DESCRIPTION category is truncated, and as a consequence you cannot see the whole description. In addition, the VENDOR category seems too wide.

```
File: BegInv.lst              REPORT FORMAT              Escape: Report Menu
Report: Startup Inventory
Selection: All records

Group totals on: VENDOR
===============================================================================
--> or <--  Move cursor                 a-J  Right justify this category
 >   a   <   Switch category positions  a-K  Define a calculated category
--> a <--   Change column width         a-N  Change report name and/or title
a-A  Arrange (sort) on this category    a-O  Printer options
a-D  Delete this category               a-P  Print the report
a-G  Add/remove group totals            a-R  Change record selection rules
a-I  Insert a prev. deleted category    a-T  Add/remove category totals
-------------------------------------------------------------------------------

ITEM NAME   DESCRIPTION  VENDOR       COST         MIN.QTY.     TOTAL COST   L
-A---------- -B---------- ▯C--------- -D-------    -E--------    -F--------   e
f100        Dupe film 12 9999999999   9999999.99   9999999999   9999999.99   n
f25         Photostat sc 9999999999   9999999.99   9999999999   9999999.99   7
f30         Photostat sc 9999999999   9999999.99   9999999999   9999999.99   8
                                                                ==========
-------------------------------------------------------------------------------
Use options shown above to change report format              52K Avail.
```

Let's shorten the VENDOR category and widen the DE-
SCRIPTION category. Follow these simple steps:

1. Since the cursor is already on VENDOR, press OA-LEFT
   ARROW four times to shorten the category.

You can see the category become narrower each time you
press the key.

2. Move the cursor to DESCRIPTION.

3. Press OA-RIGHT ARROW twelve times to widen the DE-
   SCRIPTION category.

When you've finished, the text has slid off the screen slightly
so that you can no longer see the two decimal places in
TOTAL COST. To correct this,

4. Place your cursor on COST.

5. Press OA-LEFT ARROW four times.

6. Place your cursor on ITEM NAME.

7. Press OA-LEFT ARROW three times.

This will shorten the COST and ITEM NAME categories and allow room for the two decimal places in TOTAL COST to be printed.

Changing printer options.   Let's take a look at the Printer Options menu, by now a familiar screen.

1. Press OA-O for Options.

Most of the options are acceptable except for the platen width, left and right margins, and the top margin. Let's quickly change them so that the report will fit on the paper when it's printed.

2. Enter **PW** for Platen Width and press RETURN.

3. Change PW to **8.5** inches and press RETURN.

4. Enter **RM** for Right Margin and press RETURN.

5. Change RM to **.2** inches and press RETURN.

6. Enter **LM** for Left Margin and press RETURN.

7. Change LM to **.3** inches and press RETURN.

8. Enter **TM** for Top Margin and press RETURN.

9. Change TM to **2** inches and press RETURN.

You can see the changes reflected on the screen. Press ESC to return to the Report format screen. Now the report is ready to be printed and the format just created has been saved.

Printing the Report

To print the report quickly on the screen and then on the printer, follow these steps:

1. Press OA-P for Print.

2. Choose The screen by moving your cursor to that option and pressing RETURN.

3. Enter today's date and press RETURN.

The report will be printed on the screen, like this:

```
File:      BegInv.lst                                                  Page  1
Report: Startup Inventory                                             8/15/87
ITEM NAME DESCRIPTION                VENDOR     COST     MIN.QTY.   TOTAL COST
--------- ------------------------   ------    ------   ----------  ----------
f100       Dupe film 12x18              85      9.00        25        225.00
f25        Photostat screen 1/2         85     10.25        25        256.25
f30        Photostat screen 10x12       85     10.50        20        210.00
f35        Line film 1/2                85      8.00        25        200.00
f40        Line film 10x12              85      8.50        30        255.00
f50        Line film 12x18              85      9.25        15        138.75
f55        Halftone film                85     12.00        12        144.00
f70        Film photostat 1/2           85      8.00        10         80.00
f80        Film photostat 10x12         85      8.50        12        102.00
                                                                     1611.00

p01wh      8.5x11 16# white bond       102      5.20        10         52.00
p03wh      8.5x11 20# white bond       102      6.80        10         68.00
p03bl      8.5x11 20# blue  bond       102      6.80         5         34.00
p03bu      8.5x11 20# buff  bond       102      6.80         5         34.00


Press Space Bar to continue []                                     52K Avail.
```

Press the spacebar to continue scrolling through the report, screen by screen. When you decide that the report looks the way you expect it to, go ahead and print it.

4. Press OA-P for Print.

5. This time move the cursor to your printer and press RETURN to direct the output to the printer.

6. Press RETURN to accept the previously entered date.

7. Press RETURN to accept the single copy of the report AppleWorks assumes you want.

The report should now begin printing. Figure 7-3 shows what it should look like.

Saving the Report Format

To save your work in formatting the report, press OA-S, as you would for a file. After a short wait, the file and all report formats will be saved for you.

```
File:    BegInv.lst                                              Page  1
Report: Startup Inventory                                       8/15/87
ITEM NAME DESCRIPTION                  VENDOR      COST   MIN.QTY.  TOTAL COST
--------- --------------------------   ------    ------   --------  ----------
f100      Dupe film 12x18                85        9.00       25       225.00
f25       Photostat screen 1/2           85       10.25       25       256.25
f30       Photostat screen 10x12         85       10.50       20       210.00
f35       Line film 1/2                  85        8.00       25       200.00
f40       Line film 10x12                85        8.50       30       255.00
f50       Line film 12x18                85        9.25       15       138.75
f55       Halftone film                  85       12.00       12       144.00
f70       Film photostat 1/2             85        8.00       10        80.00
f80       Film photostat 10x12           85        8.50       12       102.00
                                                                      1611.00

p01wh     8.5x11 16# white bond         102        5.20       10        52.00
p03wh     8.5x11 20# white bond         102        6.80       10        68.00
p03bl     8.5x11 20# blue  bond         102        6.80        5        34.00
p03bu     8.5x11 20# buff  bond         102        6.80        5        34.00
p03go     8.5x11 20# gold  bond         102        6.80        5        34.00
p03iv     8.5x11 20# ivory bond         102        6.80       15       102.00
p07wh     8.5x11 60# white bond         102       11.82       12       141.84
p07bl     8.5x11 60# blue  bond         102       11.82       10       118.20
p07go     8.5x11 60# gold  bond         102       11.82       10       118.20
p07iv     8.5x11 60# ivory bond         102       11.82        7        82.74
                                                                       784.98

                                                                      2395.98*
```

Figure 7-3.   Final inventory startup list

This concludes our work with AppleWorks' data base. You have learned to handle many of the more advanced data base functions and are ready to organize and enter your own lists and tables. If you choose to continue now, proceed either to Chapter 5 for beginning spreadsheet concepts or to Chapter 8 for advanced spreadsheet uses.

8

Expanding Your Spreadsheet Skills

The spreadsheet of AppleWorks may be your most valued component in terms of productivity. Certainly when it comes to preparing budgets, there is no comparison between manual and automated spreadsheets. Even when compared to all the other tasks you can perform using AppleWorks, budgeting is high on the list as a powerful and useful tool.

In Chapter 8 you will create a budget and, in the process, learn a great deal more about AppleWorks' spreadsheet component. For easy data entry and retrieval, you'll learn how to work with windows, how to freeze the row and column headings as you work, and how to copy text across rows and columns. You will learn more about setting standard values, setting protection, using formulas and functions, and changing the recalculation of formulas and functions so that it occurs only on demand.

The budget you will build in this chapter will be used to assess the cost of adding a new retail store to your company. In Chapter 9, you will integrate this budget with the business plan from Chapter 6.

Let's take a close look at this hypothetical budget and see what it is intended to do.

About the Budget

Suppose that your company, ABC Company, is adding a new retail store in 1988. A budget is required so that you can project

```
File:   Newstore88.bud                                                      Page  1
                                  A B C   C O M P A N Y                      8/15/87
                                  BUDGET TO ADD STORE 1988

===================================ASSUMPTIONS=======================
EMPLOYEES        NUMBER  SALARIES      1ST GWTH   8.0%       RENT     2000
  STORE MANAGER      1    2500         2ND GWTH  12.0%       UTIL.     400
  ASST. MANAGER      1    2000         3RD GWTH  12.0%       MAINT.    500
  SENIOR CLERK       1    1600         4TH GWTH  15.0%       DEPREC.   750
  JUNIOR CLERK       4    1200         RETURNS    2.0%       INSUR.    250
          .                           C O S     63.0%       PHONE     150
TOTAL SALARIES   10,900               P/R TAX   15.0%       MISCEL.   150
                                      FRINGE     7.0%
                                      POST/FGT   1.0%
                                      EXC.TAX     .5%


===================================BUDGET============================================
BUDGET CATEGORY    JAN     FEB     MAR     QTR1     QTR2     QTR3     QTR4    TOTAL  % SALES
----------------------------------------------------------------------------------------
REVENUE
  SALES             0   35,000  37,800  72,800 127,008 142,249 163,586 505,643   102.0%
  RETURNS           0      700     756   1,456   2,540   2,845   3,272  10,113     2.0%
     NET SALES      0   34,300  37,044  71,344 124,468 139,404 160,315 495,530   100.0%

  COST OF SALES     0   21,609  23,338  44,947  78,415  87,825 100,998 312,184    63.0%

GROSS PROFIT        0   12,691  13,706  26,397  46,053  51,579  59,316 183,346    37.0%


EXPENSES
  SALARIES      10,900  10,900  10,900  32,700  32,700  32,700  32,700 130,800    26.4%
  PAYROLL TAXES  1,635   1,635   1,635   4,905   4,905   4,905   4,905  19,620     4.0%
  FRINGE BENEFITS  763     763     763   2,289   2,289   2,289   2,289   9,156     1.8%
    SUBTOTAL LABOR 13,298 13,298 13,298 39,894  39,894  39,894  39,894 159,576    32.2%

  STORE RENT     2,000   2,000   2,000   6,000   6,000   6,000   6,000  24,000     4.8%
  UTILITIES        400     400     400   1,200   1,200   1,200   1,200   4,800     1.0%
  MAINTENANCE      500     500     500   1,500   1,500   1,500   1,500   6,000     1.2%
  DEPRECIATION     750     750     750   2,250   2,250   2,250   2,250   9,000     1.8%
  ADVERTISING    1,500   1,500   1,500   4,500   2,000   1,750   1,500   9,750     2.0%
  POSTAGE & FREIGHT  0     343     370     713   1,245   1,394   1,603   4,955     1.0%
  INSURANCE        250     250     250     750     750     750     750   3,000      .6%
  TELEPHONE        150     150     150     450     450     450     450   1,800      .4%
  EXCISE TAXES       0     172     185     357     622     697     802   2,478      .5%
  MISCELLANEOUS    150     150     150     450     450     450     450   1,800      .4%
    SUBTOTAL NONLAB 5,700  6,214   6,256  18,170 16,467  16,441  16,505  67,583    13.6%

TOTAL EXPENSE   18,998  19,512  19,554  58,064  56,361  56,335  56,399 227,159    45.8%

NET PROFIT     (18,998) (6,822) (5,847)(31,667)(10,308) (4,756)  2,918 (43,813)   -8.8%
```

Figure 8-1. The budget to be created

what that year will look like. The plan is for the store to be profitable within the first eight months.

Figure 8-1 shows the budget as it will be finally developed. You can see that it is divided into two main parts: an Assumptions section and a Budget section. Separating the assumptions from the budget itself makes it easier to manipulate the budget and measure the impacts of changing values on it. It's always a good idea, in fact, to think about your budget assumptions first and then separate them from the actual budget figures in the spreadsheet. When the baseline numbers are isolated, you can change them throughout the spreadsheet simply by setting up pointers to the cells containing those numbers. In this way, you can avoid having to hunt for numbers that may be dispersed in formulas throughout the spreadsheet and that would have to be located and changed individually in order to vary the assumed scenario.

Since this is an important point for building efficient spreadsheet models, an example may be helpful. Suppose that in planning a budget, you have assumed that sales will increase by a growth rate that changes each quarter. Then after you've developed the budget, you receive new information suggesting growth rates that differ from those first anticipated. If you have not isolated your assumptions about growth rates within the spreadsheet, you will have to find and change every formula in the spreadsheet that contains or depends on a growth rate figure. However, if you have put the initial growth rate figures in cells at the top of the spreadsheet, you need only change the figures in those cells and put pointers to those cells in the formulas instead of the actual growth rate figures. Thus you can change the growth rate everywhere in the spreadsheet by altering only the assumption, and the change will be effective for all the formulas that point to it.

The assumptions in the budget can be divided into three groups: those about employees, percentages, and fixed expenses. The employee assumptions include the type of employee that the store will employ, the number of each type of employee, and the salary per type per month. By multiplying the number of each employee type by the salary for that type and adding them together, you have the total salaries for the store. Assume that the number of employees will remain constant throughout the year. That's not to say that there won't be turnover, but the number will remain constant for budgeting purposes.

The percentage assumptions will be used for several purposes. First there are the growth percentages for each quarter's sales. During the first three months, sales will grow at a monthly rate of 8.0% because of the momentum of the early sales promotions. The second quarter's growth of 12.0% looks higher but is actually lower, since it is based on a quarterly period rather than the monthly period of the first quarter's sales. Assume that there will be 2.0% returns in the merchandise, which will thus reduce sales by that amount. Also assume that the cost of sales (COS) is 63.0% of sales. Payroll taxes (P/R TAX) and fringe benefits (FRINGE) are labor expenses that are estimated to be 15.0% and 7.0% respectively. Postage and freight (POST/FGT) expenses are estimated to be about 1.0% of net sales. Finally, excise tax will be 0.5% of net sales.

Fixed expenses are the expenses that are the same amount every month, or that at least can be assumed to be the same for budgeting purposes. You should assume constant amounts for rent, utilities, maintenance (building and equipment), depreciation (which, by the way, would normally be calculated from another spreadsheet), insurance, phone, and miscellaneous expenses. The last category, miscellaneous (MISCEL.), is made up of several expenses too small to budget individually. All of the amounts are rounded to the nearest dollar, since cents are often meaningless in a budget, which is, after all, only someone's best guess.

The budget covers one year's time. The first quarter is unique because of the startup situation, and is therefore budgeted in detail by month. You'll notice that expenses begin in January, the month in which you're preparing to open the store, even though the store doesn't actually open until February. After the first three months, the budget is figured by quarters. In addition to the estimates for each quarter, the budget contains both a total column that sums the dollars for the year and a percent of sales column that determines what percent each budget category is of the net sales.

The procedure in this chapter will be similar to that in Chapter 5. You will enter the budget by first entering the spreadsheet standard values. Then you will modify the cell standard values for those rows or columns that differ from the spreadsheet standards. Next, you will enter the assumption headings, assumptions, budget headings, formulas and functions, and finally the data.

Setting Up the Budget Spreadsheet

To start, bring up AppleWorks, change the disk assignment to drive 2 if necessary, and insert the AppleWorks2 disk containing the business plan. Create a file by selecting option 5, Make a new file for the: Spreadsheet, from the Add Files menu. From the Spreadsheet menu, select the first option, From scratch, and name your file **Newstore88.bud**. The blank Review/Add/Change screen will be displayed. You are now ready to enter standard values into the spreadsheet.

Assigning Spreadsheet Standard Values

In Chapter 5 you learned that spreadsheet standard values are design tools governing the size of columns, whether labels are to be centered or right- or left-justified, how values are to be formatted and with how many decimal places, and so on. Take a quick look at the current standard value settings in order to remind yourself just what the defaults are and which ones you should change.

You can see the current settings of standard values by looking at the end of the Help menu, which is displayed by pressing OA-?, and then pressing the DOWN ARROW 43 times.

```
File: Newstore88.bud                HELP            Escape: Review/Add/Change
===============================================================================
                    @-Arrows       Move to another full screen

                    0-9 + - .      Type a value

                    " or letters   Type a label

                    @-1            Go to beginning of file
                      through        through
                    @-9            Go to end of file

                    Current settings of standard values
                    =====================================

                    Protection is       On
                    Label format is     Left justify
                    Value format is     Appropriate
                    Frequency is        Automatic
                    Order is            Columns
-------------------------------------------------------------------------------

Use arrows to see remainder of Help __                      56K Avail.
```

Looking at the screen, you'll notice that the Protection feature is On, indicating that you may protect cells from being changed if you choose. Remember, however, that the Protection feature is ineffective until you take the second step of defining exactly which cells you wish to protect. You can also see that the Label formats are to be left-justified and that the Value formats are set at Appropriate, meaning that the numbers are formatted exactly as they're entered. Finally, the Help menu shows that the Frequency of recalculation is set to Automatic and that the Order of recalculation is by columns first rather than by rows. (Remember that the @ sign represents the OA key in our depiction of the screen.)

There are several values that will need to be changed from their default status. First the Value format must be changed to Comma, with zero decimal places. You are rounding to dollars only and do not have room for the dollar sign, but you need a comma to separate thousands. Also, the Frequency of recalculation should be changed to the Manual setting, since performing recalculations every time you enter a number will be too time-consuming. The Order of recalculation, in this case, can be by either rows or columns; since it makes no difference, leave the order as is. Left-justified labels will be correct for most of the labels, so you can leave that standard value as it is; later you'll change the few that should be centered. Finally, the column width must be changed from the default setting of 9 characters to 8 characters.

If you have not already done so, press ESC to return to the Review/Add/Change screen. Since you've set standard values for the spreadsheet before, the following necessary steps are just a review:

1. Press OA-V for Value.

2. Press RETURN to request the Value format.

3. Enter **C** for Commas, and press RETURN for zero decimal places.

4. Press OA-V again.

5. Enter **C** for Column width.

6. Press OA-LEFT ARROW one time to reduce the column width to 8 characters, and then press RETURN.

7. Press OA-V once more.

8. Enter **R** for Recalculate.

9. Enter **F** for Frequency and then **M** for Manual.

The standard values have now been changed. To verify the new settings, return to the end of the Help menu and see that they are changed. Press ESC to exit the Help menu.

Assigning Cell Standard Values

The one column that does not conform to our standard width of eight characters is column A, the BUDGET category. Change the column width of column A to 20 characters, wide enough to contain the budget categories. Do this now.

1. Move your cursor to column A and press OA-L for Layout.

2. Enter C for Columns.

3. Press RETURN to acknowledge that the correct column is highlighted.

4. Enter C for Column width.

5. Press OA-RIGHT ARROW 12 times, and then press RETURN.

Column A has been widened to 20 characters. Now enter the title of the budget.

Entering the Title

The title of the spreadsheet needs to be centered. If you enter the first line of the title in column D indented two spaces and the second line in column D with no indentation, the lines will be nicely centered as they are in Figure 8-1.

Follow these steps to enter the two-line title:

1. Move your cursor to D1 and press the CAPS LOCK key.

Remember that to indent you must inform AppleWorks that you are using a label that does not start with the letter of the alphabet, but with a space. The spaces are, of course, not letters and must therefore be preceded with a quotation mark (").

2. Enter a quotation mark ("), two spaces, and then the name of the company, allowing one space between each letter and two spaces between the words ABC and COMPANY, like this: " A B C   C O M P A N Y.

3. Press RETURN to signal AppleWorks that the entry is correct.

4. Move your cursor to cell D2.

5. Enter **BUDGET TO ADD STORE 1988** and press RETURN.

Your screen should look like this:

```
File: Newstore88.bud        REVIEW/ADD/CHANGE              Escape: Main Menu
=============A=============B=======C=======D=======E=======F=======G====
  1|                                 A B C   C O M P A N Y
  2|                               BUDGET TO ADD STORE 1988
  3|
  4|
  5|
  6|
  7|
  8|
  9|
 10|
 11|
 12|
 13|
 14|
 15|
 16|
 17|
 18|
-------------------------------------------------------------------------
D2: (Label) BUDGET T

Type entry or use ⌕ commands __                        ⌕-? for Help
```

Now enter a double line to separate the title from the next part of the spreadsheet, the assumptions. Notice that the equal sign is another non-alphabetic label character that must be preceded by a quotation mark. Follow these steps:

6. Move your cursor to cell A3.

7. Enter a quotation mark (") and 20 equal signs (=) until cell A3 is filled, and then press RETURN.

The cell indicator will tell you that the contents of cell A3 have been repeated. This means that the equal signs, or any other characters you choose to put in the cell, will fill up columns of varying widths. Here column A is completely filled with equal signs:

```
File: Newstore88.bud        REVIEW/ADD/CHANGE             Escape: Main Menu
==============A=============B=======C=======D=======E=======F=======G====
    1|                                    A B C   C O M P A N Y
    2|                                 BUDGET TO ADD STORE 1988
    3|====================
    4|
    5|
    6|
    7|
    8|
    9|
   10|
   11|
   12|
   13|
   14|
   15|
   16|
   17|
   18|
----------------------------------------------------------------------
A3: (Label) Repeated-=

Type entry or use Ć commands __                              Ć-? for Help
```

Now copy cell A3 across the rest of row 3.

8. Press OA-C for Copy.

9. Press RETURN to verify that Within worksheet is what you want.

10. Press RETURN to verify that cell A3 is the correct source from which to copy.

11. Press the RIGHT ARROW one time to get to cell B3, press the period (.) to signal the beginning of the range for the copy operation, press the RIGHT ARROW eight times to get to cell J3, and press RETURN.

The double line will be copied across the page. Looking at Figure 8-1, however, you'll notice that the line should have the heading "ASSUMPTIONS" embedded within it to tell you that the assumptions follow. Remember when entering a heading beginning with a non-alphabetic character that you must also enter a quotation mark first and wait for Apple-Works to load the information. Follow these steps to enter the title for the Assumptions section:

12. Move the cursor to D3.

13. Enter "======ASSUMPTIONS======= (six equal signs before and seven after) and then press RETURN.

The leading and trailing equal signs ensure that the word "ASSUMPTIONS" is centered and leaves no gap in the double line. Your screen should look like the following screen.

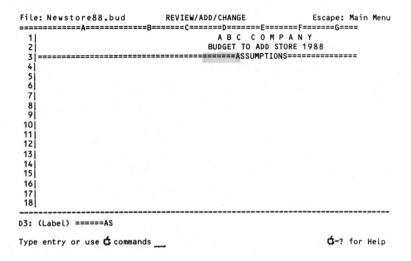

```
File: Newstore88.bud        REVIEW/ADD/CHANGE              Escape: Main Menu
=============A=============B=======C=======D=======E=======F=======G====
  1|                                    A B C  C O M P A N Y
  2|                                  BUDGET TO ADD STORE 1988
  3|=========================================ASSUMPTIONS==============
  4|
  5|
  6|
  7|
  8|
  9|
 10|
 11|
 12|
 13|
 14|
 15|
 16|
 17|
 18|
------------------------------------------------------------------------
D3: (Label) ======AS

Type entry or use ⌂ commands ___                        ⌂-? for Help
```

Now enter the assumptions for the budget.

Entering the Assumptions

You can see from Figures 8-1 and 8-2 that the assumptions occupy the upper third of the budget—rows 5 through 15. In order to demonstrate and review the spreadsheet's Edit, Copy, Insert, Delete, and Blank commands, you will first enter the assumption headings in one straight line in column A and then copy them to their appropriate columns. Use Figure 8-3 as a guide to enter the assumption headings and data. To get you started, the first few steps are listed here. Then you are on your own, guided by Figure 8-3.

```
File:   Newstore88.bud                                              Page  1
                                                                   8/15/87
ROWS\COL        A        B       C        D      E      F     G       H      I      J
  1                                        A B C   C O M P A N Y
  2                                     BUDGET TO ADD STORE 1988
  3
  4       =============================ASSUMPTIONS========================================
  5       EMPLOYEES        NUMBER  SALARIES    1ST GWTH    .08    RENT      2,000
  6          STORE MANAGER      1   2,500      2ND GWTH    .12    UTIL.       400
  7          ASST. MANAGER      1   2,000      3RD GWTH    .10    MAINT.      500
  8          SENIOR CLERK       1   1,600      4TH GWTH    .15    DEPREC.     750
  9          JUNIOR CLERK       3   1,200      RETURNS     .02    INSUR.      250
 10                                            C O S       .63    PHONE       150
 11       TOTAL SALARIES                       P/R TAX     .15    MISCEL.     150
 12                                            FRINGE      .07
 13                                            POST/FGT    .01
 14                                            EXC. TAX   .005
 15
 16       =========================================================================
```

Figure 8-2. Assumptions with column and row labels

1. Move your cursor to cell A4.

2. Enter **EMPLOYEES** and press the DOWN ARROW one time.

Notice that the next four labels are indented two spaces and that you must use a quotation mark to inform AppleWorks that you are entering a label.

3. Enter a quotation mark ("), two spaces, and then **STORE MANAGER** and press the DOWN ARROW one time.

4. Enter a quotation mark ("), two spaces, and then **ASST. MANAGER** and press the DOWN ARROW one time.

Continue to enter the rest of the labels and contents in column A, as shown in Figure 8-3. You may mistakenly enter a value for a label, or a label for a value, and find you are unable to reenter the correct keys. AppleWorks protects you from entering labels when a cell is defined as a value and vice versa. In this case you simply press ESC to clear the cell and then enter the correct contents.

There are a few things you should notice as you enter the

```
File:    figure 8.3                                                              Page  1
                                                                                 8/15/87

ROWS\COL        A           B       C       D       E       F       G       H       I       J
  1                                         A B C   C O M P A N Y
  2                                      BUDGET TO ADD STORE 1988
  3         ==========================================ASSUMPTIONS============================================
  4         EMPLOYEES
  5           STORE MANAGER
  6           ASST. MANAGER
  7           SENIOR CLERK
  8           JUNIOR CLERK
  9         TOTAL SALARIES
 10         NUMBER
 11                         1
 12                         1
 13                         1
 14                         3
 15         SALARIES
 16                     2,500
 17                     2,000
 18                     1,600
 19                     1,200
 20         1ST GWTH
 21         2ND GWTH
 22         3RD GWTH
 23         4TH GWTH
 24         RETURNS
 25         C O S
 26         P/R TAX
 27         FRINGE
 28         POST/FGT
 29         EXC. TAX
 30                       .08
 31                       .12
 32                        .1
 33                       .15
 34                       .02
 35                       .63
 36                       .15
 37                       .07
 38                       .01
 39                      .005
 40         RENT
 41         UTIL.
 42         MAINT.
 43         DEPREC.
 44         INSUR.
 45         PHONE
 46         MISCEL.
 47                     2,000
 48                       400
 49                       500
 50                       750
 51                       250
 52                       150
 53                       150
 54
```

Figure 8-3.   List of assumptions to be entered

rest of the data. First of all, you may notice that the data you enter does not conform in all cases to that of Figure 8-2. Enter the data as you see it in Figure 8-3. Do not be concerned at this point about the differences. They will provide an opportunity later to review the spreadsheet editing process, which differs slightly from editing in the data base and the word processor. As you enter labels they will be left-justified in the cell as they are set in the spreadsheet standard values. The numbers, however, will be right-justified in the cells. Don't be concerned about the positioning of the numbers.

In addition, you should notice that the decimal numbers (0.08, 0.12, and so on) appear as zeros and ones as you enter them, although the cell indicator displays the correct number. This is because the column is currently formatted for only whole numbers according to the standard values set for the whole spreadsheet. AppleWorks rounds off the decimal numbers that are less than 0.5 to zero and those that are more than 0.5—in this case, only 0.63—to 1. Don't worry. You will reformat these particular cells later. Just make sure you have entered the correct numbers according to Figure 8-3 and as reflected in the cell indicator.

Enter the salary figures without commas. They will be automatically displayed on the screen because the Value format standard value is set to Commas.

Finally, notice that you must enter quotation marks before the labels 1ST GWTH, 2ND GWTH, 3RD GWTH, and 4TH GWTH to prevent AppleWorks from reading labels that begin with a number as values.

Enter the rest of the labels now. When the labels and data for the assumptions have been entered, look over the spreadsheet and make adjustments.

Inserting rows.   There are two spacing corrections that should be made at this time. The title and the separator line are too close together. A blank line between them would improve readability. Another problem in readability is how close the TOTAL SALARIES label is to the list of employee titles. The following steps show you how to insert rows in these places

1. Move your cursor to any column in row 3.

2. Press OA-I for Insert.

You will be asked whether you want to insert rows or columns.

3. Press RETURN to accept the Rows default.

4. Enter **1** to insert one row and press RETURN.

A blank row separating the title from the separator line will be inserted in the spreadsheet above the row the cursor was on.

5. Move your cursor to row 10.

6. Press OA-I.

7. Press RETURN to select the Rows default.

8. Enter **1** to insert a single row and press RETURN.

Another blank row will be inserted above TOTAL SALARIES.

Copying data.   If you compare Figures 8-2 and 8-3, you will notice that all the data that should be spread out over columns A through I is currently in column A. To remedy this, copy the data from column A to columns B, C, E, F, H, and I. Follow these steps:

1. Move your cursor to cell A12, which contains the label NUMBER.

The NUMBER label is in cell A12 now instead of in A10 (as shown in Figure 8-3) because of the two blank rows just inserted.

2. Press OA-C for Copy.

3. Press RETURN to acknowledge that the copy is Within worksheet.

4. Press the DOWN ARROW four times to reach cell A16 and press RETURN.

5. Move your cursor to cell B5 and press RETURN.

Now copy the salaries to column C.

6. Move your cursor to cell A17, which contains the label SALARIES.

7. Press OA-C for Copy.

8. Press RETURN to acknowledge that the copy is Within worksheet.

9. Press the DOWN ARROW four times to reach 1,200 and press RETURN.

10. Move your cursor to cell C5 and press RETURN.

Using the following guide, proceed in the same manner to copy the rest of the data from column A to the other columns. The columns that differ from what you want will be edited to conform after the copy operation is complete. Remember that you can use the OA-UP, DOWN, LEFT, and RIGHT ARROW keys to move quickly through the spreadsheet.

Copy From	Copy To
A22 containing 1ST GWTH for 9 cells down	E5
A32 containing .08 for 9 cells down	F5
A42 containing RENT for 6 cells down	H5
A49 containing 2000 for 6 cells down	I5

At this point your screen looks rather untidy with the original data still in column A.

Blanking cells and deleting rows.   There are two ways that you can erase the original labels and data that you entered into column A: by blanking or by deleting them. Blanking erases the contents but leaves the cells intact. Deleting eliminates a row or column altogether. *All* data in a deleted row or column is lost.

You could use the Blank command to erase all of the labels in column A. However, to use both the Blank and the Delete commands, you will use the Blank command to erase cells A12 through A16 and the Delete command to delete cells A17 through A55. It is necessary to use the Blank command on cells A12 through A16 because rows 12 through 16 contain copied labels that you want to preserve. Deleting would eliminate the rows entirely, including that data. However, since rows 17 through 55 contain no other data, those rows can be safely eliminated.

Follow these steps to blank the original labels.

1. Move your cursor to cell A12.

2. Press OA-B for Blank.

3. Enter B for Block.

4. Press the DOWN ARROW four times and press RETURN.

The contents of cells A12 to A16 will be erased. Now you can erase the rest using the Delete command. Remember that you can use the OA-DOWN and UP ARROW keys to move vertically through the spreadsheet.

5. Move your cursor to column A17.

6. Press OA-D for Delete.

7. Press RETURN to acknowledge that you want to delete rows.

8. Move your cursor down until you see row 55 in the cell indicator; then press RETURN.

The unnecessary data has been removed and now you can finish your assumptions by formatting the percent column and entering a formula to calculate total salaries.

Your screen now looks like this:

```
File: Newstore88.bud        REVIEW/ADD/CHANGE            Escape: Main Menu
=============A=============B=======C=======D=======E=======F=======G====
  1|                              A B C   C O M P A N Y
  2|                            BUDGET TO ADD STORE 1988
  3|
  4|=================================ASSUMPTIONS==============
  5|EMPLOYEES          NUMBER  SALARIES       1ST GWTH   0
  6|  STORE MANAGER       1     2,500         2ND GWTH   0
  7|  ASST. MANAGER       1     2,000         3RD GWTH   0
  8|  SENIOR CLERK        1     1,600         4TH GWTH   0
  9|  JUNIOR CLERK        3     1,200         RETURNS    0
 10|                                          C O S      1
 11|TOTAL SALARIES                            P/R TAX    0
 12|                                          FRINGE     0
 13|                                          POST/FGT   0
 14|                                          EXC. TAX   0
 15|
 16|
 17|
 18|
   -----------------------------------------------------------------------
A1

Type entry or use ⌂ commands __                          ⌂-? for Help
```

Formatting the decimal numbers column. Column F should contain the percentages of growth and of costs in relation to total sales. But the column is currently formatted according to the standard values set for the spreadsheet as a whole, which means that decimal numbers are rounded either up to one or down to zero.

Follow these steps to reformat column F so that the data can be presented correctly.

1. Move your cursor to F5.

2. Press OA-L for Layout.

3. Enter **B** for Block.

4. Press the DOWN ARROW nine times to reach F14 and press RETURN.

5. Press RETURN for Value format.

6. Enter **P** for Percent and **1** for decimal places, and then press RETURN.

Each of the zeros will be transformed into the appropriate percent. The percent format multiplies each number entered by 100 in order to display it as a percent. Thus, for example, because you entered .08 earlier on, it is now correctly displayed as 8.0%.

Your screen should now look like this:

```
File: Newstore88.bud        REVIEW/ADD/CHANGE          Escape: Main Menu
=========≈======A==============B=======C=======D=======E=======F=======G====
  1|                                A B C   C O M P A N Y
  2|                              BUDGET TO ADD STORE 1988
  3|
  4|========================================ASSUMPTIONS===============
  5|EMPLOYEES           NUMBER  SALARIES      1ST GWTH   8.0%
  6|  STORE MANAGER        1     2,500        2ND GWTH  12.0%
  7|  ASST. MANAGER        1     2,000        3RD GWTH  10.0%
  8|  SENIOR CLERK         1     1,600        4TH GWTH  15.0%
  9|  JUNIOR CLERK         3     1,200        RETURNS    2.0%
 10|                                          C O S     63.0%
 11|TOTAL SALARIES                            P/R TAX   15.0%
 12|                                          FRINGE     7.0%
 13|                                          POST/FGT   1.0%
 14|                                          EXC. TAX    .5%
 15|
 16|
 17|
 18|
------------------------------------------------------------------------
F5: (Value, Layout-P1) .08

Type entry or use ⌂ commands __                        ⌂-? for Help
```

Now let's enter the formula for TOTAL SALARIES.

Entering a Formula.   The formula for calculating total salaries multiplies the number of employees of each type by the salaries for that type and adds them together. Follow these steps to enter the formula:

1. Move your cursor to cell B11.

The formula will begin with a left parenthesis, which tells AppleWorks that it is dealing with a value, not a label. The formula addresses each cell individually. The parentheses group elements to be calculated together, just as they do in algebraic equations. If you make an obvious error, such as forgetting a parenthesis, AppleWorks will beep and wait for you to correct the mistake.

2. Enter **(B6∗C6)+(B7∗C7)+(B8∗C8)+(B9∗C9)** and press RETURN.

Your screen now looks like this:

```
File: Newstore88.bud        REVIEW/ADD/CHANGE              Escape: Main Menu
=============A=============B=======C=======D=======E=======F=======G====
   1|                                    A B C   C O M P A N Y
   2|                                    BUDGET TO ADD STORE 1988
   3|
   4| ======================================ASSUMPTIONS==============
   5|EMPLOYEES           NUMBER  SALARIES      1ST GWTH    8.0%
   6|  STORE MANAGER        1    2,500         2ND GWTH   12.0%
   7|  ASST. MANAGER        1    2,000         3RD GWTH   10.0%
   8|  SENIOR CLERK         1    1,600         4TH GWTH   15.0%
   9|  JUNIOR CLERK         3    1,200         RETURNS     2.0%
  10|                                          C O S      63.0%
  11|TOTAL SALARIES        9,700               P/R TAX    15.0%
  12|                                          FRINGE      7.0%
  13|                                          POST/FGT    1.0%
  14|                                          EXC. TAX     .5%
  15|
  16|
  17|
  18|
-----------------------------------------------------------------------
B11: (Value) (B6∗C6)+(B7∗C7)+(B8∗C8)+(B9∗C9)

Type entry or use ⌂ commands __                      ⌂-? for Help
```

Your screen reflects the new value that has been calculated in cell B11. The cell indicator recounts what formula was used.

Now let's get to the actual budget.

Entering the Budget

Entering the budget consists of entering the data for the year in the proper rows and columns. In doing this you will learn several additional spreadsheet functions, such as using windows and freezing the column and row headings on the screen.

Your first task will be to enter the row and column headings.

Entering the Column Headings

In addition to entering the ten column headings, you must change the formatting of nine of them so that they are centered instead of left-justified. The Budget section will be separated from the Assumptions section by a double line; the headings will be separated from the budget by a single line.

Follow these steps to enter and format the headings and the Budget section title:

1. Move your cursor to A16.

2. Enter a quotation mark (") and 20 equal signs (=) to fill cell A16, and then press RETURN.

3. Press OA-C for Copy.

4. Press RETURN to verify that the copy is to be Within worksheet.

5. Press RETURN to verify that cell A16 is the correct source.

6. Press the RIGHT ARROW once, type a period (.), press the RIGHT ARROW eight times to reach cell J16, and press RETURN.

7. Move your cursor to cell E16, a midpoint for the budget title.

8. Enter **BUDGET==** in uppercase with two trailing equal signs, and press RETURN.

Now that you have entered the separator line and the title, enter the column headings. Then adjust the headings for the numeric columns B through J, which look off-center after having been left-justified according to the spreadsheet standard values.

9. Move your cursor to cell A17.

10. Enter **BUDGET CATEGORY** and press the RIGHT ARROW once.

11. Enter **JAN**, **FEB**, **MAR**, **QTR1**, **QTR2**, **QTR3**, **QTR4**, and **TOTAL** in the same way.

12. Enter "**% SALES** in cell J17 (the leading quotation mark indicates a non-alphabetic label), and press RETURN.

13. Using OA-LEFT ARROW, move your cursor to B17 to center the headings.

14. Press OA-L for Layout.

15. Enter **B** for Block.

16. Press the OA-RIGHT ARROW to reach cell J17 and press RETURN.

17. Enter **L** for Label format and **C** for Center.

The column headings are now entered and your value headings are centered. Finally, you need to end the headings with the single line separator.

18. Move your cursor to cell A18.

19. Enter a quotation mark (") and then 20 dashes (-) until cell A18 is filled.

20. Copy cell A18 across the row to cell J18.

Your screen should look like this:

```
File: Newstore88.bud          REVIEW/ADD/CHANGE               Escape: Main Menu
=============A=============B=======C=======D======E=======F=======G====
  1|                                     A B C   C O M P A N Y
  2|                                   BUDGET TO ADD STORE 1988
  3|
  4|=================================================ASSUMPTIONS==============
  5|EMPLOYEES          NUMBER  SALARIES        1ST GWTH   8.0%
  6|   STORE MANAGER        1   2,500          2ND GWTH  12.0%
  7|   ASST. MANAGER        1   2,000          3RD GWTH  10.0%
  8|   SENIOR CLERK         1   1,600          4TH GWTH  15.0%
  9|   JUNIOR CLERK         3   1,200          RETURNS    2.0%
 10|                                           C O S     63.0%
 11|TOTAL SALARIES      9,700                  P/R TAX   15.0%
 12|                                           FRINGE     7.0%
 13|                                           POST/FGT   1.0%
 14|                                           EXC. TAX    .5%
 15|
 16|=================================================BUDGET==================
 17|BUDGET CATEGORY     JAN    FEB    MAR    QTR1    QTR2    QTR3
 18|----------------------------------------------------------------------
--------------------------------------------------------------------------
A18: (Label) Repeated--

Type entry or use ⌘commands__                            ⌘-? for Help
```

Entering the Row Headings

There are 24 row headings that must be entered. These name the budget categories of revenue and expense items. Figure 8-4 shows the row headings exactly as they should be entered.

As you enter the labels, remember that those that are indented require a quotation mark to inform AppleWorks that they are labels and not values. Also notice that there are blank rows between some labels; be sure to space your labels the same way. Otherwise, entering the labels only entails entering each label in uppercase, and then pressing the

```
File:   Newstore88.bud                              Page  1
                                                    8/15/87
ROWS\COL          A              B     C     D
   16 ==================================================
   17 BUDGET CATEGORY        JAN   FEB   MAR
   18 --------------------------------------------------
   19 REVENUE
   20   SALES
   21   RETURNS
   22     NET SALES
   23
   24      COST OF SALES
   25
   26 GROSS PROFIT
   27
   28 EXPENSES
   29   SALARIES
   30   PAYROLL TAXES
   31   FRINGE BENEFITS
   32     SUBTOTAL LABOR
   33
   34   STORE RENT
   35   UTILITIES
   36   MAINTENANCE
   37   DEPRECIATION
   38   ADVERTISING
   39   POSTAGE & FREIGHT
   40   INSURANCE
   41   TELEPHONE
   42   EXCISE TAXES
   43   MISCELLANEOUS
   44     SUBTOTAL NONLAB
   45
   46 TOTAL EXPENSE
   47
   48 NET PROFIT
```

Figure 8-4. Budget row headings to be entered

DOWN ARROW key once (or twice if you have to skip over a blank row) to get to the next row.

When you are finished, verify that the positions of your labels correspond with the row numbers in Figure 8-4, or you'll find that the formulas you'll be entering soon will not be correct.

If you printed your spreadsheet at this point, it would look like this:

```
                            A B C   C O M P A N Y
                        BUDGET TO ADD STORE 1988


=========================================ASSUMPTIONS=========================================
EMPLOYEES        NUMBER  SALARIES    1ST GWTH    8.0%    RENT      2,000
  STORE MANAGER     1     2,500      2ND GWTH   12.0%    UTIL.       400
  ASST. MANAGER     1     2,000      3RD GWTH   10.0%    MAINT.      500
  SENIOR CLERK      1     1,600      4TH GWTH   15.0%    DEPREC.     750
  JUNIOR CLERK      3     1,200      RETURNS     2.0%    INSUR.      250
                                     C O S      63.0%    PHONE       150
TOTAL SALARIES    9,700              P/R TAX    15.0%    MISCEL.     150
                                     FRINGE      7.0%
                                     POST/FGT    1.0%
                                     EXC. TAX     .5%


=============================================================================================
BUDGET CATEGORY    JAN    FEB    MAR    QTR1   QTR2   QTR3   QTR4   TOTAL  % SALES
---------------------------------------------------------------------------------------------

REVENUE
  SALES
  RETURNS
    NET SALES

    COST OF SALES

GROSS PROFIT

EXPENSES
  SALARIES
  PAYROLL TAXES
  FRINGE BENEFITS
    SUBTOTAL LABOR

  STORE RENT
  UTILITIES
  MAINTENANCE
  DEPRECIATION
  ADVERTISING
  POSTAGE & FREIGHT
  INSURANCE
  TELEPHONE
  EXCISE TAXES
  MISCELLANEOUS
    SUBTOTAL NONLAB

TOTAL EXPENSE

NET PROFIT
```

Notice that the budget is getting rather long. In order to see it all, you'll need to scroll back and forth through the file. Let's use a more efficient way to view the budget.

Using the Windows

It's particularly important to be able to look at more of the spreadsheet right now because you are about to enter the formulas. As you enter the formulas, you'll want to refer to the assumptions constantly, even though they are in another part of the spreadsheet and not visible to you.

Fortunately, AppleWorks provides a solution to this problem: its Window feature. The Window feature allows you to divide your screen into two images, either side by side, or one on top of the other. You can view one part of your spreadsheet (such as the assumptions) as one image, and another part (such as the budget) as the other image. You can easily switch your cursor from one image to the other, and while your cursor is in that window, you have the full capabilities of AppleWorks at your command within that window.

Invoke the Window command now to divide the screen into two parts. First move the cursor to the spot where the screen is to be split. In this case you want most of the assumptions to show, but you also want most of the screen to be dedicated to the budget image.

1. Move the cursor so that cell A5 is at the top left-hand corner of the screen.

2. Move your cursor to row 10.

Your screen should look like this:

```
File: Newstore88.bud        REVIEW/ADD/CHANGE            Escape: Main Menu
=============A=============B=======C=======D=======E=======F=======G====
    5|EMPLOYEES         NUMBER  SALARIES       1ST GWTH   8.0%
    6|   STORE MANAGER      1    2,500         2ND GWTH  12.0%
    7|   ASST. MANAGER      1    2,000         3RD GWTH  10.0%
    8|   SENIOR CLERK       1    1,600         4TH GWTH  15.0%
    9|   JUNIOR CLERK       3    1,200         RETURNS    2.0%
   10|                                         C O S     63.0%
   11|TOTAL SALARIES     9,700                 P/R TAX   15.0%
   12|                                         FRINGE     7.0%
   13|                                         POST/FGT   1.0%
   14|                                         EXC. TAX    .5%
   15|
   16|==================================BUDGET==================
   17|BUDGET CATEGORY     JAN    FEB    MAR    QTR1   QTR2   QTR3
   18|-----------------------------------------------------------
   19|REVENUE
   20|  SALES
   21|  RETURNS
   22|   NET SALES
-----------------------------------------------------------------
A10

Type entry or use ⌘ commands __                     ⌘-? for Help
```

You can see that if the screen splits on row 10, you will be able to see those assumptions above row 10, while most of the screen remains below row 10 where you can place the budget.

3. Press OA-W for Windows.

You will be asked whether you want the screen to be split into side-by-side images or top and bottom images. You want top and bottom images.

4. Enter **T** for Top and bottom.

Your screen will immediately be split into two images, like this:

```
File: Newstore88.bud          REVIEW/ADD/CHANGE              Escape: Main Menu
==============A==============B=======C=======D=======E=======F=======G====
   5|EMPLOYEES          NUMBER  SALARIES       1ST GWTH    8.0%
   6|  STORE MANAGER       1    2,500          2ND GWTH   12.0%
   7|  ASST. MANAGER       1    2,000          3RD GWTH   10.0%
   8|  SENIOR CLERK        1    1,600          4TH GWTH   15.0%
   9|  JUNIOR CLERK        3    1,200          RETURNS     2.0%
==============A==============B=======C=======D=======E=======F=======G====
  10|                                          C O S      63.0%
  11|TOTAL SALARIES       9,700                P/R TAX    15.0%
  12|                                          FRINGE      7.0%
  13|                                          POST/FGT    1.0%
  14|                                          EXC. TAX     .5%
  15|
  16|=================================================BUDGET=================
  17|BUDGET CATEGORY     JAN    FEB     MAR    QTR1     QTR2     QTR3
  18|----------------------------------------------------------------------
  19|REVENUE
  20|  SALES
  21|  RETURNS
--------------------------------------------------------------------------
A10

Type entry or use ⌕ commands _                         ⌕-? for Help
```

The screen is split between rows 9 and 10 into two windows. Each window is headed by the line designating the column letter names. Thus you will be able to view the assumptions in the top window while you are working in the bottom window. Regardless of which window you're in, you can move the cursor and perform all functions exactly as if there were only one window. Your cursor is in the bottom window. Let's see how easily you can jump from one window to the other.

5. Press OA-J for Jump.

The cursor jumped to the top window. To make the cursor

jump back to the bottom window, simply press OA-J again: the command works like a toggle. Use the OA-J command several times until you are comfortable with it. Leave the cursor in the bottom window when you are through.

What if you want to see more of the budget than you can currently see in the bottom window? It's easy: you are able to thumb through the screen containing the cursor.

Thumbing Through the Budget

As you may recall, the OA-1 through OA-9 commands allow you to thumb through the spreadsheet very quickly. You can move your cursor through the text at distances proportional to the numbers 1 through 9. For example, OA-1 will position you at the beginning of the spreadsheet, OA-9 at the end, and OA-4 at the beginning of the budget categories. Try this command now. Notice that as you scroll through the lower half of the split screen, the top half remains fixed. Similarly, if your cell cursor is in the top half of the screen (that is, in the Assumptions section), you can scroll through it and the bottom will remain fixed.

At this point, having entered the row and column labels for the Budget section and having learned how to look at the Assumptions section while entering the budget, you might want to review some aspects of the concept of *values* in a spreadsheet before actually entering the formulas and functions that will calculate your budget.

Reviewing Values

As you will recall from Chapter 5, you can enter values into the budget cells in a variety of ways. You can enter values in the form of numbers: for example, the number of employees in the assumptions. Values can also be pointers, which get their values from other cells. Values can be entered as formulas, which you use to define the calculations to be performed in your spreadsheet. Finally, values can be functions, which are predefined calculations, like the @SUM function you entered in Chapter 5.

Let's take a closer look for a moment at formulas and functions. Formulas calculate values according to equations. They can be made up of any combination of numbers and arithmetic operators, which are the plus (+), minus (−), multiply (∗), and divide (/) signs. Pointers may be included in formulas, and so can functions. Formulas in AppleWorks begin with plus or minus signs, numbers, left parentheses, or, in the case of functions, with the at (@) sign.

Functions are coded statements that perform calculations on a single value, a list of values, or a range of values. Functions begin with the at sign (@) and the name of the function. In addition to the @SUM and @CHOOSE functions, which you have used, AppleWorks provides several others, such as @SQRT for performing a square root, @MAX and @MIN for selecting the maximum value or the minimum value, @AVG for calculating the average value of a list of items, and @COUNT for counting the non-blank entries in a list.

AppleWorks has two unusual functions called @NA and @ERROR. You use the @NA function when you have an incomplete value — one that will be completed later. It serves as a reminder to you. AppleWorks also recognizes and uses this function to notify you of other cells trying to use data from the original NA cell.

The @ERROR function flags errors by displaying the word ERROR in any cell you designate. AppleWorks recognizes this and will display ERROR in other cells trying to use that same information. By flagging cells you want to trace with @ERROR, you can use this function to help uncover errors in your spreadsheet.

If you are interested in learning more about the variety of functions available to you and how to use them, refer to the

AppleWorks *Reference Manual.*

In the next several pages, you will learn more about how to enter and use values. You will learn how to look at each cell and determine its relationship to the total spreadsheet and how AppleWorks gives you the flexibility to customize the spreadsheet to your exact needs.

You are ready now to enter the formulas according to category: first the REVENUE, then the EXPENSES, and finally, the NET PROFIT and % SALES.

Entering Values for REVENUE

Revenue is one of the most complex entries for several reasons. First of all, sales for ABC Company won't actually start until February, when the store opens, which distorts the first quarter's sales figures. Second, you have estimated that sales will increase each quarter by the percent entered in the assumptions. The first quarter, which seems to have the lowest growth percent, is actually the fastest since it is based on month-to-month growth. This faster growth is partly attributable to the heavy advertising done during the first quarter. The third quarter is rather slow, since business is off a bit during the summer months.

Each month's or quarter's sales are composed of the prior month's or quarter's sales multiplied by the growth percentage for that month or quarter. In the assumptions, the percent growth was expressed as a fractional percent (for example, entered as 0.08 and displayed as 8.0%) to ease data entry. For your company to achieve growth, each month or quarter must see an 8% gain in addition to the complete revenue for that period. That is, you will need to add 1 to the fractional percent to make it a growth factor (displayed as 108%).

Follow these steps to enter the values projected for sales (ignore the TOTAL and % SALES columns until later):

1. Move your cursor to cell B20, January sales.

2. Enter **0** and press the RIGHT ARROW one time.

3. Enter **35000** for February sales and press the RIGHT ARROW once.

Next you will enter a formula for calculating the monthly amount for March, which will be placed into cell D20. To do this, you will multiply February sales by the growth percent in the first quarter growth assumptions (cell F5), having first converted it to a growth factor by adding 1 to the percent.

4. Enter the formula **+C20∗(1+F5)** and press the RIGHT ARROW once.

5. Enter the first quarter's sales with the function **@SUM (B20...D20)** and press the RIGHT ARROW once.

Your screen should look like this:

```
File: Newstore88.bud           REVIEW/ADD/CHANGE              Escape: Main Menu
==============A=============B=======C=======D=======E=======F=======G====
   5|EMPLOYEES        NUMBER  SALARIES        1ST GWTH    8.0%
   6|  STORE MANAGER      1    2,500          2ND GWTH   12.0%
   7|  ASST. MANAGER      1    2,000          3RD GWTH   10.0%
   8|  SENIOR CLERK       1    1,600          4TH GWTH   15.0%
   9|  JUNIOR CLERK       3    1,200          RETURNS     2.0%
==============A=============B=======C=======D=======E=======F=======G====
  13|                                         POST/FGT    1.0%
  14|                                         EXC. TAX     .5%
  15|
  16| ================================================BUDGET=================
  17|BUDGET CATEGORY    JAN     FEB     MAR     QTR1    QTR2    QTR3
  18| --------------------------------------------------------------------
  19|REVENUE
  20|  SALES             0   35,000  37,800  72,800
  21|  RETURNS
  22|    NET SALES
  23|
  24|    COST OF SALES
  --------------------------------------------------------------------------
F20

Type entry or use ⌘ commands___                              ⌘-? for Help
```

The three month's sales have been summed and placed in cell E20.

Next you will enter the second quarter's sales. Since the first quarter does not represent a typical quarter's sales, you will take the sales figure for March and multiply it by three to arrive at an estimate of a normal quarter's sales and then multiply that figure by the growth rate for the second quarter.

6. Enter the second quarter's sales with the equation +D20*3*(1+F6) and press the RIGHT ARROW once.

The third and fourth quarters' sales can be calculated in the same manner, by multiplying the previous quarter's sales by the growth percentage.

7. Enter the formula +F20*(1+F7) and press the RIGHT ARROW.

8. Enter the formula +G20*(1+F8) and press RETURN.

Now enter the formulas for returns of merchandise, net sales, cost of sales, and gross profit. The RETURNS row can be calculated by multiplying the assumed percent of returns times sales. The numbers in the NET SALES row are the result of subtracting returns from sales for each month or quarter. COST OF SALES is calculated by multiplying the assumed cost of sales percent (COS) by net sales. Finally, GROSS PROFIT is the net sales amount less the cost of sales. In all cases, the first quarter's values will be the sum of the first three months' values.

Follow these steps to finish entering the revenue part of the budget.

9. Move your cursor to cell B21.

10. Enter the formula +B20*F9 and press RETURN.

Now copy this formula to the rest of the RETURNS row, except for the last two columns.

11. Press OA-C for Copy.

12. Press RETURN twice to verify that you want to copy Within worksheet and that the correct source is highlighted.

13. Press the RIGHT ARROW once, enter a period (.), press the RIGHT ARROW five times, and press RETURN.

14. Enter **R** to indicate that the copy should be Relative for the B20 cell.

15. Press RETURN to indicate that the copy should be No change for the F9 cell.

Your screen will show all zeros, which is incorrect. This is because you turned off the automatic recalculation feature. You can force the recalculation to be done by pressing OA-K for Calculate.

16. Press OA-K.

The values will be calculated as shown:

```
File: Newstore88.bud          REVIEW/ADD/CHANGE               Escape: Main Menu
===========A============B======C=======D=======E======F=======G====
   5|EMPLOYEES           NUMBER  SALARIES      1ST GWTH    8.0%
   6|  STORE MANAGER        1    2,500         2ND GWTH   12.0%
   7|  ASST. MANAGER        1    2,000         3RD GWTH   10.0%
   8|  SENIOR CLERK         1    1,600         4TH GWTH   15.0%
   9|  JUNIOR CLERK         3    1,200         RETURNS     2.0%
======B======C=======D======E======F=======G=======H=======I=======J====
  13|                           POST/FGT    1.0%
  14|                           EXC. TAX     .5%
  15|
  16|=====================BUDGET=======================================
  17| JAN     FEB     MAR    QTR1    QTR2    QTR3    QTR4   TOTAL   %SALES
  18|-----------------------------------------------------------------
  19|
  20|    0   35,000  37,800  72,800 127,008 139,709 160,665
  21|    0      700     756   1,456   2,540   2,794   3,213
  22|
  23|
  24|
-------------------------------------------------------------------
B21: (Value) +B20*F9

Type entry or use É commands __                          É-? for Help
```

Now enter the other three formulas in the same way: for NET SALES (beginning in cell B22), enter +B20−B21; for COST OF SALES (beginning in cell B24), enter +B22*F10; for GROSS PROFIT (beginning in cell B26), enter +B22−B24. Copy the three formulas across to the QTR4 column. In all cases, the budget cells (those in column B) should be copied Relative, while the cells located in the assumption part of the spreadsheet (those in column F) should be copied with No change.

Position your cursor in cell H26 and press OA-K. This is what your screen should look like with all revenue figures entered.

```
File: Newstore88.bud            REVIEW/ADD/CHANGE              Escape: Main Menu
============A===========B=======C=======D========E=======F=======G====
 5|EMPLOYEES          NUMBER  SALARIES        1ST GWTH    8.0%
 6|  STORE MANAGER        1    2,500          2ND GWTH   12.0%
 7|  ASST. MANAGER        1    2,000          3RD GWTH   10.0%
 8|  SENIOR CLERK         1    1,600          4TH GWTH   15.0%
 9|  JUNIOR CLERK         3    1,200          RETURNS     2.0%
======B=======C=======D=======E=======F=======G=======H=======I=======J====
15|
16|=====================BUDGET=========================================
17| JAN    FEB     MAR     QTR1    QTR2    QTR3    QTR4    TOTAL   %SALES
18|--------------------------------------------------------------------
19|
20|   0  35,000  37,800  72,800 127,008 139,709 160,665
21|   0     700     756   1,456   2,540   2,794   3,213
22|   0  34,300  37,044  71,344 124,468 136,915 157,452
23|
24|   0  21,609  23,338  44,947  78,415  86,256  99,195
25|
26|   0  12,691  13,706  26,397  46,053  50,658  58,257
--------------------------------------------------------------------
H26: (Value) +H22-H24

Type entry or use Ć commands__                          Ć-? for Help
```

Briefly check the numbers in your spreadsheet to make sure they are the same as shown here. If not, double-check the formulas.

Now total the last two columns, TOTAL and % SALES.

Entering the TOTAL and % SALES Figures

The TOTAL and % SALES columns are used for informational purposes. The TOTAL sales column is derived from a function that sums sales for the four quarters. Enter the function with these steps:

1. Move your cursor to I20 and enter the function @SUM
   (E20...H20).

As you will recall, this function sums the range of cells defined within the parentheses — in this case cells E20, F20, G20, and H20.

The % SALES column tells you what percent of net sales a budget category is. It is calculated by dividing the total for a budget category by total NET SALES (I22). In this way you can judge what part of your net sales goes to each category.

2. Move your cursor to cell J20, the % SALES for SALES.

3. Enter the formula +I20/I22 and press RETURN.

The word ERROR will appear in the cell. Don't be concerned about it now. You'll fix it in a minute.

Once the year's budgeted amounts have been entered, the TOTAL and % SALES formulas will be accurate for all the values calculated in columns I and J, regardless of budget category. Copy the formulas to all rows in those two columns.

4. Move your cursor to I20.

5. Press OA-C for Copy.

6. Press RETURN to confirm that the copy is Within worksheet.

7. Press the RIGHT ARROW one time to highlight both cells I20 and J20 and press RETURN to verify that the correct source is highlighted.

8. Press the DOWN ARROW once, enter a period (.) to anchor the copy, and press the OA-DOWN ARROW three times

and the UP ARROW two times until you reach cell I48;
then press RETURN.

9. Enter **R** three times and press RETURN once to indicate
that the two source cells in the TOTAL and the first in
the % SALES are to be copied in the Relative manner
and that the last source cell in the % SALES is to be
copied with No change.

The functions will be copied to all the cells. You will see
erroneous amounts in the TOTAL column and the word
ERROR in the % SALES column. This is because you have
not yet entered the values making up many of the totals and
percents. Ignore the incorrect numbers and error messages.
They will be corrected as the values are entered and recalculated. You will also notice that the wrong numbers and error
messages exist in cells that should be blank. These will be
erased later and can be ignored for now.

Formatting % SALES

The values in column J, % SALES, are percentages and must
be formatted as such. Doing so will correct some of the
erroneous results now on the screen. Follow these steps:

1. Move your cursor to J20 and press OA-L for Layout.

2. Enter **B** for Block, and press the DOWN ARROW until
cell J48 is highlighted; then press RETURN.

3. Press RETURN for Value format.

4. Enter **P** for Percent and **1** for 1 decimal place; then
press RETURN.

Entering the First Quarter Formula

Another formula that is the same for all budget categories is
the first quarter column. In all cases, that column is the sum
of values for the first three months. (You will see later how to

change some of these to simplify data entry.) Cells E21, E22, E24, and E26 already contain formulas that you previously had copied into them. But in order to save you some work in entering formulas for rows 28 to 48, you can go ahead and overwrite these existing formulas, since they achieve the same result as adding the first three months' figures.

1. Place your cursor on cell E20 and press OA-C for Copy.

2. Press RETURN to verify that the copy is to be made within the spreadsheet.

3. Press RETURN again to verify that E20 is the correct source.

4. Press the DOWN ARROW once, enter a period (.), and press the DOWN ARROW again until the cursor rests on cell E48; then press RETURN.

5. Type **R** twice to signify a Relative copy.

Not only will inaccurate totals be placed in the cells, but cells that should be blank will contain totals. Press OA-K and see how the values are corrected for you. This is what your screen should look like:

```
File: Newstore88.bud            REVIEW/ADD/CHANGE              Escape: Main Menu
=============A=============B======C=======D=======E=======F=======G====
   5|EMPLOYEES          NUMBER  SALARIES       1ST GWTH    8.0%
   6|   STORE MANAGER      1    2,500          2ND GWTH   12.0%
   7|   ASST. MANAGER      1    2,000          3RD GWTH   10.0%
   8|   SENIOR CLERK       1    1,600          4TH GWTH   15.0%
   9|   JUNIOR CLERK       3    1,200          RETURNS     2.0%
======B======C======D=======E=======F=======G======H======I======J====
  18| -----------------------------------------------------------------
  19|
  20|    0  35,000  37,800  72,800 127,008 139,709 160,665 500,182  102.0%
  21|    0     700     756   1,456   2,540   2,794   3,213  10,004    2.0%
  22|    0  34,300  37,044  71,344 124,468 136,915 157,452 490,178  100.0%
  23|                            0                              0     0.0%
  24|    0  21,609  23,338  44,947  78,415  86,256  99,195 308,812   63.0%
  25|                            0                              0     0.0%
  26|    0  12,691  13,706  26,397  46,053  50,658  58,257 181,366   37.0%
  27|                            0                              0     0.0%
  28|                            0                              0     0.0%
  29|                            0                              0     0.0%
---------------------------------------------------------------------
E20: (Value) @SUM(B20...D20)

Type entry or use ⌂ commands ___                        ⌂-? for Help
```

Now look at the top and the left side of the bottom window.

Freezing the Titles

The headings at the top and left side of the budget window have moved out of view. This is annoying because you cannot know what value you're entering without seeing the headings. You are able to correct this by freezing the titles in the bottom window in place.

1. Move your cursor so that the column headings in row 17 are in the upper-left corner of the window and column A is visible. Then move your cursor to cell B19.

The column and row headings should appear at the top and left edge of the bottom window, like this:

```
File: Newstore88.bud           REVIEW/ADD/CHANGE              Escape: Main Menu
=============A=============B=======C=======D=======E=======F=======G====
   5|EMPLOYEES           NUMBER   SALARIES           1ST GWTH     8.0%
   6|  STORE MANAGER          1    2,500            2ND GWTH    12.0%
   7|  ASST. MANAGER          1    2,000            3RD GWTH    10.0%
   8|  SENIOR CLERK           1    1,600            4TH GWTH    15.0%
   9|  JUNIOR CLERK           3    1,200            RETURNS      2.0%
=============A=============B=======C=======D=======E=======F=======G====
  17|BUDGET CATEGORY      JAN      FEB      MAR      QTR1     QTR2     QTR3
  18|-----------------------------------------------------------------
  19|REVENUE
  20|  SALES                  0   35,000   37,800   72,800  127,008  139,709
  21|  RETURNS                0      700      756    1,456    2,540    2,794
  22|    NET SALES            0   34,300   37,044   71,344  124,468  136,915
  23|                                                   0
  24|    COST OF SALES        0   21,609   23,338   44,947   78,415   86,256
  25|                                                   0
  26|GROSS PROFIT             0   12,691   13,706   26,397   46,053   50,658
  27|                                                   0
  28|EXPENSES                                           0
-----------------------------------------------------------------
B19

Type entry or use ⌘ commands __                        ⌘-? for Help
```

Cell B19 is immediately to the right of the row headings and below the column headings. It marks the upper leftmost corner of the window that is to remain unfrozen. Follow these steps to freeze the headings:

2. Press OA-T for Titles.

3. Enter **B** to indicate that you wish Both top and left-side titles to be frozen.

Now move your cursor down using OA-DOWN ARROW. You'll see that the column headings do not disappear. No matter what row you are on, you can still see the column headings. Now return to the top using the OA-UP ARROW.

Move your cursor to the right using OA-RIGHT ARROW. See how the row headings do not disappear even though you have moved off the first screen. No matter what column you move to, you can still see the row heading. Return to the left by using the OA-LEFT ARROW.

You may notice that your headings are duplicated on the screen if you move too far to the left. This is only a visual effect; the spreadsheet still has only one set of row and column headings. AppleWorks provides this means of allowing you to change the headings if you want to, since the cursor cannot otherwise get to them in their frozen state. If you move your cursor down and to the right, the duplicate headings will disappear. However, for purposes of preparing a budget, you won't want to alter the row headings, but rather to protect them from being changed.

Protecting the Row Headings

By default, the standard value for the Protection feature is On. This means that if you want to protect any cells from accidental change or erasure, you can do so simply by taking one more step. Follow these steps to protect the row headings from being changed:

1. Move your cursor to column A, row 19.

2. Press OA-L for Layout.

3. Enter **B** for Block, press the DOWN ARROW until cell A48 is highlighted, and then press RETURN.

You will be asked which of several formatting tasks you want to define standards.

4. Enter **P** for Protection.

You will be asked to define the extent of the protection that you want—from no protection, which would allow any changes, to total protection, which would allow no changes. You want total protection.

5. Enter **N** for Nothing.

Now no changes can be made to the row headings in the budget area of the spreadsheet.

Entering Values for the EXPENSES

You will be entering three kinds of values for expenses: those that are constant amounts from month to month; those that vary from month to month but are not based on any other figures; and those that are based on other values and consequently are calculated from formulas and functions. Enter the constant values first.

Constant value expenses.   The constant values you will be entering in the EXPENSES column of the budget are based upon the constant values entered in the Assumptions section. Move your cursor to the assumptions window using the OA-J command and find the cell containing the TOTAL SALARIES amount. This is cell B11. With that cell number in mind, move into view the assumptions defining the constant values for the rent, utilities, and other expenses in column I, rows 5 through 9. When you can see as many assumptions as possible in these columns (you should be able to see from RENT to INSUR.), jump back to the budget window and follow these steps.

1. Move your cursor to cell B29, SALARIES, under the EXPENSES category.

2. Enter **+B11** to point to the constant value in the Assumptions section and press the RIGHT ARROW.

3. Enter the same value in cells C29 and D29.

The formula for the first quarter's salaries has already been entered, so move on to the second quarter's salaries, cell F29.

4. Enter the formula +B11*3 to multiply the month's salaries, which are fixed, by 3 to get the quarter's salaries.

5. Enter the same formula into the third and fourth quarters' salary cells.

Now let's enter the constant RENT expense, which is also fixed, in a slightly different way by copying the formulas to the appropriate cells.

6. Move your cursor to cell B34, STORE RENT for January.

7. Enter the value +I5, which points to the rent assumption.

8. Copy this cell to C34 and D34, copying the pointer with No change.

The formula for the first quarter's rent has been entered for you, but now you need to establish the rent for the rest of the quarters.

9. Move your cursor to cell F34, the second quarter's rent.

10. Enter +I5*3 to multiply the constant assumption value by 3, and then press RETURN.

11. Copy the formulas to the third and fourth quarters, copying the constant value with No change.

The entire RENT expense is now entered. Now enter the rest of the constant expenses: UTILITIES, MAINTENANCE, DEPRECIATION, INSURANCE, TELEPHONE, and MISCELLANEOUS. The values for the first quarter have already been established. Thus, for the months of January, February, and March, you should either directly enter or copy the pointer to the value in the Assumptions section for these six expenses. If you're not sure of the location of the values in the Assumptions section or can't see them in the top window, use the Jump command to move to the top window, place your cursor on the assumption you want, and then jump back and enter the cell coordinates.

For the other quarters, either enter the formula to multiply the constant value by 3, or copy the formula. Because the TOTAL column has been previously calculated, move on to the next expense item when you reach the TOTAL column.

When you're finished, press OA-K to calculate the values. The budget should now look like this:

File: Newstore88.bud

Page 1
8/15/87

A B C   C O M P A N Y
BUDGET TO ADD STORE 1988

=======================================ASSUMPTIONS=======================================

EMPLOYEES	NUMBER	SALARIES	1ST GWTH	8.0%	RENT	2,000
STORE MANAGER	1	2,500	2ND GWTH	12.0%	UTIL.	400
ASST. MANAGER	1	2,000	3RD GWTH	10.0%	MAINT.	500
SENIOR CLERK	1	1,600	4TH GWTH	15.0%	DEPREC.	750
JUNIOR CLERK	3	1,200	RETURNS	2.0%	INSUR.	250
			C O S	63.0%	PHONE	150
TOTAL SALARIES	9,700		P/R TAX	15.0%	MISCEL.	150
			FRINGE	7.0%		
			POST/FGT	1.0%		
			EXC. TAX	.5%		

==BUDGET==

BUDGET CATEGORY	JAN	FEB	MAR	QTR1	QTR2	QTR3	QTR4	TOTAL	%SALES
REVENUE									
SALES	0	35,000	37,800	72,800	127,008	139,709	160,665	500,182	102.0%
RETURNS	0	700	756	1,456	2,540	2,794	3,213	10,004	2.0%
NET SALES	0	34,300	37,044	71,344	124,468	136,915	157,452	490,178	100.0%
				0				0	0.0%
COST OF SALES	0	21,609	23,338	44,947	78,415	86,256	99,195	308,812	63.0%
				0				0	0.0%
GROSS PROFIT	0	12,691	13,706	26,397	46,053	50,658	58,257	181,366	37.0%
				0				0	0.0%
EXPENSES				0				0	0.0%
SALARIES	9,700	9,700	9,700	29,100	29,100	29,100	29,100	116,400	23.7%
PAYROLL TAXES				0				0	0.0%
FRINGE BENEFITS				0				0	0.0%
SUBTOTAL LABOR				0				0	0.0%
				0				0	0.0%
STORE RENT	2,000	2,000	2,000	6,000	6,000	6,000	6,000	24,000	4.9%
UTILITIES	400	400	400	1,200	1,200	1,200	1,200	4,800	1.0%
MAINTENANCE	500	500	500	1,500	1,500	1,500	1,500	6,000	1.2%
DEPRECIATION	750	750	750	2,250	2,250	2,250	2,250	9,000	1.8%
ADVERTISING				0				0	0.0%
POSTAGE & FREIGHT				0				0	0.0%
INSURANCE	250	250	250	750	750	750	750	3,000	.6%
TELEPHONE	150	150	150	450	450	450	450	1,800	.4%
EXCISE TAXES				0				0	0.0%
MISCELLANEOUS	150	150	150	450	450	450	450	1,800	.4%
SUBTOTAL NONLAB				0				0	0.0%
				0				0	0.0%
TOTAL EXPENSE				0				0	0.0%
				0				0	0.0%
NET PROFIT				0				0	0.0%

Check your figures on your screen against these and correct any discrepancies.

Fluctuating expenses.   Some expenses cannot be based on a constant value and are not based upon other values in the budget. The ADVERTISING expense is this type of expense; it must be estimated from your experience and intuition. In this case it has been decided that the advertising will be fairly heavy during the startup months and then taper down through the year. Follow these steps to enter the ADVERTISING expenses:

1. Move your cursor to cell B38.

2. Enter **1500** in the January, February, and March advertising cells.

3. Enter **2000, 1750,** and **1500** in the second, third, and fourth quarters' cells respectively.

4. Press OA-K to calculate the values.

Formulas and functions.   The rest of the expenses are based upon values in other budget categories and can be calculated by formulas and functions. Let's enter them now.

First enter the PAYROLL TAXES, FRINGE BENEFITS, and SUBTOTAL LABOR expenses. PAYROLL TAXES are based upon a percentage, which is stated in the Assumptions section, multiplied by the salaries for the month or quarter. In several cases you will be overwriting the formula in the first quarter cell with a new one. Either formula gives you exactly the same result.

1. Move your cursor to the PAYROLL TAXES expense for January, in cell B30.

2. Enter the formula **+B29*F11** and copy it across the row to the fourth quarter's cell (H30), copying the

SALARIES pointer (B29) Relatively and the Assumptions pointer (F11) with No change.

The fringe benefits are very similar to the payroll taxes. They are estimated to be a percent of the salary expenses for the same period.

3. Move your cursor to cell B31, the FRINGE BENEFITS expense for January.

4. Enter the formula +B29*F12 and copy it across the row to the fourth quarter's cell, copying the SALARIES pointer (B29) Relatively and the Assumptions pointer (F12) with No change.

The SUBTOTAL LABOR expense is simply the sum of salaries, payroll taxes, and fringe benefits.

5. Move your cursor to cell B32, the SUBTOTAL LABOR expense for January.

6. Enter the function @SUM(B29...B31).

7. Copy the function to all other cells in the SUBTOTAL LABOR row, copying both pointers Relatively.

POSTAGE & FREIGHT are the next expenses to be entered. They are estimated using an assumed percentage of NET SALES for the same period. Using 0A-J, jump to the top window and bring the postage and freight and the excise tax percentages into view. Then jump back to the bottom window.

8. Enter the formula +B22*F13 in cell B39, the January POSTAGE & FREIGHT cell.

9. Copy the formula to all cells up to the fourth quarter, copying the NET SALES pointer Relatively and the Assumptions pointer with No change.

The EXCISE TAXES are calculated in the same way. They are estimated by assumed percent of NET SALES.

10. Enter the formula +**B22∗F14** in cell B42, the January EXCISE TAXES expense cell.

11. Copy the formula to all cells up to the fourth quarter, copying the NET SALES pointer Relatively and the Assumptions pointer with No change.

The final three formulas for SUBTOTAL NONLABOR, TOTAL EXPENSE, and NET PROFIT are all very similar and can be entered and then copied at one time, saving some effort. Follow these steps:

12. Enter the function @**SUM(B34...B43)** in the January SUBTOTAL NONLABOR expense, cell B44.

13. Enter the formula +**B32+B44** in the January TOTAL EXPENSE, cell B46.

14. Enter the formula +**B26−B46** in the January NET PROFIT, cell B48.

15. Now return to cell B44 and press OA-C for Copy.

16. Press RETURN to verify Within worksheet.

17. To define the source cells, press the DOWN ARROW four times until cells B44, B45, B46, B47, and B48 are highlighted, and press RETURN.

18. To define the destination for the copy operations, press the RIGHT ARROW once, enter a period(.), press the RIGHT ARROW five times until the cursor reaches the fourth quarter's cells, and press RETURN.

19. Enter **R** six times to copy all the pointers Relatively.

Now move your cursor to cell J48 and press OA-K to perform the calculations. See how rows 44, 46, and 48 are filled in for you, like this:

File: Newstore88.bud

A B C   C O M P A N Y
BUDGET TO ADD STORE 1988

==ASSUMPTIONS==

EMPLOYEES	NUMBER	SALARIES					
STORE MANAGER	1	2,500	1ST GWTH	8.0%	RENT	2,000	
ASST. MANAGER	1	2,000	2ND GWTH	12.0%	UTIL.	400	
SENIOR CLERK	1	1,600	3RD GWTH	10.0%	MAINT.	500	
JUNIOR CLERK	3	1,200	4TH GWTH	15.0%	DEPREC.	750	
			RETURNS	2.0%	INSUR.	250	
			C O S	63.0%	PHONE	150	
TOTAL SALARIES	9,700		P/R TAX	15.0%	MISCEL.	150	
			FRINGE	7.0%			
			POST/FGT	1.0%			
			EXC. TAX	.5%			

==BUDGET==

BUDGET CATEGORY	JAN	FEB	MAR	QTR1	QTR2	QTR3	QTR4	TOTAL	%SALES
REVENUE									
SALES	0	35,000	37,800	72,800	127,008	139,709	160,665	500,182	102.0%
RETURNS	0	700	756	1,456	2,540	2,794	3,213	10,004	2.0%
NET SALES	0	34,300	37,044	71,344	124,468	136,915	157,452	490,178	100.0%
				0				0	0.0%
COST OF SALES	0	21,609	23,338	44,947	78,415	86,256	99,195	308,812	63.0%
				0				0	0.0%
GROSS PROFIT	0	12,691	13,706	26,397	46,053	50,658	58,257	181,366	37.0%
				0				0	0.0%
EXPENSES				0				0	0.0%
SALARIES	9,700	9,700	9,700	29,100	29,100	29,100	29,100	116,400	23.7%
PAYROLL TAXES	1,455	1,455	1,455	4,365	4,365	4,365	4,365	17,460	3.6%
FRINGE BENEFITS	679	679	679	2,037	2,037	2,037	2,037	8,148	1.7%
SUBTOTAL LABOR	11,834	11,834	11,834	35,502	35,502	35,502	35,502	142,008	29.0%
				0				0	0.0%
STORE RENT	2,000	2,000	2,000	6,000	6,000	6,000	6,000	24,000	4.9%
UTILITIES	400	400	400	1,200	1,200	1,200	1,200	4,800	1.0%
MAINTENANCE	500	500	500	1,500	1,500	1,500	1,500	6,000	1.2%
DEPRECIATION	750	750	750	2,250	2,250	2,250	2,250	9,000	1.8%
ADVERTISING	1,500	1,500	1,500	4,500	2,000	1,750	1,500	9,750	2.0%
POSTAGE & FREIGHT	0	343	370	713	1,245	1,369	1,575	4,902	1.0%
INSURANCE	250	250	250	750	750	750	750	3,000	.6%
TELEPHONE	150	150	150	450	450	450	450	1,800	.4%
EXCISE TAXES	0	172	185	357	622	685	787	2,451	.5%
MISCELLANEOUS	150	150	150	450	450	450	450	1,800	.4%
SUBTOTAL NONLAB	5,700	6,214	6,256	18,170	16,467	16,404	16,462	67,503	13.8%
								0	0.0%
TOTAL EXPENSE	17,534	18,048	18,090	53,672	51,969	51,906	51,964	209,511	42.7%
								0	0.0%
NET PROFIT	(17,534)	(5,358)	(4,383)	(27,275)	(5,916)	(1,247)	6,293	(28,145)	-5.7%

It is now time to tidy up the spreadsheet.

Tidying Up

Several rows contain zero values where none should be. You can clear these rows by blanking the cells using the OA-B command, just as you did in Chapter 5. Since you're familiar with the command, we will just review it here once, and then you may continue with the cleanup on your own.

1. Move your cursor to row 23.

2. Press OA-B for Blank.

3. Enter **R** for Rows.

4. Press RETURN to verify that row 23 is appropriately highlighted.

Because you protected the row headings earlier, you will be asked whether you really want to clear protection now. The screen looks like this:

```
File: Newstore88.bud              BLANK          Escape: Review/Add/Change
======C=======D=======E=======F=======G=======H=======I=======J=======K====




                        You are about to clear
                        or remove protected cells.




----------------------------------------------------------------------------
B23

Do you really want to do this?  No  Yes
```

5. Enter **Y** for Yes.

Row 23 will be cleared. Now continue to clear rows 25, 27, 28 (only columns B to J, not the whole row), 33, 45, and 47 in the same way.

Now that you've built your spreadsheet, let's briefly explore its potential before printing the final product.

Playing What-If Games

One of the most powerful capabilities of spreadsheets is the opportunity they afford to vary assumptions and see how the results affect the base line calculations. Let's play a short "what-if" game and see how this works.

Suppose you have just interviewed a most promising young person for the position of junior clerk in your store. Although you have already hired your maximum number of employees, this individual has good experience, is very intelligent, has ambition, and is married to the boss's son. What if you were to hire this individual in the new store? How would it affect your plans to break even in eight months?

1. Press OA-9 and move the cursor to J48 to view the bottom right corner of the spreadsheet.

The critical part of the budget is now showing. If you should change an assumption, you will immediately see the results on the bottom line, the third quarter's net profits.

2. Press OA-J to jump to the Assumptions window.

If necessary, move your cursor so that the screen looks like this:

```
File: Newstore88.bud        REVIEW/ADD/CHANGE           Escape: Main Menu
=============A=============B=======C=======D=======E=======F=======G====
 7|  ASST. MANAGER      1    2,000        3RD GWTH   10.0%
 8|  SENIOR CLERK       1    1,600        4TH GWTH   15.0%
 9|  JUNIOR CLERK       3    1,200        RETURNS     2.0%
10|                                       C O S      63.0%
11|TOTAL SALARIES       9,700             P/R TAX    15.0%
=============A=============E=======F=======G=======H=======I=======J====
17|BUDGET CATEGORY     QTR1    QTR2    QTR3    QTR4   TOTAL    %SALES
18|--------------------------------------------------------------------
44|    SUBTOTAL NONLAB 18,170  16,467  16,404  16,462  67,503   13.8%
45|
46|TOTAL EXPENSE       53,672  51,969  51,906  51,964 209,511   42.7%
47|
48|NET PROFIT         (27,275) (5,916) (1,247)  6,293 (28,145)  -5.7%
49|
50|
51|
52|
53|
--------------------------------------------------------------------------
A11: (Label) TOTAL SALARIES

Type entry or use Ú commands __                        Ú-? for Help
```

3. Move your cursor to the employee NUMBER column.

4. Change the number of junior clerks from 3 to 4.

5. Press OA-K to recalculate the results.

Voila! The impact of an additional junior clerk is immediately reflected. You can see the TOTAL SALARIES change to 10,900 from 9,700 in the top window. And in the bottom window you see the effect this increase has on NET PROFIT and % SALES. In each quarter the total expense increased by $4392 so the net profit declined by the same amount.

```
File: Newstore88.bud          REVIEW/ADD/CHANGE              Escape: Main Menu
=============A=============B=======C=======D=======E=======F=======G====
     7|  ASST. MANAGER          1    2000      3RD GWTH    10.0%
     8|  SENIOR CLERK            1    1600      4TH GWTH    15.0%
     9|  JUNIOR CLERK            4    1200      RETURNS      2.0%
    10|                                         C O S       63.0%
    11|TOTAL SALARIES         10,900             P/R TAX    15.0%
=============A=============E=======F=======G=======H=======I=======J====
    17|BUDGET CATEGORY        QTR1    QTR2    QTR3    QTR4   TOTAL  % SALES
    18|------------------------------------------------------------------
    44|     SUBTOTAL NONLAB  18,170  16,467  16,404  16,462  67,503   13.8%
    45|
    46|TOTAL EXPENSE         58,064  56,361  56,298  56,356 227,079   46.3%
    47|
    48|NET PROFIT          (31,667)(10,308) (5,639)  1,901 (45,713)   -9.3%
    49|
    50|
    51|
    52|
    53|
---------------------------------------------------------------------------
J53

Type entry or use ⌘ commands __                        ⌘-? for Help
```

Suppose you decide that sales may not in fact decline in the third quarter. Despite the fact that declines in sales are normal in summer, there is a great demand for your product in the immediate vicinity of your store, and the decline may not be experienced. To make the change in the projection for third-quarter growth, follow these steps.

6. Change the 3RD GWTH from 10.0% to 12.0% (remember to enter it as **.12**).

7. Press OA-K and watch the results.

Even with the increased growth rate, the cost of the new employee substantially dampens the profit figures for the year. You must make a decision to reduce the costs if your planned breakeven point is to be achieved. Using the method just used to change the variables for the number of employees and the third quarter's sales projections, experiment with adjusting some of the costs to see how these variations affect overall profits for the year. The power to adjust variables and instantly see the results is one of the great advantages of spreadsheets.

As with all other files, it is important to save the file at this point. Press OA-S for Save.

Now let's take a quick look at the printer options before you print the file.

Printing the Budget

Press OA-O to get the Printer Options menu:

```
File: Newstore88.bud        PRINTER OPTIONS        Escape: Review/Add/Change
===============================================================================


      -------Left and right margins-------      ------Top and bottom margins------
PW: Platen Width              8.0 inches    PL: Paper Length         11.0 inches
LM: Left Margin               0.0 inches    TM: Top Margin            0.0 inches
RM: Right Margin              0.0 inches    BM: Bottom Margin         0.0 inches
CI: Chars per Inch           10             LI: Lines per Inch        6

    Line width                8.0 inches        Printing Length      11.0 inches
    Char per Line (est)      80                 Lines per page        66

              -------------------Formatting options-------------------
      SC:  Send Special Codes to printer                        No
      PH:  Print report Header at top of each page              Yes
           Single, Double or Triple Spacing (SS/DS/TS)          SS



-------------------------------------------------------------------------------
Type a two letter option code __                              51K Avail.
```

You have worked with most of the options listed on this menu. Here are the two options with which you may be only somewhat familiar.

The first is the SC option—Send Special Codes to printer. This option allows you to embed special characters in your spreadsheet that direct the printer to perform certain actions not supported by AppleWorks' spreadsheet formatting. For example, you might want to print certain values in boldface or to underline them. The default for the SC option is No.

The second option is PH, Print report Header at top of each page. The PH option allows you to decide whether printing the filename and date as headers is appropriate for each spreadsheet or not. The default is Yes.

Now change some basic options. Specifically, you'll want to print the spreadsheet on one 8 1/2- by 11-inch page, if possible, with comfortable margins. As you can see, the platen width is 8.0 inches—too narrow for the spreadsheet. Change the platen width to 8.5 inches. Since you can only get 85 characters on a line at that width, and you need room for at least 92, you must also change the Characters per Inch (CI) to 12. (In your current worksheet there are 9 columns of 8 characters each plus 1 column of 20 characters, which equals 92 characters.) By changing the CI to 12 characters per inch, you will be able to squeeze 102 characters on a line, which will be just fine for the printout of the spreadsheet.

You should also change the top and bottom margins to 1.0 inch. The left margin should be changed to 0.3 inches, the right margin to 0.2 inches. You'll note that you have room for four extra characters on each line of print, which is not so many that you're wasting space on the page or so few that you're unable to fit everything on the page.

Now you are ready to print the spreadsheet. Press ESC to return to the Review/Add/Change screen.

Press OA-P to print the spreadsheet. You want to print All of the budget. After selecting your named printer on the Print menu, type in today's date and request one copy.

The spreadsheet should now be printing. Your results should look like those shown at the beginning of the chapter, in Figure 8-1. Save your file by pressing OA-S.

Verifying the Results

Compare the results of your spreadsheet with those in Figure 8-1. If they are not the same, you need to find out why. The differences can be the result of three factors: (1) your rows and columns may not correspond to those shown in the figure; (2) your entered values, such as the constants and number values, may not be the same; (3) the formulas, functions, or pointers may not be correct.

Track down any error and correct it; perform the recalculation again. Continue to do this until your spreadsheet exactly matches Figure 8-1. Remember to save your final copy.

In this chapter you have learned the more complex spreadsheet functions, such as windows, freezing titles, and entering varied and detailed formulas and functions. You are now ready to learn to tie AppleWorks' three components together and how to use a mailing program tailored to AppleWorks to generate customized letters to your customers.

Integration and Mail Merge: The Final Step

Integration, as you will recall, is the ability to combine information from different components easily and quickly. Integration allows you to use the right component for the task at hand. For example, you could use the word processor to create a spreadsheet, but doing so would be time-consuming and awkward. The word processor, which handles word processing very well, simply isn't designed to handle the functions needed to create a spreadsheet. Through integration, however, you can use the spreadsheet to create the type of material it does best and then move or copy the information to the word processor so that it can be merged with the text created there. In this way you have the best of both worlds.

Within AppleWorks you can integrate by using one of three techniques to transfer information: moving or copying information to the Clipboard using cut and paste motions, "printing" information to the Clipboard, or "printing" to DIF files.

The first technique is used when you are transferring information between two files created by the same component; for example, when you want to move text from one word processing file to another. You cut text (from a word processing file), records (from a data base file), or lines (from the spreadsheet) by temporarily moving or copying whatever you've defined onto the Clipboard. You paste the data by moving or copying it from the Clipboard into the second file. When you *move* part of a file, the original is permanently erased and placed somewhere else. When you *copy*, the original remains intact and a duplicate of it is placed somewhere else.

The second technique is used to transfer information from the spreadsheet or data base components to the word processor. In this case, you format a report that contains the information you want and then "print" it to the Clipboard rather than to the printer. Then, you move or copy the report from the Clipboard into your word processing file.

The third technique is used when you are transferring information from the data base to the spreadsheet, or vice versa. In this case, you also format and print a report, but this time to a DIF file rather than to the Clipboard. Once you have "printed" the file you wish to integrate to the DIF file, you switch to the other component and call up the DIF file as the source of a new data base or spreadsheet. If you want to copy or move information after the new file has been edited, you can use the normal cut and paste to the Clipboard technique.

Table 9-1 summarizes the various techniques for transferring information.

In this chapter you will do two different exercises to demonstrate integration in AppleWorks. In the first, you will combine the data base inventory list created in Chapter 7 and the spreadsheet budget for adding the new store created in Chapter 8 with the business plan text created in Chapter 6. The second exercise will demonstrate another type of integration that is very useful to most people: merging a form letter with a name and address list. This kind of *mail merge* operation allows you to create a common but personalized letter for all the names on a mailing list without retyping each letter. In the exercise illustrating the mail merge operation, you will combine the letter you created in Chapter 2 with the customer list you created in Chapter 4 to produce personalized letters that could be sent to customers.

Table 9-1. Transferring Information Between Components

From:	To:	Use This Technique:
Spreadsheet	Spreadsheet	Move or copy to and from the Clipboard using OA-M or OA-C
Data Base	Data Base	Move or copy to and from the Clipboard using OA-M or OA-C
Word processor	Word Processor	Move or copy to and from the Clipboard using OA-M or OA-C
Spreadsheet	Word Processor	Print to the Clipboard using OA-P
Data Base	Word Processor	Print to the Clipboard using OA-P
Spreadsheet	Data Base	Print to a DIF file using OA-P
Data Base	Spreadsheet	Print to a DIF file using OA-P

For the two exercises, you will need all three of the disks that you formatted in Chapter 2: AppleWorks1, containing the files from Chapters 2, 3, 4, and 5; AppleWorks2, containing the files from Chapters 6, 7, and 8; and AppleWorks3, as yet unused.

Let's get started by building the business plan. For this first exercise you will need the files you created in Chapters 6, 7, and 8. Specifically, they are the word processing Busplan88.unf, the data base BegInv.lst, and the spreadsheet Newstore88.bud. All of these should be on the AppleWorks2 disk. When you have this disk in hand, start up your computer, make drive 2 your current drive, insert the AppleWorks2 disk, and get to the Main Menu.

Integrating Data Base and Word Processing Files

You will start by combining your data base Inventory List with your business plan. After placing both the word processing and data base files on the Desktop, you will format a data base report. Since you do not want all the detailed records from the data base within the business plan, you will format the report to print only the lines containing totals, not all the lines. You will print the report to the Clipboard. Then, in the word processing file, you will find the markers you left in the business plan to mark the place for the data base information, and you will move the report from the Clipboard into the business plan.

Putting the Files on the Desktop

Your first task is to place the two files that you will be working with, Busplan88.unf and BegInv.lst, on the Desktop. In the future, you may have files that are too large to place on the Desktop at one time. When this happens, you will have to place the files on the Desktop one at a time. After each step you will erase the file from the Desktop so that you can place the next file on the Desktop. This process is slower and more cumbersome, but having the ability to integrate information from various components when you need it makes the process worthwhile, regardless of the effort.

Another task you may face is retrieving your files from more than one disk. You will have to insert one disk into the drive, add one file to the Desktop, and then change disks and add the next file to the Desktop. Fortunately, both of your files will fit on the Desktop at one time, and both are contained on the same disk, so the task is simplified.

Add the two files onto the Desktop memory now. Go to the Review/Add/Change screen and view the BegInv.1st file so that you can format the data base report.

Formatting the Data Base Report

You are going to create a simple report from the data base Inventory List. The list now consists of detailed inventory records. You will create a report that consists only of the lines showing totals by vendor of the inventory items, since the business plan is not an appropriate place to list detailed records. Of course, an actual business plan would have many

more lines than the three that this plan will have.
Follow these steps to format the report:

1. Press OA-P for Print.

You already have a report for the BegInv.lst file named Start-up Inventory. Since that report contains much of what you want, create a copy and then modify it.

2. Choose option 4, Duplicate an existing format, and when prompted, press RETURN to verify the name of the report to be duplicated.

3. Name the new report format **Inventory Totals**, and press RETURN.

The Report Format screen will be displayed.

```
File: BegInv.lst              REPORT FORMAT              Escape: Report Menu
Report: Inventory Totals
Selection: All records


Group totals on: VENDOR
===============================================================================
--> or <--  Move cursor                    a-J  Right justify this category
  >  a  <    Switch category positions     a-K  Define a calculated category
--> a <--   Change column width            a-N  Change report name and/or title
a-A  Arrange (sort) on this category       a-O  Printer options
a-D  Delete this category                  a-P  Print the report
a-G  Add/remove group totals               a-R  Change record selection rules
a-I  Insert a prev. deleted category       a-T  Add/remove category totals
-------------------------------------------------------------------------------

ITEM NAME DESCRIPTION               VENDOR   COST     MIN.QTY.      TOTAL COST
=A------- -B--------------------- -C---- -D---- -E-------- -F--------
f100      Dupe film 12x18           999999   999.99   9999999999    9999999.99
f25       Photostat screen 1/2      999999   999.99   9999999999    9999999.99
f30       Photostat screen 10x12    999999   999.99   9999999999    9999999.99
                                                                    ==========
----------------------------------------------------------------------- More --->
Use options shown above to change report format               51K Avail.
```

The current report contains group totals by vendor number, as noted on the screen immediately above the double line. You want to keep the group totals, but you must redefine the feature so that it only prints total lines, not the detail lines as well. This requires that you cancel the current group total and replace it with another one.

4. Move your cursor to column C, VENDOR.

5. Press OA-G for Group to remove the current group total definition.

6. Press OA-G again to create a new group total definition.

7. Enter **Y** for Yes to print group totals only.

The message above the options should now read, "Group totals only on: VENDOR."

Now change one of the printer options so that the data base page headers are not printed. The business plan has its own headers that are more appropriate. Also, you want to make sure that the platen width and margins are wide enough for the 79 characters in the report (you can tell how wide your report is by looking at the LEN setting at the right edge of the screen).

8. Press OA-O for Options so that you can alter some printing options.

9. Enter **PH** for Page Header and press RETURN.

The default for the page header has been changed from Yes to No, which is what you want, and the platen width and margins are already ample for 79 characters. The rest of the options are not important since they will be removed from the file when you move it from the Clipboard to the word processor file, so exit and print the report.

10. Press ESC to exit the Printer Options menu.

11. Press OA-P for Print.

12. Select the option, The Clipboard (for the Word Processor), and press RETURN.

A message will be displayed informing you that the report has been printed to the Clipboard.

13. Press the spacebar to continue.

14. Press ESC twice to return to the Review/Add/Change screen.

Combining the Data Base
With the Word Processing File

Your report is on the Clipboard, ready to be inserted into the word processing business plan. You must bring up the business plan, find the spot where the report is to be inserted, and move it there from the Clipboard. Follow these steps to do this:

1. Press OA-Q to get a Quick index of what is presently on the Desktop.

2. Move the cursor to Busplan88.unf and press RETURN.

The word processing file should now be in front of you. You must find the marker you inserted in the text for the data base. If you recall, this marker is called Marker 1.

3. Press OA-F for Find.

4. Enter **M** for Marker and **1** for marker number, and press RETURN.

This screen will be displayed:

```
File: Busplan88.unf                    FIND              Escape: Review/Add/Change
=====|====|====|====|====|====|====|====|====|====|====|====|====|====|====|===
the Renton store.▓
▓
     The rest of the employees will be hired especially for
the new store.  The details concerning the number of persons
hired and the skills needed are described under the
Financial Plan.▓
▓
     The list of startup inventory items which will be used
to initially stock the store is as follows:▓
--------Set a Marker: 1
▓
(from data base)▓
▓
- - - - - - - - - - - - - End of Page 15- - - - - - - - - - - - - - - -
^Marketing Plan^▓
     Advertising will begin one month prior to opening.
There will be weekly 1/2 page advertisements in the leading
Bellevue newspapers.  In addition, a direct mail campaign
will be used to distribute announcements to Bellevue
businesses.  One week before the opening, a daily radio ad
---------------------------------------------------------------------------
Find next occurrence?  No  Yes
```

5. Press RETURN for No to discontinue the search for more number 1 markers.

You can now delete the comment "(from data base)," which is no longer needed. After that, insert the report from the Clipboard.

6. Press the DOWN ARROW to move the cursor to "(from data base)."

7. Press OA-D for Delete.

8. Press the DOWN ARROW once, the LEFT ARROW once, and press RETURN so that you can easily move the report from the Clipboard to this spot.

9. Press OA-M for Move.

10. Enter F for From Clipboard.

You will instantly see the following data base report on your screen.

```
File: Busplan88.unf          REVIEW/ADD/CHANGE          Escape: Main Menu
=====|====|====|====|====|====|====|====|====|====|====|====|====|====|====|===
the Renton store.※
※
     The rest of the employees will be hired especially for
the new store.  The details concerning the number of persons
hired and the skills needed are described under the
Financial Plan.※
※
     The list of startup inventory items which will be used
to initially stock the store is as follows:※
--------Set a Marker: 1
[]                                           85
          1611.00※
                                            102
           784.98※

          2395.98*※
--------------------------------------------------------------------------
Type entry or use ⌂ commands          Line 64  Column  1      ⌂-? for Help
```

You can also see that there are a couple of problems.

Modifying the Merged Data Base

One difficulty with the newly merged text is that there is a word wrap problem. The lines have wrapped around so that you cannot tell which numbers belong on which lines. You will now correct that and enter some titles for the numbers as well.

1. Press OA-1 to get to the beginning of the file.

2. Press OA-O to get to the Printer Options.

3. Change the Platen Width to **8.5** inches, the Right Margin to **.5** inches, and the Left Margin to **.5** inches.

4. Press ESC to return to the Review/Add/Change screen.

5. Press OA-6 to return to the text just above the merged data.

Although changing the platen width and margins for the data base report does not completely solve the word wrap problem, it does improve the situation. To solve the problem completely, however, you must make changes directly to the lines that have wrapped incorrectly.

You are going to correct the format of the report by deleting 24 spaces from each line. Then you are going to make the report more intelligible by adding a description to each total line and putting a dollar sign ($) in front of the dollar amounts.

6. Move your cursor to the left margin of the line immediately below -------- Set a Marker: 1, which contains the number 85.

7. Using OA-E to put your cursor in overstrike mode (the cursor will be a flashing block), enter the phrase **Film products from vendor:**.

8. Press the RIGHT ARROW ten times to move the cursor toward the vendor number, 85.

Your screen looks like this:

```
File: Busplan88.unf              REVIEW/ADD/CHANGE              Escape: Main Menu
=====|====|====|====|====|====|====|====|====|====|====|====|====|====|===
product lines that Office Mart carries.▨
 ▨
        Many of the startup personnel will initially be transferred from
the Renton store.  These employees will be returned to the Renton
store after two weeks time, except for the store manager who is to be
permanently promoted from the Renton store.▨
 ▨
        The rest of the employees will be hired especially for the new
store.  The details concerning the number of persons hired and the
skills needed are described under the Financial Plan.▨
 ▨
        The list of startup inventory items which will be used to
initially stock the store is as follows:▨
--------Set a Marker: 1
 ▨
Film products from vendor:           []   85
1611.00▨
                                          102
784.98▨
-------------------------------------------------------------------------------
Type entry or use Ć commands          Line 61  Column 37        Ć-? for Help
```

9. Press the DELETE key ten times to move the vendor number to the correct position.

10. Move your cursor to the first character in the number 1611.00 and press the DELETE key 14 times to position the column listing the prices to the right of the vendor number.

11. Move your cursor to the character preceding 1611.00 and type in a dollar sign (**$**).

With the dollar sign preceding the number 1611.00 and everything on one line, the first line should now be clearer. Now correct the next line.

12. Press the DOWN ARROW twice and then OA-LEFT ARROW twice to get to the left margin of the next report total line.

13. Enter **Paper products from vendor:**.

14. Move your cursor ten spaces to the right.

15. Press the DELETE key ten times.

16. Move the cursor to the first character in the price column and press DELETE 14 times to align it with the price above.

The second line is now corrected. Finally, correct the bottom line in the same way.

17. Press the DOWN ARROW twice and OA-LEFT ARROW once to move your cursor to the beginning of the last line (the blank line above the number 2395.98).

18. Enter **Total**.

19. Move the cursor ten spaces to the right.

20. Delete ten spaces from the line so that the total dollars are on the same line as the title.

21. Move the cursor to the first character of the dollar amount and press DELETE 14 times.

22. Place a dollar sign (**$**) in front of the total dollars, $2395.98.

Your screen should look like this:

```
File: Busplan88.unf          REVIEW/ADD/CHANGE              Escape: Main Menu
=====|====|====|====|====|====|====|====|====|====|====|====|====|====|===
The details concerning the number of persons hired and the skills needed are
described under the Financial Plan.※
※
     The list of startup inventory items which will be used to initially
stock the store is as follows:※
※
--------Set a Marker: 1
Film products from vendor:     85           $1611.00 ※
※
Paper products from vendor: 102              784.98 ※
※
Total                                    $2395.98* ※
※
※
^Marketing Plan^※
     Advertising will begin one month prior to opening.  There will be weekly
1/2 page advertisements in the leading Bellevue newspapers.  In addition, a
direct mail campaign will be used to distribute announcements to Bellevue
businesses.  One week before the opening, a daily radio ad will announce the
opening of om.  The ads will be timed to reach the Bellevue business during
---------------------------------------------------------------------------
Type entry or use @ commands          Line 64  Column 46      @-? for Help
```

You have now successfully transferred the data base information to the word processing file and edited it to fit nicely within the business plan.

The next task is the integration of the spreadsheet budget.

Integrating Your Spreadsheet With Your Word Processing File

Integrating the spreadsheet data will be accomplished in the same way that you integrated the data base records. You will put the spreadsheet file on the Desktop and create a new report for it. Then you will print the report to the Clipboard.

Preparing the Desktop

Although at this point you may not need to clear the Desktop in order to make room for the budget, in real practice you'll eventually experience not having enough memory to hold all your files at once on the Desktop. To practice what to do in this situation, it will be assumed that you are currently out of space on the Desktop.

To clear the Desktop area, first save your files and then remove them from the Desktop. Follow these steps:

1. Return to the Main Menu.

2. Select option 4, Remove files from the Desktop, and press RETURN.

3. For each of the two files on the Desktop, press the RIGHT ARROW to mark the files to be removed from the Desktop and then press RETURN.

For each of the files, a screen will be displayed that looks like this:

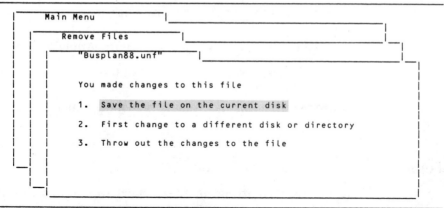

```
Disk: Disk 2                    "BUSPLAN88.UNF"           Escape: Remove Files
_____
 _____
|    Main Menu                  |                                           |
|  _____     |
| |    Remove Files             |                                     |     |
| |  _____   |_|     |
| | |    "Busplan88.unf"          |                             |  |_|      |
| | |                                                           |  |        |
| | |    You made changes to this file                          |  |        |
| | |    1.  [Save the file on the current disk]                |  |        |
| | |    2.  First change to a different disk or directory      |  |        |
| | |    3.  Throw out the changes to the file                  |  |        |
| | |                                                           |  |        |
|_|_|                                                           |  |        |
  | |                                                           |  |        |
  |_|_____|  |        |
    |_____|_|        |
_____
Type number, or use arrows, then press Return□               50K Avail.
```

You are informed that you want to remove a file that has had changes made to it and you are asked how you wish to dispose of the files. First, you can save the file, which will cause the current file on the disk to be overwritten (unless you change the name of the file). Second, you can change to a different disk. You do want to save these files on another disk since you want to preserve the original versions of your files for other purposes. So you'll replace the AppleWorks2 disk with the blank AppleWorks3 disk. Your third option is to throw out the changes that would result in the erasure of the Desktop copies without duplicates saved on disk.

4. Select option 2, First change to a different disk or directory.

5. Insert the AppleWorks3 disk into drive 2.

6. Select option 2, Disk 2, to tell AppleWorks where to expect the different disk.

7. Press RETURN to save Busplan88.unf on the new disk.

8. Press RETURN to save BegInv.lst.

Now you'll want to place the spreadsheet budget on the Desk-top so that you can begin working with it.

9. Replace the AppleWorks3 disk with AppleWorks2.

10. Add Newstore88.bud to the Desktop.

You are ready to format your spreadsheet report.

Formatting the Spreadsheet Report

You will be formatting another report to print to the Clip-board. But one of your first tasks will be to do away with the two windows that you created in the process of generating the budget and which were saved with the Newstore88.bud file. It's important to do away with the windows at this point so that you can see the information more easily.

1. Press OA-W for Window.

2. Press RETURN to verify that you only want one window.

As with the data base report, you want to eliminate the spreadsheet headers from the report. The other printing options are unimportant since the move to the word process-ing file will remove most of them.

3. Press OA-O to get the Printer Options menu.

4. Enter **PH** to change the Page Header option from Yes to No and press RETURN.

5. Press ESC to exit from the Printer Options menu.

Having eliminated the spreadsheet headers, you next want to ensure that only the budget portion of the file, and not the assumptions at the beginning, are printed. The assumptions are important when building and analyzing the spreadsheet, but for the business plan you want to show only the results of the financial projections you've made. To eliminate the Assumptions section, specify that only the block of the spreadsheet that contains the Budget section should be printed.

6. Move your cursor to A16.

7. Press OA-P for Print.

8. Enter **B** for Block.

9. Press the RIGHT ARROW nine times, the OA-DOWN ARROW two times, and then the DOWN ARROW as many times as necessary to put your cursor on cell J48. Then press RETURN to complete the definition of the block to be printed.

You will be given a choice of where to direct the output of the print operation.

10. Move your cursor to The Clipboard (for the Word Processor) and press RETURN.

You will see the message informing you that your report is now on the Clipboard.

11. Press the spacebar to continue, as advised, and then ESC to return to the Main Menu.

You must again remove the file from the Desktop so that you can bring in the Busplan88.unf file and move the budget into it.

12. From the Main Menu select option 4, Remove files from Desktop.

13. Press RETURN to verify that you want to remove Newstore88.bud from the Desktop.

This time you don't need to save the changes you made in the file. You just want to throw them away, realizing that the budget is safely stored on the disk and that you will only be discarding a copy on the Desktop that you don't want. (You saved the data base because it contained a new report format that you wanted to keep. The spreadsheet does not contain report formats that are stored with the file.)

14. Select option 3, Throw out the changes, press RETURN, and then verify that you really want to do this by entering **Y** for Yes.

Combining the Spreadsheet With the Word Processing File

You are ready for the last step in integrating your files. Insert the AppleWorks3 disk into drive 2, place Busplan88.unf on the Desktop, and follow these next steps to combine the contents of the Clipboard with the file.

1. Press OA-F for Find.

2. Enter **M** for Marker and **2** for marker number, and press RETURN.

3. Press RETURN to verify that you do not want the search to continue.

You are now at the marker for the spreadsheet. Below it is the comment line, "(from spreadsheet)," that should be deleted.

4. Delete the whole line "(from spreadsheet)."

After the line is deleted, you can move the budget from the Clipboard.

6. Press OA-M for Move.

7. Enter **F** for From Clipboard.

Your screen looks like this:

```
File: Busplan88.unf            REVIEW/ADD/CHANGE            Escape: Main Menu
=====|====|====|====|====|====|====|====|====|====|====|====|====|====|===
to Bellevue businesses.  One week before the opening, a daily radio ad will
announce the opening of Office Mart.  The ads will be timed to reach the
Bellevue business during the noon news hour.  The financial costs are
described under the Financial Plan.※
※
FINANCE PLAN※
      The following budget covers the new store for one year beginning one
month prior to the opening:※
※
--------Set a Marker: 2
▮==========================================BUDGET==========================
================※
BUDGET CATEGORY     JAN    FEB    MAR    QTR1    QTR2    QTR3    QTR4
TOTAL    %SALES※
----------------------------------------------------------------------------
------------------※
REVENUE ※
  SALES             0   35,000 37,800 72,800 127,008 142,249 163,586
505,643   102.0%※
  RETURNS           0      700    756  1,456   2,540   2,845   3,272
----------------------------------------------------------------------------
Type entry or use @ commands          Line 81  Column  1      @-? for Help
```

You can see that the budget also has a word wrap problem, but it can be corrected in a way other than the one used to fix the alignment problem in the data base.

Modifying the Budget Data

This time you will not correct the word wrap on the screen, but only as it's printed. That is, you will define the printing options so that the budget is accurately printed. Follow these steps:

1. Move your cursor up one line, to the line with --------Set a Marker: 2 on it.

2. Press OA-O to get the Printer Options menu.

3. Enter CI for Characters per Inch and press RETURN.

4. Enter 12 for Chars, and then press RETURN.

5. Change both the Right Margin and the Left Margin to .2 inches.

6. Press ESC to exit from the Printer Options menu.

Now print the business plan and see how the word wrap problem has been corrected.

Printing the Business Plan

The business plan will be printed accurately even though the screen image is still distorted. This is because AppleWorks allows you to vary the characters per inch in one file. The first part of the business plan is printed at 10 characters per inch, and the last part at 12 characters per inch. This feature is very helpful since you otherwise would be faced with deleting characters in each line of the budget, a formidable task.

Follow these familiar steps to print the report.

1. Press OA-P for Print.

2. Press RETURN to ask for a printout of the whole file from the beginning.

3. Move the cursor to the name of your printer and specify it as the destination by pressing RETURN.

4. Press RETURN to verify that you want only one copy.

Your report should look like Figure 9-1. As you can see, the budget is nicely spaced on the second page.

Before continuing, change the name of the file and save it. The plan is now finished, and the name should distinguish it from the unfinished version.

5. Press OA-N for Name.

6. Enter **Busplan88.txt** and press RETURN.

Return to the Main Menu and remove the files from the Desktop one more time, saving the renamed copy of the busi-

```
                         ABC COMPANY

                   Plan to Add Store, 1988

          This section of the business plan addresses the opening of an
     additional store in 1988.
                              OBJECTIVE
          ABC Company plans to open one new retail store in 1988 which is
     to be profitable within eight months from opening.
                              THE PLAN
          The plan is composed of three sections: a description of the new
     store, the startup plans, and the financial plan.

     DESCRIPTION
          ABC Company's new store will be named Office Mart.  It will
     appeal to small businesses in and near the city of Bellevue,
     Washington.  Office Mart will sell office supplies and accessories.
     Paper and film products will be stressed in the product lines sold.

     STARTUP PLAN
          The startup plan for Office Mart involves two areas:  the
     physical startup and the marketing plans.

     Physical Startup
          One month prior to opening the store, space will be leased.  At
     that time the new equipment, inventory, and displays will be moved
     into the store.  Also the new personnel training will begin.  The
     training will teach the new employees about ABC Company and about the
     product lines that Office Mart carries.

          Many of the startup personnel will initially be transferred from
     the Renton store.  These employees will be returned to the Renton
     store after two weeks time, except for the store manager who is to be
     permanently promoted from the Renton store.

          The rest of the employees will be hired especially for the new
     store.  The details concerning the number of persons hired and the
     skills needed are described under the Financial Plan.

          The list of startup inventory items which will be used to
     initially stock the store is as follows:

     Film products from vendor:   85            $1611.00

     Paper products from vendor: 102             784.98

     Total                                      $2395.98*


     CONFIDENTIAL                                PAGE 15
```

Figure 9-1.   Final printed business plan

ABC COMPANY

Marketing Plan
        Advertising will begin one month prior to opening. There will be
weekly 1/2 page advertisements in the leading Bellevue newspapers. In
addition, a direct mail campaign will be used to distribute
announcements to Bellevue businesses. One week before the opening, a
daily radio ad will announce the opening of Office Mart. The ads will
be timed to reach the Bellevue business during the noon news hour.
The financial costs are described under the Financial Plan.

FINANCE PLAN
        The following budget covers the new store for one year beginning
one month prior to the opening:

```
===============================================BUDGET==============================================
BUDGET CATEGORY     JAN     FEB     MAR     QTR1    QTR2    QTR3    QTR4    TOTAL   % SALES
---------------------------------------------------------------------------------------------------
REVENUE
  SALES              0     35,000  37,800  72,800 127,008 142,249 163,586 505,643  102.0%
  RETURNS            0        700     756   1,456   2,540   2,845   3,272  10,113    2.0%
    NET SALES        0     34,300  37,044  71,344 124,468 139,404 160,315 495,530  100.0%

  COST OF SALES      0     21,609  23,338  44,947  78,415  87,825 100,998 312,184   63.0%

GROSS PROFIT         0     12,691  13,706  26,397  46,053  51,579  59,316 183,346   37.0%

EXPENSES
  SALARIES       10,900   10,900  10,900  32,700  32,700  32,700  32,700 130,800   26.4%
  PAYROLL TAXES   1,635    1,635   1,635   4,905   4,905   4,905   4,905  19,620    4.0%
  FRINGE BENEFITS   763      763     763   2,289   2,289   2,289   2,289   9,156    1.8%
    SUBTOTAL LABOR 13,298  13,298  13,298  39,894  39,894  39,894  39,894 159,576   32.2%

  STORE RENT      2,000    2,000   2,000   6,000   6,000   6,000   6,000  24,000    4.8%
  UTILITIES         400      400     400   1,200   1,200   1,200   1,200   4,800    1.0%
  MAINTENANCE       500      500     500   1,500   1,500   1,500   1,500   6,000    1.2%
  DEPRECIATION      750      750     750   2,250   2,250   2,250   2,250   9,000    1.8%
  ADVERTISING     1,500    1,500   1,500   4,500   2,000   1,750   1,500   9,750    2.0%
  POSTAGE & FREIGHT   0      343     370     713   1,245   1,394   1,603   4,955    1.0%
  INSURANCE         250      250     250     750     750     750     750   3,000     .6%
  TELEPHONE         150      150     150     450     450     450     450   1,800     .4%
  EXCISE TAXES        0      172     185     357     622     697     802   2,478     .5%
  MISCELLANEOUS     150      150     150     450     450     450     450   1,800     .4%
    SUBTOTAL NONLAB 5,700   6,214   6,256  18,170  16,467  16,441  16,505  67,583   13.6%

TOTAL EXPENSE    18,998   19,512  19,554  58,064  56,361  56,335  56,399 227,159   45.8%

NET PROFIT      (18,998) (6,822) (5,847)(31,667)(10,308) (4,756)  2,918 (43,813)   -8.8%
```

Figure 9-1. Final printed business plan (*continued*)

ness plan on AppleWorks3. You are now ready to begin working with the mail merge capability.

Performing a Mail Merge

If you have not upgraded your AppleWorks programs to version 2.0, you will not have the Mail Merge feature. In that case you can purchase one of several mail merge packages for AppleWorks. Even if you have version 2.0, you may want to investigate other mail merge packages since some of them offer more comprehensive capabilities than those that come with version 2.0 of AppleWorks. For example, the size of the Clipboard allows only 253 database records at a time to be merged with a document. If you have files with several thousand records you will want a mail merge package that handles large files more efficiently.

AppleWorks' Mail Merge feature allows you to combine a data base file, such as a name and address list, with a word processing file. To explore the potential of this important feature, you will use the customer information file (CIF.LST) created in Chapter 4 and the Opening.ltr file created in Chapter 2 to generate personalized letters announcing the opening of a new store. The names and addresses from the CIF file will be merged with copies of the letters so that letters informing customers about the opening don't have to be typed and addressed individually.

First you will work with the data base and then with the word processing file. Next you will print a test letter to make sure the format is correct. Finally, you will print the merged announcement letters.

Preparing the Data Base File

There are two tasks involved in preparing the data base for the mail merge. In the data base you will create a report containing only the records that you want to merge: customers from Bellevue. Then you will "print" the report (it must be a table-style report) to the Clipboard. This is similar to what you did earlier to integrate the elements of the business plan.

Creating the Data Base Report

Insert AppleWorks1 into drive 2 and add both the CIF.LST and Opening.ltr files to the Desktop. Bring up the Review/Add/Change screen to view the data base file, CIF.LST. Replace the AppleWorks1 disk with AppleWorks3. Now follow these steps to format the data base report:

1. Press OA-P.

2. Select Create a new "tables" format, and name the report **Mailing List**.

You will see the Report Format screen, which looks like this:

```
File: CIF.LST                    REPORT FORMAT              Escape: Report Menu
Report: Mailing List
Selection: All records



===============================================================================
--> or <--  Move cursor                   a-J  Right justify this category
   >  a  <    Switch category positions   a-K  Define a calculated category
--> a  <--  Change column width           a-N  Change report name and/or title
a-A  Arrange (sort) on this category      a-O  Printer options
a-D  Delete this category                 a-P  Print the report
a-G  Add/remove group totals              a-R  Change record selection rules
a-I  Insert a prev. deleted category      a-T  Add/remove category totals
-------------------------------------------------------------------------------

CUST          CUSTOMER NAM STREET 1     STREET 2     CITY         STATE       Z
-A---------   -B---------- -C---------- -D---------- -E---------- -F--------- -
1             Aires Quick  1345 South 8              Bellevue     WA          9
10            Best and Mar Department C 10476 NE 8th Bellevue     WA          9
8             Bo's Print M 7264 Northru              Bellevue     WA          9
-------------------------------------------------------------- More --->
Use options shown above to change report format                52K Avail.
```

Sorting the records. To benefit from savings offered by the post office if you batch your letters in ZIP code sequence, you are going to sort the records first by customer name and then by ZIP code. This will arrange your records alphabetically by customer name within ZIP codes.

1. Move your cursor to the CUSTOMER NAME category and press OA-A to "arrange" the records.

2. Press RETURN to arrange the records alphabetically in ascending sequence.

3. Move your cursor to the ZIP CODE category and press OA-A again.

4. Move your cursor to option 3, From 0 to 9, and press RETURN.

Although you cannot see the results right now, your records have been sorted.

Selecting the records. You plan to mail the letters to your Bellevue customers because the new store is likely to appeal only to them. You will use the Record Selection command to select the customer records that you want merged with the letter. Follow these steps:

1. Press OA-R for Record Selection.

2. Move your cursor to the CITY category. Do not press RETURN.

Your screen will look like this:

```
File: CIF.LST                    SELECT RECORDS          Escape: Report Format
Report: Mailing List
Selection:


===============================================================================
  1.   CUST
  2.   CUSTOMER NAME
  3.   STREET 1
  4.   STREET 2
  5.   CITY
  6.   STATE
  7.   ZIP CODE
  8.   TELEPHONE
  9.   CONTACT NAME
 10.   CREDIT LIMIT
 11.   PRODUCT TYPE
 12.   1ST ORDER DATE


-------------------------------------------------------------------------------
Type number, or use arrows, then press Return__          52K Avail.
```

Now examine your category names. Although there are none in this file, note that duplicate names cannot be used by Mail Merge. If you were working with your own files and had a duplicate category name, you would have to give each category a unique name before proceeding.

3. Press RETURN.

You will see a screen that asks you to describe the conditions under which the data will be selected. You want to select those customers whose CITY category equals Bellevue.

4. Press RETURN to request the Equals option.

5. When prompted for comparison information, type **Bellevue** and press RETURN.

6. Press ESC to leave the Record Selection command.

When the report is printed, only the Bellevue customers will be included.

Printing the Data Base List

Before you can merge the data base list with the word processing letter, you must print the newly formed Mailing List report to the Clipboard. This procedure is familiar to you since you have recently integrated spreadsheet and data base reports into the word processing Busplan88.txt report.

As with copying or moving data to the Clipboard, when you print data to it you cannot use the Clipboard again until the mail merge operation is completed, or the data (in this case, the Mailing List report) will have to be printed to the Clipboard again.

Follow these steps to print the Mailing List report to the Clipboard:

1. Press OA-P for printing.

2. Choose option 5, The Clipboard (for Mail Merge) and press RETURN. Yours may be a different option number depending on the number of printers you have added to AppleWorks.

3. Press the spacebar when prompted by the message that tells you your report is now on the Clipboard.

4. Press ESC twice to return to the Review/Add/Change screen.

Your data base report is now waiting on the Clipboard, and you can prepare your word processing form letter.

Preparing the Word Processing File

Pull the Opening.ltr file onto the screen by pressing OA-Q for the Quick Index and then requesting that the letter be displayed. This screen will appear:

```
File: Opening.ltr              REVIEW/ADD/CHANGE           Escape: Main Menu
=====|====|====|====|====|====|====|====|====|====|====|====|====|====|===
—



Aires Quick Copy
1345 South 8th
Bellevue, WA   98004

Dear Larry Aires,

ABC COMPANY is pleased to announce the opening of a new
retail outlet, the Office Mart.  It will be located in the
Evergreen Northwest Shopping Mall, in Bellevue, Washington.

The grand opening will be on February 4, 1988 and you are
invited to attend.  We will be showing off our new line of
paper products.  Wine and cheese will be served and there
will be a drawing for a door prize.  Be sure to attend!

-----------------------------------------------------------------------------
Type entry or use @ commands            Line 1  Column  1        @-? for Help
```

You can see that the letter is already addressed to Aires Quick Copy. The first step is to remove references to the specific customer and replace them with the name of the data base category to be used instead.

Follow these steps to delete the current addressee:

1. Move your cursor to the first letter of the addressee, to the A in Aires. Press OA-D for delete.

2. Press the DOWN ARROW key three times and the LEFT ARROW key once to highlight the address to be deleted. Press RETURN to make the deletion.

Now that the address is deleted, tell AppleWorks what to put in its place. From the Options screen select the Mail Merge option which informs AppleWorks that a data base list is on the Clipboard.

3. Press OA-O, enter **MM**, and then press RETURN to request the Mail Merge option.

If you get the message, "There's no Mail Merge data on the Clipboard," you'll have to print the data base report to the Clipboard again. This would occur if you had moved, copied, or printed any other text to the Clipboard after printing the data base records.

To replace the customer's name and address, request that the CUSTOMER NAME, STREET1, STREET2, CITY, STATE, and ZIP CODE categories be inserted in specific locations. You are presented with the list of data base categories from which to choose the one to be inserted next. The screen looks like this:

```
File: Opening.ltr              MAIL MERGE          Escape: Printer Options
=====|====|====|====|====|====|====|====|====|====|====|====|====|====|====|===

Select a data base category

   1.  CUST
   2.  CUSTOMER NAME
   3.  STREET 1
   4.  STREET 2
   5.  CITY
   6.  STATE
   7.  ZIP CODE
   8.  TELEPHONE
   9.  CONTACT NAME
  10.  CREDIT LIMIT
  11.  PRODUCT TYPE
  12.  1ST ORDER DATE




-----------------------------------------------------------------------------
Type number, or use arrows, then press Return__           51K Avail.
```

4. Press the DOWN ARROW key and then RETURN to indicate that the CUSTOMER NAME category is to be inserted where your cursor currently points.

An arrow points to CUSTOMER NAME indicating that you have chosen it as the category to be inserted.

At the bottom of the screen, a prompt asks you whether to omit a line if the record being merged has no data for that category. For example, if the address has no STREET2, answering Yes to the question would "close up" the address so that there would be no blank line between STREET1 and CITY when the letter is printed. In the case of CUSTOMER NAME, you want to retain the blank line by accepting the default.

5. Press RETURN to retain the line if it is blank.

6. Press ESC and then RETURN to leave the option screen and move down one line.

Your screen now looks like this:

```
File: Opening.ltr              REVIEW/ADD/CHANGE              Escape: Main Menu
=====|====|====|====|====|====|====|====|====|====|====|====|====|====|====|===


^<CUSTOMER NAME>

Dear Larry Aires,

ABC COMPANY is pleased to announce the opening of a new
retail outlet, the Office Mart.  It will be located in the
Evergreen Northwest Shopping Mall, in Bellevue, Washington.

The grand opening will be on February 4, 1988 and you are
invited to attend.  We will be showing off our new line of
paper products.  Wine and cheese will be served and there
will be a drawing for a door prize.  Be sure to attend!

Sincerely,
-----------------------------------------------------------------------------
Type entry or use @ commands        Line 7   Column  1        @-? for Help
```

Before the category name is a caret (^), which indicates that a data base category immediately follows. You can see that the category name, CUSTOMER NAME, is enclosed in braces <>. This tells you that AppleWorks is not going to remove a line if the record being printed has no data for the name.

Continue to add the remaining address lines by following these steps:

7. Press OA-O and then enter **MM** and press RETURN for Mail Merge.

8. Press the DOWN ARROW key twice to move to the STREET1 category and then press RETURN.

9. Move the cursor to Yes and press RETURN to tell AppleWorks to remove the line if a record has no data in this category.

10. Press ESC and then RETURN to leave the Options screen and move down one line.

You'll notice that the category name is now enclosed in square brackets ([ ]). This tells AppleWorks that the line is to be deleted if no data exists for STREET1 in the record being merged.

Continuing in the same way, add the STREET2 category. The line for STREET2 should be omitted if there is no data for it.

After you have again escaped from the Options screen and moved down one line, add the CITY, STATE, and ZIP CODE categories one after another on the same line. Do not leave the Options screen until you have specified all three category names. You'll want to retain this line, so accept the line omission default for all three of these categories.

Don't be concerned about the spacing between categories because AppleWorks automatically inserts one space between categories.

After you have entered the three category names, escaped the Options screen, and moved down one line, your screen will look like this:

```
File: Opening.ltr              REVIEW/ADD/CHANGE              Escape: Main Menu
=====|====|====|====|====|====|====|====|====|====|====|====|====|====|====|===




^<CUSTOMER NAME>
^[STREET 1]
^[STREET 2]
^<CITY> ^<STATE> ^<ZIP CODE>

Dear Larry Aires,

ABC COMPANY is pleased to announce the opening of a new
retail outlet, the Office Mart.  It will be located in the
Evergreen Northwest Shopping Mall, in Bellevue, Washington.

The grand opening will be on February 4, 1988 and you are
invited to attend.  We will be showing off our new line of
paper products.  Wine and cheese will be served and there
will be a drawing for a door prize.  Be sure to attend!
-------------------------------------------------------------------
Type entry or use a commands           Line 10  Column  1      a-? for Help
```

Next, you must replace the name in the greeting with the CONTACT NAME category. First delete the current name and then insert the category name. Follow these steps to do so:

11. Move the cursor to the "L" in *Larry*.

12. Press OA-D and move the cursor to the last letter of *Aires* to highlight the name you want to delete. Press RETURN.

13. Choose the Mail Merge option by pressing OA-O for the Options screen, entering **MM** for Mail Merge and then pressing RETURN.

14. Press the DOWN ARROW key until the cursor rests on CONTACT NAME and then press RETURN to indicate your choice of category name.

15. Type **Y** for Yes to omit the line.

16. Leave the Options screen by pressing ESC, but do not space down yet.

AppleWorks, you will remember, places a space after each category name. In this case, you want the space between the name and the comma removed.

17. Press DELETE to delete the space.

The screen now looks like this:

```
File: Opening.ltr              REVIEW/ADD/CHANGE             Escape: Main Menu
=====|====|====|====|====|====|====|====|====|====|====|====|====|====|===


^<CUSTOMER NAME>
^[STREET 1]
^[STREET 2]
^<CITY> ^<STATE> ^<ZIP CODE>

Dear ^[CONTACT NAME],

ABC COMPANY is pleased to announce the opening of a new
retail outlet, the Office Mart.  It will be located in the
Evergreen Northwest Shopping Mall, in Bellevue, Washington.

The grand opening will be on February 4, 1988 and you are
invited to attend.  We will be showing off our new line of
paper products.  Wine and cheese will be served and there
will be a drawing for a door prize.  Be sure to attend!
------------------------------------------------------------------------------
Type entry or use @ commands          Line 11  Column 21       @-? for Help
```

Save your letter at this point. Use the fast method: press OA-S.

Printing the Letter

Printing the letter is very straightforward. A new feature allows you to print a test page to see if the categories are lined up as you want them to be. No data will be merged with the test page. Print a test page as follows:

1. Press OA-P, for print.

2. Press RETURN to indicate that you want to print the whole letter.

3. Move the cursor to the name of your printer and press RETURN.

4. Move your cursor to option 2, Print document without merging, and press RETURN.

5. To verify that you want one copy, press RETURN.

The test letter should look like Figure 9-2. After you make sure that yours matches, print the merged letters by following these steps:

1. Press OA-P and then RETURN to indicate that you want to print the file from the beginning.

```
^<CUSTOMER NAME>
^[STREET 1]
^[STREET 2]
^<CITY> ^<STATE> ^<ZIP CODE>

Dear ^[CONTACT NAME],

ABC COMPANY is pleased to announce the opening of a new
retail outlet, the Office Mart.  It will be located in the
Evergreen Northwest Shopping Mall, in Bellevue, Washington.

The grand opening will be on February 4, 1988 and you are
invited to attend.  We will be showing off our new line of
paper products.  Wine and cheese will be served and there
will be a drawing for a door prize.  Be sure to attend!

Sincerely,



Your Name
```

Figure 9-2. A sample test letter

```
Aires Quick Copy
1345 South 8th
Bellevue WA 98004

Dear Larry Aires,

ABC COMPANY is pleased to announce the opening of a new
retail outlet, the Office Mart.  It will be located in the
Evergreen Northwest Shopping Mall, in Bellevue, Washington.

The grand opening will be on February 4, 1988 and you are
invited to attend.  We will be showing off our new line of
paper products.  Wine and cheese will be served and there
will be a drawing for a door prize.  Be sure to attend!

Sincerely,



Your Name
```

Figure 9-3. A finished letter created with Mail Merge

At this point you can specify that you want the merged letters to be printed to disk as a text file. Do this if you want to print the letters later.

2. Press RETURN to verify that your printer is to be used.

3. Press RETURN to indicate that you want the data base items merged with the letter.

4. Press RETURN for one copy of each letter.

Your letter should now be printed seven times, once for each record selected from the data base. Figure 9-3 shows a sample of a finished letter.

Conclusion

This concludes *AppleWorks Made Easy*. It is hoped you'll find that this book continues to be useful as a handy reminder of the steps involved when you are covering infrequently used AppleWorks procedures and as a helpful guide when starting up new processes. Many of the procedures explained in this book are adaptable to your particular business needs.

Best wishes in your efforts.

Setting Up
Your Printer

AppleWorks allows you a broad choice of printers to use with its three components. If you have an ImageWriter and will only be using this one printer, you don't need to do anything special at all to install it; AppleWorks has already done so. Chapter 2 explains the simple procedure for printing if you have this printer.

However, there are 11 other printers that AppleWorks is programmed to recognize once you tell it you have one of them. These printers are listed for you, and all you need to do is let AppleWorks know that you want to use one of them. The process is simple and straightforward.

You may have a printer that AppleWorks doesn't yet recognize. In this case, you must give AppleWorks certain information about the printer. AppleWorks calls these printers "custom," since they will be defined just for you by you. If you have a custom printer, you may have to supply information found in the printer's technical manuals. So have the manuals handy as you proceed.

This appendix will guide you in setting up your printer if you have one of the 11 recognized printers or if you have a custom printer. In either of those cases, you need to get to the screens where you define the printer specifications. Follow these steps to get started:

1. From the Main Menu, select option 5, Other Activities.

2. On the Other Activities menu, select option 7, Specify information about your printer(s).

The Printer Information menu will be displayed.

```
Disk: Disk 2                    PRINTER INFORMATION      Escape: Other Activities
_____

|        Main Menu              |_____|
|   |                                                                     |
|   |     Other Activities      |_____|
|   |   |                                                               |
|   |   |     Printer Information  |_____|__
|   |   |                                                               |
|   |   |                                                               |
|   |   |   Change standard values                                      |
|   |   |   1.  Open-Apple-H printer   ImageWriter (Slot 1)             |
|   |   |                                                               |
|   |   |   Add or remove a printer                                     |
|   |   |   2.  Add a printer (maximum of 3)                            |
|   |   |   3.  Remove a printer                                        |
|   |   |                                                               |
|   |   |   Change printer specifications                               |
|___|   |   4.  ImageWriter (Slot 1)                                    |
    |   |                                                               |
    |___|                                                               |
        |_____|

_____
Type number, or use arrows, then press Return__               56K Avail.
```

The Printer Information menu displays four options: (1) you can define which printer is to be used to print hard copies of screen images, (2) you can add up to three printers to use within AppleWorks, (3) you can remove a printer that currently is in use within AppleWorks, and (4) you can change printer definitions for the printer in use.

The first option is used to describe to AppleWorks which printer will be used to print copies of screen images with the OA-H command. This is used when you want to keep a copy of exactly what you see on the screen. This is not the same as printing a report or file listing.

The second and third options are used to identify the printers you will be using or removing from use. When you add a printer, you simply add it to a list of up to three printers that you may specify for AppleWorks. A printer must be on this list in order for AppleWorks to recognize it. When you remove a printer, you take it off the list of three printers.

The fourth option allows you to change printer options for a printer already on the list of three printers. You may find that a specification is invalid for a printer, and these options allow you to make a change.

You want to add a printer to the list of three possibilities, so

3. Select option 2, Add a printer (maximum of 3).

You will be shown the list of printers that are already handled by AppleWorks, as seen on the following screen.

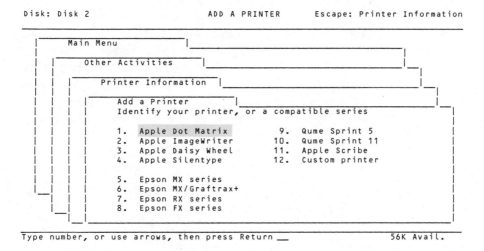

```
Disk: Disk 2                     ADD A PRINTER       Escape: Printer Information

|     Main Menu            |
|   |  Other Activities        |
|   |   |  Printer Information   |
|   |   |   |  Add a Printer          |
|   |   |   |  Identify your printer, or a compatible series
|   |   |   |
|   |   |   |  1.  Apple Dot Matrix      9.  Qume Sprint 5
|   |   |   |  2.  Apple ImageWriter    10.  Qume Sprint 11
|   |   |   |  3.  Apple Daisy Wheel    11.  Apple Scribe
|   |   |   |  4.  Apple Silentype      12.  Custom printer
|   |   |   |
|   |   |   |  5.  Epson MX series
|   |   |   |  6.  Epson MX/Graftrax+
|   |   |   |  7.  Epson RX series
|   |   |   |  8.  Epson FX series

Type number, or use arrows, then press Return __          56K Avail.
```

The list consists of Apple, Epson, and Qume printers that have already been defined for AppleWorks to use. If you have one of these printers, then all you have to do is to tell Apple-Works which one, and AppleWorks will retrieve the preestablished specifications for that printer from its program disk. If you have a Custom printer (option 12 on the list), setting up your printer for AppleWorks requires only slightly more effort as you'll see.

The instructions for adding a custom printer are in the section entitled "Adding a Custom Printer" later in this appendix. If you have a custom printer, however, you'll still want to read the following section, "Adding a Supported Printer," because some of the screens will be identical to those explained in the following section.

Adding a Supported Printer

If you see your printer on the list of 11, the basic procedure is to identify it to AppleWorks and verify that the specifications that AppleWorks already has for your printer are correct. The Qume Sprint 5 printer is used in these examples. Follow these steps:

1. Select the printer option you want by typing in the number of the option or by using the DOWN ARROW to move to it, and pressing RETURN.

You will be asked to give your printer a name so that you will recognize it when you see it called out on the screen. Use a name that you can easily recall and associate with the printing tasks. The name becomes especially important if you have more than one printer you want to use with Apple-Works. You may use up to 15 characters in the name.

2. Type a name for your printer and press RETURN.

When you enter the printer name, a list of slot numbers will be displayed, like this:

```
Disk: Disk 2                    ADD A PRINTER       Escape: Printer Information
_____
 |-----Main Menu-----------|_____
 |  |-----Other Activities-----|_____|_
 |  |  |----Printer Information--|_____|_
 |  |  |  |----Add a Printer-------|_____|_
 |  |  |  |                                                             |
 |  |  |  |   How is the printer accessed?                              |
 |  |  |  |                                                             |
 |  |  |  |   1.  Slot 1                                                |
 |  |  |  |   2.  Slot 2                                                |
 |  |  |  |   3.  Slot 4                                                |
 |  |  |  |   4.  Slot 5                                                |
 |  |  |  |   5.  Slot 6                                                |
 |__|  |  |   6.  Slot 7                                                |
    |__|  |   7.  Print onto disk or on another Apple                  |
       |__|                                                             |
_____
Type number, or use arrows, then press Return__              56K Avail.
```

AppleWorks is asking for the slot number on the main circuit board inside the Apple computer in which the printer's accessory card (Parallel Interface Card, Super Serial Card, or equivalent) is inserted. You may indicate one of six slot numbers. Normally your printer will be accessed through slot 1. Option 7, Print onto disk or on another Apple, tells AppleWorks that you intend to print a file to disk rather than to the printer. The Print onto disk option is what you would use to telecommunicate formatted files, for example.

To print to disk, you would first add the printer type that you intend to use eventually to print the file. Then you would assign the slot number to option 7, the disk.

3. Select the slot number through which the printer is electronically accessed by the Apple computer and then press RETURN.

At this point you will be shown five printer specifications that contain default values that AppleWorks has already established and which you must verify about the new printer. These items tell AppleWorks how the printer handles some formatting and paper-handling functions. If you don't know whether the defaults are correct, assume that they are and try them out. If your printer does not print correctly, refer to your printer manual and correct the specifications.

```
Disk: Disk 2                    ADD A PRINTER        Escape: Printer Information
_____
 _____
|    Main Menu                |_____
|  _____|                                                |
| |    Other Activities       |_____ |
| |  _____|                                              | |
| | |    Printer Information  |_____  |_|
| | |  _____|                                           |_| |
| | | |    Add a Printer      |_____  |_| |
| | | |  _____|                                        |_| | |
| | | |                                                                 | | | |
| | | |    Printer name: Qume 5 (Slot 1)                                | | | |
| | | |                                                                 | | | |
| | | |    Printer type: Qume Sprint 5                                  | | | |
| | | |                                                                 | | | |
| | | |    1.  Needs line feed after each Return        No             | | | |
| | | |    2.  Accepts top-of-page commands             Yes            | | | |
| | | |    3.  Stop at end of each page                 No             | | | |
| |_| |    4.  Platen width                             13.2 inches    | | | |
|   |_|    5.  Interface cards                                         | | | |
|     |_____| | |
|       |_____| |
|_____|
_____
Type number, or use arrows, then press Return _              56K Avail.
```

The first option specifies whether the printer automatically skips to the next line when it encounters a carriage return character. If it doesn't, AppleWorks will have to generate a line feed for it. If your printer is adding extra blank lines, set this option to No to prevent this. If your printer prints each line over the previous line, set this option to Yes.

The second option tells AppleWorks whether your printer can recognize a Top-of-page command. This is a command to advance the paper immediately to the top of the next page. There are two ways to advance the paper: a printer can immediately skip to the top of the page, or it can print the number of blank lines needed to advance the paper to the top of the page. If your printer accepts Top-of-page commands, the option should be set to Yes.

The third option tells AppleWorks whether your printer must stop at the end of each page. You might have a printer that cannot use continuous form paper, or you might want to print on letterhead stationery. If your printer should stop at the end of each page, the option should be set to Yes.

The fourth option tells AppleWorks how many inches wide the platen on your printer is. The platen width is the distance that the printer head will travel from the left to the right edges of the page. This width must be the maximum width you will be printing with the printer.

The fifth option allows you to specify the standard setting for an interface card other than the Apple II Parallel Interface Card or the Super Serial Card.

To change one of the first three specifications, follow these steps:

4. Type the number of the option (**1**, **2**, or **3**) and press RETURN.

5. When prompted with the message Change the value?, select **Yes**.

AppleWorks will change the value for you from No to Yes or vice versa. Option 4 works a little differently. To change the platen width,

6. Type **4** and press RETURN.

7. Enter the platen width in inches as prompted and press RETURN.

To enter the interface setting (option 5) for a nonstandard parallel or serial accessory card,

8. Type **5** and press RETURN.

The following screen will be displayed, which informs you that the standard interface setting is "Control-I 80N." This tells AppleWorks that the line length is 80 characters and that the automatic repeat to the screen (also called *echo*) should be turned off, so that what is printed on the printer is not echoed on the screen as well. If you use a nonstandard accessory card, you will have to go to that card's manual to find out what the interface setting is. If you have the Apple Parallel Interface or Super Serial Card, you don't need to change the setting.

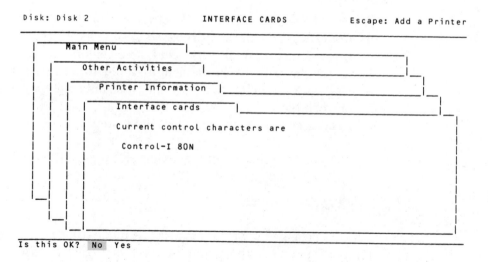

```
Disk: Disk 2                    INTERFACE CARDS          Escape: Add a Printer
_____

|----Main Menu----------|_____
|                       |                                                  |
|   |----Other Activities----|_____|_
|   |                        |                                             |
|   |   |----Printer Information----|_____|
|   |   |                           |                                      |
|   |   |   |----Interface cards----|_____|_ |
|   |   |   |                       |                                    | |
|   |   |   | Current control characters are                            | |
|   |   |   |                                                           | |
|   |   |   | Control-I 80N                                             | |
|   |   |   |                                                           | |
|   |   |   |                                                           | |
|   |_  |   |                                                           | |
|       |   |                                                           | |
|     |_|   |                                                           | |
|       |   |_____| |
|_____|_____|

Is this OK?  No  Yes
_____
```

9. If your interface card uses the "Control-I 80N" interface

code, select Yes to accept the standard setting; otherwise, select No.

If you entered No, you will be requested to enter the interface setting that is required for your printer. You must type in the exact control characters, being careful not to enter any extra characters (including an ESC or a RETURN), since extra characters will be considered a part of the control sequence.

10. Enter the interface setting and end it with a caret (^).

You will be returned to the Add a Printer menu.

11. Press ESC to return to the Printer Information menu.

Your newly added printer will be listed under the Change printer specifications option on this menu. Press ESC twice to return to the Main Menu.

Adding a Custom Printer

You may have a printer that is not listed as one of the printers AppleWorks is already prepared to support. In that case, you must tell AppleWorks that you have a custom printer and define its characteristics. Although AppleWorks recognizes as many as three printers at any one time, only one may be a custom printer.

To add a custom printer, follow these steps:

1. From the Add a Printer screen, select option 12, Custom printer, and press RETURN.

2. Type in the name of the custom printer.

You will be asked to specify the access mode (that is, the slot number) in which the printer's accessory card is inserted into the main circuit board.

3. Select the slot number through which the custom printer is accessed.

You will be shown some printer specifications that must be set for the new printer.

> 4. Verify that the printer specifications 1 through 4 are correct and change any that are wrong for your custom printer.

If you are using a non-Apple parallel or serial interface card, you must specify the interface setting code to AppleWorks if it is not the standard setting of "Control-I 80N."

> 5. Select option 5 and when prompted, enter the setting control sequence for the nonstandard interface card.

Option 6 allows you to define the exact codes that your printer will be expecting in order to perform certain functions.

> 6. Select option 6 (option 5 if you have an Apple IIc), Printer Codes.

This screen will be displayed:

```
Disk: Disk 2              PRINTER CODES           Escape: Add a Printer
_____
| | Main Menu                  |_____
| |   Other Activities           |_____ |
| | |   Printer Information         |_____ | |
| | | |  Printer codes               |_____ | | |
| | | |                                                          | | | |
| | | |   1.  Characters per inch                                | | | |
| | | |                                                          | | | |
| | | |   2.  Lines per inch                                     | | | |
| | | |                                                          | | | |
| | | |   3.  Boldface, Subscript and Superscript                | | | |
| | | |                                                          | | | |
| | | |   4.  Underlining                                        | | | |
| | | |                                                          | | | |
| |_| |                                                          | | | |
|   |_|                                                          | | | |
|     |_____| | | |
|_____| | |
_____
Type number, or use arrows, then press Return__        56K Avail.
```

You now must give AppleWorks information about the four

printing functions listed on the screen. For the first option, tell AppleWorks how many characters per inch are to be printed per line on your custom printer. This may be a number from 2 to 24. Normally it will be 10 or 12 characters per inch.

Options 2, 3, and 4 expect you to supply them with the actual control codes that are instructions to the printer. In the case of the second option, Lines per inch, you must also supply a choice between 6 and 8 lines per inch. Follow these steps to change the printer codes.

7. Press RETURN to change the Characters per inch option.

8. Enter the number of characters per inch supported by your printer and press RETURN.

A second screen will be displayed for you to enter the control characters for the characters per inch.

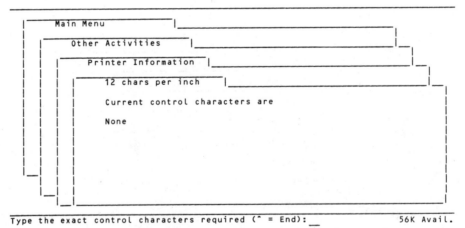

```
Disk: Disk 2                    12 CHARS PER INCH
_____
| ┌─ Main Menu ────────┐|_____ |
| |  ┌─ Other Activities ─┐|_____ |_
| |  |  ┌─ Printer Information ─┐|_____ |_
| |  |  |  ┌─ 12 chars per inch ─┐|_____ |_
| |  |  |  |  Current control characters are                   |
| |  |  |  |  None                                             |
| |  |  |  |                                                   |
| |  |  |  |                                                   |
| |  |  |  |                                                   |
| |__|  |  |                                                   |
|    |__|  |_____ |
|_____|_____|
_____
Type the exact control characters required (^ = End): _    56K Avail.
```

Enter the exact control code and end it with a caret (^). Do not enter an ESC or a RETURN as it will be considered part of the control code sequence. If you make a typing mistake, use the DELETE key to back up and correct it.

9. Enter the control code and type a caret (^) to exit.

10. Press ESC to return to the Printer Codes menu.

Now to set the Lines per inch for your custom printer,

11. Enter 2 to change the Lines per inch setting and press RETURN.

12. Move your cursor to the correct lines per inch, 6 or 8, and press RETURN.

13. Enter the control codes and type a caret (^) to exit.

14. Press ESC to return to the Printer Codes menu.

To specify the control codes for performing the character formatting of Boldface, Subscript, and Superscript, follow these steps:

15. Enter 3 and press RETURN.

This screen will be displayed.

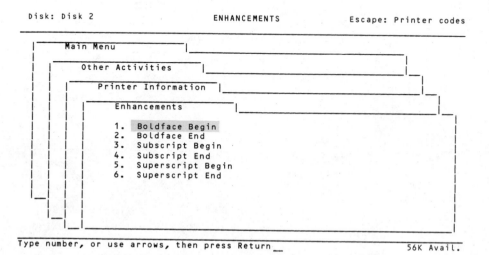

```
Disk: Disk 2                    ENHANCEMENTS           Escape: Printer codes
_____

| Main Menu                |_____
|                          |                                            |
|  | Other Activities      |_____|  |_
|  |                       |                                         |    |
|  |  | Printer Information |_____|  |_  |
|  |  |                     |                                      |     | |
|  |  |  | Enhancements     |_____|  |_    ||
|  |  |  |                  |                                   |    |   |||
|  |  |  |  1.  Boldface Begin                                  |    |   |||
|  |  |  |  2.  Boldface End                                   |    |    |||
|  |  |  |  3.  Subscript Begin                                |    |    |||
|  |  |  |  4.  Subscript End                                  |    |    |||
|  |  |  |  5.  Superscript Begin                              |    |    |||
|  |  |  |  6.  Superscript End                                |    |    |||
|  |  |  |                                                     |    |    |||
|  |__|  |                                                     |    |    |||
|     |  |                                                     |    |    |||
|     |__|                                                     |    |    |||
|        |_____|    |    ||
_____
Type number, or use arrows, then press Return__              56K Avail.
```

For each option that you want to select, you must supply the exact control code. Follow these steps for each one.

16. Move your cursor to the option you want and press RETURN.

17. Enter only the exact control characters and type a caret (^) to exit.

18. When you are finished entering the options, press ESC to return to the Printer Codes menu.

Underlining is the last printer code that needs to be set.

19. Enter **4** and press RETURN to define the underlining control codes.

This screen will be displayed so that you can specify how your printer handles underlining.

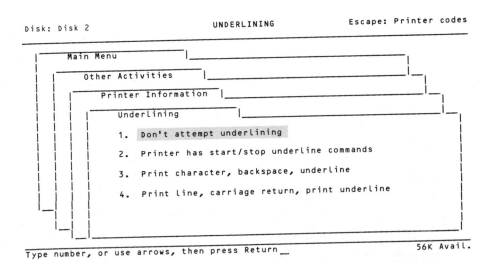

The first option instructs AppleWorks not to underline text. If you choose this option, any underlined text will be ignored by the printer. You may choose this option because your printer cannot underline text at all, or because the technique it uses for underlining differs from the techniques available in options 2, 3, and 4.

Option 2 indicates that your printer uses the technique of flagging the beginning and ending of the text to be underlined with special characters. When the printer comes to the start character, it knows to underline the following characters until the end character is encountered. If you specify this option, you will be asked to supply AppleWorks with the information about the beginning and ending control characters.

Option 3 indicates that the printer uses a character-by-character technique to underline text. Essentially, when the printer comes to an underlined character, it prints the character, backspaces one character, prints an underline character, and then continues to the next character where it goes through the same procedure.

Option 4 may be selected if the other options cannot be used to underline text on your custom printer. In this case the printer prints the line of text that contains underlined characters, returns the printhead to the beginning of the same line (without performing a line feed), and prints the underline character wherever it is needed in that line.

For the option of your choice, follow these steps:

20. Enter the option number and press RETURN.

21. If prompted for the beginning and ending underline characters, enter them and type the caret (^) to exit.

22. Press ESC to return to the Printer Codes screen.

If you have an Apple IIc, you will see an option 5 on the Printer Codes menu allowing you to change the serial interface setting. If you need to change the serial interface setting, refer to the section "Apple IIc Serial Interface Settings" in Chapter 12 of *Using AppleWorks*.

23. Press ESC twice to return to the Printer Information menu.

The screen should now list your custom printer as one of the recognized printers under the Change printer specifications options on the Printer Information menu.

Printer manuals vary considerably as to how they express the codes that the printer needs in order to perform certain functions. Some express the codes as decimal numbers. Others express the code as a hexadecimal number value. Still others express the codes as character names. Finally, some manuals express the codes as one or more keypresses.

The AppleWorks program expects the printer data to be entered in the form of keypresses. If your printer manual expresses the code in this fashion, all you have to do is follow the manual specifications for the desired function.

If your printer manual expresses the codes by one of the alternative methods, or by some combination of them, you will need to convert the values. Table A-1 lists the potential decimal and hexadecimal codes and the key or keys to press to generate these codes. (Note that if the key press column shows "CONTROL + <key>", hold the CONTROL key down while pressing and releasing the other key.

If you have further questions about adding a printer, refer to *Using AppleWorks*, your printer manual, or the manual that came with your interface card.

Table A-1. Printer Codes

Decimal	Hexadecimal	Alternative Name	Key(s) to Press
1	01	SOH	CONTROL + A
2	02	STX	CONTROL + B
3	03	ETX	CONTROL + C
4	04	EOT	CONTROL + D
5	05	ENQ	CONTROL + E
6	06	ACK	CONTROL + F
7	07	BEL	CONTROL + G

Table A-1.   Printer Codes (*continued*)

Decimal	Hexadecimal	Alternative Name	Key(s) to Press
8	08	BS	CONTROL + H
9	09	HT	CONTROL + I
10	0A	LF	CONTROL + J
11	0B	VT	CONTROL + K
12	0C	FF	CONTROL + L
13	0D	CR	CONTROL + M
14	0E	SO	CONTROL + N
15	0F	SI	CONTROL + O
16	10	DLE	CONTROL + P
17	11	DC1	CONTROL + Q
18	12	DC2	CONTROL + R
19	13	DC3	CONTROL + S
20	14	DC4	CONTROL + T
21	15	NAK	CONTROL + U
22	16	SYN	CONTROL + V
23	17	ETB	CONTROL + W
24	18	CAN	CONTROL + X
25	19	EM	CONTROL + Y
26	1A	SUB	CONTROL + Z
27	1B	ESC	ESC
28	1C	FS	CONTROL +
29	1D	GS	CONTROL +]
30	1E	RS	CONTROL + SHIFT + 6
31	1F	US	CONTROL + SHIFT + -
32	20		Spacebar
33	21		!
34	22		"
35	23		#
36	24		$
37	25		%
38	26		&
39	27		'
40	28		(
41	29		)
42	2A		*
43	2B		+
44	2C		,
45	2D		-
46	2E		.
47	2F		/
48	30		0

Table A-1. Printer Codes (*continued*)

Decimal	Hexadecimal	Alternative Name	Key(s) to Press
49	31		1
50	32		2
51	33		3
52	34		4
53	35		5
54	36		6
55	37		7
56	38		8
57	39		9
58	3A		:
59	3B		;
60	3C		<
61	3D		=
62	3E		>
63	3F		?
64	40		@
65	41		A
66	42		B
67	43		C
68	44		D
69	45		E
70	46		F
71	47		G
72	48		H
73	49		I
74	4A		J
75	4B		K
76	4C		L
77	4D		M
78	4E		N
79	4F		O
80	50		P
81	51		Q
82	52		R
83	53		S
84	54		T
85	55		U
86	56		V
87	57		W
88	58		X

Table A-1. Printer Codes (*continued*)

Decimal	Hexadecimal	Alternative Name	Key(s) to Press
89	59		Y
90	5A		Z
91	5B		[
92	5C		\
93	5D		]
94	5E		^
95	5F		—
96	60		\
97	61		a
98	62		b
99	63		c
100	64		d
101	65		e
102	66		f
103	67		g
104	68		h
105	69		i
106	6A		j
107	6B		k
108	6C		l
109	6D		m
110	6E		n
111	6F		o
112	70		p
113	71		q
114	72		r
115	73		s
116	74		t
117	75		u
118	76		v
119	77		w
120	78		x
121	79		y
122	7A		z
123	7B		{
124	7C			
125	7D		}
126	7E		
127	7F	DEL	DELETE

Trademarks

The italicized names are trademarks of the following companies. Registered trademarks are noted with an ®.

Apple®	Apple Computer, Inc.
AppleWorks	Apple Computer, Inc.
dBASE II®	Ashton-Tate
DIF	Software Arts, Inc.
Epson	Epson America, Inc.
ProDOS	Apple Computer, Inc.
ProFile	Apple Computer, Inc.
Quick File	Apple Computer, Inc.
Qume®	Qume Corporation
Silentype®	Apple Computer, Inc.
VisiCalc®	VisiCorp
WordStar®	MicroPro International Corporation

Index

The manuscript for this book was prepared and submitted to Osborne/McGraw-Hill in electronic form.

The acquisitions editor for this project was Jeffrey Pepper. The technical reviewer was Michael Fischer. Lyn Cordell was the project editor.

The typeface is Century Expanded. Display typeface is Eurostype Bold.

Cover art is by Bay Graphics Design Associates. Cover supplier is Phoenix Color Corporation. This book was printed and bound by R. R. Donnelley & Sons Company, Crawfordsville, Indiana.

Here's More Help From the Experts

Now that you've developed even better computer skills with *Apple-Works Made Easy*, let us suggest the following related titles that will help you use your computer to greater advantage.

AppleWorks®: The Pocket Reference
by Carole Boggs Matthews

Picture yourself working away efficiently on the computer when all of a sudden ... that AppleWorks® command you need just slips out of your mind and into space. Computer user's memory loss is a common ailment that plagues even the most competent Apple-Works aficionado. Now, Osborne/McGraw-Hill has a remedy that's guaranteed for immediate results — *AppleWorks®: The Pocket Reference*. All essential AppleWorks functions and commands are arranged alphabetically and described in a few paragraphs. Options are also listed in this invaluable resource for quick reference.

$5.95 p
0-07-881405-7, 128 pp., 4¼ x 7

AppleWorks™ Tips & Traps
by Dick Andersen, Janet McBeen, and Janice M. Gessin

Every AppleWorks™ user will find helpful tips and trap solutions in this book that are guaranteed to save hours of frustration and computing time on the Apple® II Plus, IIe, and IIc. *AppleWorks™ Tips & Traps* shows you how to gain maximum benefit from each AppleWorks environment — database, spreadsheet, and word processing. You'll find practical information on handling files and disks, integrating data in different files, setting up useful home and office applications, and transferring data from other programs into AppleWorks. Like all the books in the *Tips & Traps* series, this is an indispensable dictionary of shortcuts to your software.

$18.95 p
0-07-881207-0, 250 pp., 7⅜ x 9¼

AppleWorks™ Applications
by Lauren Flast and Robert Flast

Twenty-five AppleWorks™ models for business and finance are at your fingertips in *AppleWorks™ Applications*. Apple's best-selling integrated software package for the Apple® II Plus, IIe, and IIc provides database, spreadsheet, and word processing capabilities that can be combined in a variety of applications. In these pages you'll find ready-to-run models for balance sheets, income statements, cash flow analyses, monthly sales summaries, payroll databases, plus many other applications. Each model is briefly described and followed by complete program listings that you can quickly key into your Apple. Add your own data ... and obtain immediate results.

$9.95 p
0-07-881236-4, 125 pp., 7⅜ x 9¼

Extending AppleWorks™: Advanced Features & Techniques
by Mary Campbell and David R. Campbell, Jr.

Extending AppleWorks,™ a sequel to the enormously successful *AppleWorks™ Made Easy*, quickly guides experienced users to advanced-level techniques. Mary Campbell, a regular columnist for *IBM PC UPDATE* and *ABSOLUTE REFERENCE*, and David Campbell show you how to push AppleWorks to the limit using sophisticated spreadsheet, word processing, and database features. You'll also find out how to extend the program's capabilities with utilities such as UniDisk,™ a disk drive that increases the Apple IIe's storage capacity; Catalyst,® a program that allows users to load and run up to four applications simultaneously; and Pinpoint,™ a desktop accessory that provides a handy appointment calendar and merges graphics with AppleWorks. Filled with numerous applications and examples, *Extending AppleWorks™* considers all the finer points of manipulating this popular software. Includes trouble-shooting tips and command cards.

$16.95 p
0-07-881246-1, 250 pp., 7⅜ x 9¼

AppleWriter™ II Made Easy
by Leah Freiwald

This step-by-step tutorial teaches you how to use AppleWriter™ II, the best-selling, powerful word processing system for your Apple® IIe and IIc computer. Written to include AppleWriter II, version 2.0, *AppleWriter™ II Made Easy* provides you with hands-on experience you need to produce business letters, sales reports, memos, and much more. Application exercises show you how to use specific features of AppleWriter II to develop glossaries and handle mail merge. Complete explanations of system commands, helpful screen displays, and convenient appendixes guide you smoothly through the program and make this book the perfect complement to your AppleWriter II package.

$16.95 p
0-07-881166-X, 210 pp., 7⅜ x 9¼

Apple® II User's Guide For Apple® II Plus and Apple® IIe, Third Edition
by Lon Poole, Martin McNiff and Steven Cook

The all-time best-selling *Apple® II User's Guide*, with more than 500,000 copies in print, is now available in a third edition. Apple expert Lon Poole has revised the text to show you how to use the enhanced Apple® IIe, as well as the Apple II, Apple II Plus, Apple IIe, and all peripherals. You'll also find complete instructions for using the ProDOS® and DOS 3.3 operating systems. With Poole's easy-to-follow tutorials in BASIC programming, you'll learn how to utilize all the sound and graphics capabilities of your Apple, including the double high-resolution feature of the enhanced Apple IIe. As a handy reference for years of computing with your Apple, the *Apple® II User's Guide* is an undisputed classic.

$18.95 p
0-07-881176-7, 512 pp., 6⅞ x 9¼

Apple® IIc User's Guide
by Lon Poole

The top-selling Osborne/McGraw-Hill title, *Apple® II User's Guide*, has been adapted by Lon Poole for the Apple IIc computer. Following the original easy-to-use format, the *Apple IIc User's Guide* introduces you to the computer and its peripherals. A comprehensive tutorial on Applesoft® BASIC is provided, along with instructions for using your Apple IIc's color graphics and sound features. You'll find the most up-to-date information on ProDOS® Apple's latest operating system. In addition, helpful appendixes provide convenient summaries and tables for long-term reference. The *Apple IIc User's Guide* is an extensive hands-on resource book for all Apple IIc users.

$18.95 p
0-07-881156-2, 480 pp., 6½ x 9¼

Apple® IIGS™ Technical Reference
by Michael Fischer

Osborne announces **the** book on Apple's hot new computer, the *Apple® IIGS™ Technical Reference*. Michael Fischer, the same author who wrote the acclaimed *65816/65802 Assembly Language Programming*, now looks inside the Apple IIGS and gives serious programmers detailed information on all aspects of its architecture. All three operating modes are clearly explained so you can write software that runs on 8-, 16-, or 32-bit systems. Fischer's insights on software and firmware, the Apple IIGS' powerful toolbox. Programming with color graphics, sound, desk accessories, AppleTalk™, and other enhancements are thoroughly covered. The *Apple® IIGS™ Technical Reference* shows you how to upgrade from your Apple® II, design elegant software, and wholly understand the inner workings of Apple's incredible IIGS.

$19.95 p
0-07-881009-4, 697 pp., 6⅜ x 9¼

Desktop Publishing From A to Z
by Bill Grout, Irene Athanasopoulos, and Rebecca Kutlin

As a desktop publisher, you can use your microcomputer to create your own newsletters, catalogs, conference brochures, news releases, and more. *Desktop Publishing From A to Z* helps you choose the software, equipment, and procedures you need to achieve professional results. Grout discusses software packages and hardware that are available for desktop publishing, from project-management programs to page makeup programs, from the Macintosh™ and the IBM® PC to the LaserWriter™ printer. You'll find out how to establish a publishing plan, control costs and profits, handle printing and binding, promotion, and distribution.

$19.95 p
0-07-881212-7, 225 pp., 7⅜ x 9¼

The Practical Guide to Local Area Networks
by Rowland Archer

Deciding which local area network is right for you doesn't have to be a difficult process. With *The Practical Guide to Local Area Networks,* you'll be prepared to evaluate and select the LAN that's best for your business needs. LAN specialist Rowland Archer guides you through the process of planning your LAN installation, pointing out the advantages and potential pitfalls every step of the way. Archer then applies the criteria he has developed to five of the most popular LANs available for the IBM® PC and compatible computers: 3Com Ethernet® Corvus Omninet® Orchid PCnet® Novell NetWare,™ and IBM® PC Network and Token Ring.

$21.95 p
0-07-881190-2, 250 pp., 6½ x 9¼

1-2-3® Made Easy
by Mary Campbell

Osborne's famous "Made Easy" format, which has
helped hundreds of thousands of WordStar® users
master word processing, is now available to Lotus®
1-2-3® beginners. *1-2-3® Made Easy* starts with the
basics and goes step by step through the process of
building a worksheet so you can use Lotus' spreadsheet with skill and confidence. Each chapter provides
a complete 1-2-3 lesson followed by practical "hands-
on" exercises that help you apply 1-2-3 immediately to
the job. When you've got worksheets down, you'll
learn to create and print graphs, manipulate 1-2-3's
data management features, use advanced file features
. . . even design keyboard macros. As the author of *1-
2-3®: The Complete Reference*, and a former
columnist for IBM® PC UPDATE, ABSOLUTE REFERENCE,
and CPA JOURNAL, Mary Campbell has plenty of
experience with 1-2-3. With her know-how, you'll soon
be handling 1-2-3 like a pro.

$18.95 p
0-07-7881293-3, 400 pp., 7³/₈ x 9¹/₄

dBASE III PLUS™ Made Easy
by Miriam Liskin

Liskin's *Advanced dBASE III PLUS™* and Jones'
Using dBASE III PLUS™ have been so successful
that we're filling in the gap for beginners with *dBASE
III PLUS™ Made Easy*. Learning dBASE III PLUS™
couldn't be simpler. You'll install and run the program,
enter and edit data. Discover all the features of using
dBASE III PLUS at the dot prompt. Each concept is
clearly explained and followed by examples and
exercises that you can complete at your own speed.
Liskin discusses sorting and indexing, performing
calculations, and printing reports and labels. Multiple
databases are emphasized, and Liskin presents
strategies for working with them. You'll also find
chapters on customizing the working environment and
exchanging data with other software. If you're curious
about higher-level use, Liskin's final chapter shows
how to combine the commands you've learned into
batch programs so you can begin to automate your
applications. (Includes two command cards for quick
reference.)

$18.95 p
0-07-881294-1, 350 pp., 7³/₈ x 9¹/₄

DOS: Power User's Guide
by Kris Jamsa

Professional DOS users and programmers with an
interest in OS/2™, this book is a must for you! Jamsa,
the author of the best-selling *DOS: The Complete
Reference*, now shows experienced DOS users how
to wield this operating system in powerful ways. If
you're already familiar with C or Pascal, you'll gain
even more insight from Jamsa's expertise. As a
special highlight, the advanced features of DOS are
compared with those of the new OS/2 operating
system throughout the book. *DOS: Power User's
Guide* shows you how to utilize fully the DOS pipe,
memory map, system services, and subdirectories.
Learn how to adapt the DOS environment to meet your
specific needs. DOS pretender commands, disk layout,
and system configuration are additional topics that
Jamsa covers as he instructs you in the art of
becoming a truly sophisticated user.

$22.95 p
0-07-881310-7, 700 pp., 7³/₈ x 9¹/₄

These titles available at fine book stores and computer stores
everywhere.

Or call toll-free 800-227-0900.
Use your American Express, Visa, or MasterCard

For a FREE catalog of all our current publications, call or write to
Osborne/McGraw-Hill, 2600 Tenth Street, Berkeley, CA 94710

Prices subject to change without notice.